Praise for
The Go-Between:
Jan Eliasson and th_____

"Peter Wallensteen and Isak Svensson ope_____ ınto the practice of uber diplomat Jan Eliasson, whose rich experiences ın Africa, the Middle East, Central and Southeast Asia are the basis for case studies to test, illustrate, and expand our knowledge about the practice of mediation. The book belongs on the desk of any practitioner, scholar, or student who is serious about international conflict management."
—**Chester A. Crocker,** James R. Schlesinger Professor of Strategic Studies, Georgetown University

"The great strength of this book is its mapping of the conditions under which a go-between can most successfully define, enter, shape—and eventually exit—a principled mediation process. The cases are fascinating, ranging from the Iran-Iraq War, to a Burmese refugee crisis, to the Darfur mediation. Jan Eliasson, the main focus of the book, has earned his spot in the pantheon of international mediators, and his experiences are deeply informative."
—**Melanie Greenberg,** president, Cypress Fund for Peace and Security

"Focusing on the intermediary experiences of the renowned Swedish diplomat Jan Eliasson, this important book draws key lessons for the study and practice of diplomacy and the successful management of today's conflicts. Written in a clear, highly accessible, and engaging style, this book is a must read for any serious student or practitioner of international mediation. It is chock full of insights and wisdom that are drawn from a careful analysis of the deft diplomatic hand of its main protagonist."
—**Fen Osler Hampson,** director, The Norman Paterson School of International Affairs, Carleton University

"This volume is a valuable contribution to the literature on mediation and conflict resolution. The authors successfully bridge the gap between theory and practice, drawing heavily on Ambassador Eliasson's diaries in describing his actions in six major mediation exercises over twenty-eight years, and drawing on their own academic and more theoretical background in relating the exercises to one another."
—**Teresita C. Schaffer,** director, South Asia Program, CSIS and former U.S. ambassador to Sri Lanka

The Go-Between

The
GO-
BETWEEN

Jan Eliasson and the Styles of Mediation

Isak Svensson and Peter Wallensteen

UNITED STATES INSTITUTE OF PEACE PRESS
WASHINGTON, D.C.

United States Institute of Peace
1200 17th Street, NW, Suite 200
Washington, DC 20036-3011
www.usip.org

Library of Congress Cataloging-in-Publication Data

Svensson, Isak.
The go-between : Jan Eliasson and the styles of mediation / Isak Svensson and Peter Wallensteen.
    p. cm.
Includes index.
ISBN 978-1-60127-062-7 (alk. paper)
1. Mediation, International. 2. Mediation, International–Case studies. 3. Eliasson, Jan.
I. Wallensteen, Peter, 1945- II. Title.

JZ6045.S84 2010
341.5'2--dc22

2010022919

Contents

Preface by Kofi A. Annan xi

Introduction xii

1. One Mediator, Six Experiences 1

2. How Mediators Mediate: Styles of Mediation 11
 Mandating Mediation 11
 Styles of International Mediation 15
 Mandates and Style 24

3. Going In: The Diplomacy of Entry 25
 Giving the Mandate 25
 Requesting Mediation 30
 Offering Mediation 32
 Style and the Diplomacy of Entry 35

4. Going About: The Diagnostics of Diplomacy 37
 Assessing the Initial Situation 37
 Identifying the Issues 43
 Identifying the Actors 46
 Using the Entry 47
 Style and the Diagnostics of Mediation 49

5. Going On: The Instruments of Mediation 53
 Creating Confidence 53
 Establishing Principles 56
 Formulating Proposals 58
 Using the Media 61
 Dealing with Justice 64
 Keeping Them at the Table 67
 Reframing the Issues 68
 Style and the Instruments of Mediation 69

6. Going Together: The Context of Mediation 73
 Coping with Other Conciliators 73
 Forging Global Support 75
 Leading International Mediation 77
 Generating Global Attention 82
 Using International Norms 83
 Designing International Negotiations 84
 Inserting International Mediation 86
 Styles in Mediation Context 90

7. Going Out: The Diplomacy of Exit   95
     Threatening to Terminate   95
     Timing the Exit   97
     Finding Successors   100
     Style and the Diplomacy of Exit   101

8. Going Ahead: Lessons for Mediation Theory and Practice   105
     Mediation Mandate   106
     Mediation Outcome   109
     Mediation Resources   111
     Styles of International Mediation   114
     Comparing Mediation Styles   122
     Ten Implications for Mediation Research and Mediation Practice   128

Appendix: Chronologies of the Six Cases   137

Index   161

About the Authors   171

Preface

O ver the last two decades more wars have ended through mediation than in the previous two centuries. This is in large part because the United Nations has provided leadership, opportunities for negotiation, strategic coordination, and appropriate tools to implement peace agreements, but it is also due to the growing determination and efforts of states, regional organizations, and civil society to end the scourge of conflict.

This determination has sprung from the realization that our world has changed. While it has changed in many ways, among the most profound is our growing interdependence. We now live in a world where fragile states in the heart of Asia or Africa can come back to haunt us as safe havens for terrorists; a world where diseases like swine flu can be carried across oceans in a matter of hours; a world where a sub-prime crisis in the U.S. can lead to the worst global recession in decades; a world where a changing climate can affect global food security, increase pressures on fresh water supplies, and trigger mass movement of people. Against such threats, no nation can hope to make itself secure by seeking exclusive security. We all share responsibility for each other's security, and only by working to make each other secure can we hope to achieve lasting peace and security for ourselves.

This realization has done much to strengthen support for the idea of collective security. It has also provided a new, and powerful, rationale for peacemaking, including through mediation. As a result, the early years of the twenty-first century have seen mediation help end conflict in places such as Aceh, Northern Ireland, the Ivory Coast, Kenya, and Nepal.

Yet clearly, our scorecard is mixed. As the latest numbers from the Uppsala Conflict Data Program show, the world is far from pacific. In recent years, there were over seventy active violent conflicts, thirty-five of which involved one or more state actors. Tens of thousands of our fellow human beings are killed or maimed in war every year. And millions still have to flee their homes in search of a better life. So it is worth considering why some mediation efforts succeed and others fail. This book does so by skillfully drawing on the experiences of my dear friend and

colleague, Ambassador Jan Eliasson, who was deeply involved in many mediation attempts ranging from the Iran-Iraq War in the 1980s to the ongoing conflict
in Darfur.

The task of a mediator is seemingly straightforward. It is to help parties
develop a shared understanding of the conflict at hand and work toward building a practical and lasting solution. Successful mediation, however, depends on
many factors over which the mediator has little control, such as the geostrategic
framework, the comparative strengths of the parties to the conflict, their perception of the way the conflict is moving, their state of exhaustion or fresh hope, the
support they are getting from various external forces, the personalities of those
involved, and just plain luck.

But as Jan has proven over and over again, a skillful mediator can make a
crucial difference. It is with this difference in mind that Professors Peter Wallensteen and Isak Svensson have distilled his experience into a fascinating
journey through the process and styles of mediation. Ending in ten practical
conclusions, this journey is bound to be of great interest to practitioners and
academics alike.

—KOFI A. ANNAN
UN SECRETARY-GENERAL, 1997–2006

Introduction

In polarized situations of armed conflict and humanitarian crisis, there is often a need for a go-between, an international third-party mediator who can help to overcome barriers and divisions that keep conflicting parties apart. There is a growing awareness that international mediators can play a critical role in the process from war to peace. This book explores how mediators mediate. We examine the *styles* of international mediation. Style, we suggest, is not only a matter of manner and personality. It is more important than that. It refers to the overall priorities in the process of mediation. Style is crucial for understanding how the mediation process unfolds. Furthermore, it cannot be understood in isolation. In particular, we argue that the mandate of international mediation influences both the style employed by mediators and how that style affects the international mediation process.

One rationale for this book is the disturbing gap between the practice and theory of mediation. At its core, mediation is a practical diplomatic skill. But at the same time, mediation is the focus of a developing theoretical discussion. Knowing more about international mediation is therefore crucial for policymakers as well as academics. Yet, many policymakers are unfamiliar with the debates and insights within academia. Further, theoretical discussions are not always firmly anchored in the policymakers' reality, and conclusions arrived at are not easily transformed into practical lessons. The gap between theory and practice has to be narrowed. Mediation theory needs more input on how mediators actually mediate, and policymakers would benefit from analytical tools in deciding on optimal mediation strategies.

One reason for this gap can be found in the fact that previous mediation research has been limited to two basic types of approaches. Typically it consists of the narratives of mediators in autobiographies or tries to explain general patterns through systematic comparison of some mediators. This has resulted in descriptions that are not necessarily anchored in theory and systematic studies that do not necessarily speak to policymakers.

The unique contribution of this book is to explore the styles of mediation by a systematic analysis of the experiences of Swedish diplomat and statesman

Jan Eliasson, a key actor personally involved in several of the most contentious conflicts of the past few decades. This means combining Eliasson's political-practical insights with contemporary theoretical discussions in research on international mediation. We hope this will contribute to filling the gap between the theory and practice of mediation. In contrast to both the narrative approach and the cross-individual comparison, this book sets out to describe and compare mediation in different conflicts and crises by the same mediator.

The focus of this book is on international mediation, by which we mean diplomatic actions that aim to assist primary parties (whether states or nonstate actors) in social conflict to mitigate, manage, or settle their disagreements. Since mediation basically is a voluntary commitment by conflict actors (although the parties' enthusiasm for participating in mediation efforts may vary considerably), some degree of acceptance is necessary. The level of acceptance from the parties can help to distinguish mediation from other forms of third-party intervention, such as arbitration, which is a judicial mechanism where parties are bound by the third-party outcome. Another example is coercive intervention, such as military intervention and economic sanctions, where an outcome is forced upon the parties.

A note on the process of writing this book is needed. Jan Eliasson has been associated with the Uppsala University Department of Peace and Conflict Research for a long time. This has led to friendship and cooperation with one of the authors (Wallensteen). As will be described, the department has at certain instances played a role in some of Eliasson's efforts. More recently, as a visiting professor at and honorary doctor of Uppsala University, Eliasson has shared his understanding of international mediation with students and researchers. This book grew out of a need to not only collect and organize his experiences, but also to link them to the theoretical discussion in our field. One empirical basis for the book is a set of direct interviews with Jan Eliasson by one of the writers (Svensson). Both authors have also conducted interviews with some of Eliasson's colleagues and associates from the different missions. These include Anders Bjurner, Jörn Beckman, Paul Kavanagh, Anders Lidén, Mathias Mossberg, Giandomenico Picco, Agneta Ramberg, Helena Rietz, Iqbal Riza, Diego Cordovez, and Per Thöresson.[1] We also want to express our thanks to Professor Gerd Haverling, Uppsala University, and Bill Montross. In addition, we have had access to the archives at the Swedish Foreign Ministry as well as to some of Eliasson's own notes and excerpts from his personal diaries. Let us also make clear that although Jan Eliasson has read the manuscript, the views expressed and the interpretations made are solely those of the two authors.

1.   Anders Bjurner, Stockholm, August 22, 2008; Jörn Beckman, Stockholm, June 7, 2008; Paul Kavanagh, New York, February 20, 2009; Anders Lidén, Stockholm and New York, August 25, 2008, February 18–19, 2009; Mathias Mossberg, Uppsala, March 9, 2009; Giandomenico Picco, New York, February 18, 2009; Agneta Ramberg, Stockholm, March 6, 2009; Helena Rietz, Stockholm, October 1, 2008; Iqbal Riza, Madrid, February 2, 2009; Diego Cordovez, e-mail correspondence, February 2009; and Per Thöresson, Stockholm, August 29, 2008.

This gives the book unusual insights that are significant for analyzing the workings of an international go-between. It implies that we have information on the processes as seen from the lens of the mediator; on the conflicting parties' perspective and negotiation behavior as understood from third parties; and on the dynamics of the larger peace processes as reflected in correspondence and memos by third parties. This means that this book is written from the perspective of a third-party mediator. This is evidently only one side of a larger picture, which we do not have the aspiration to draw here. For a fuller understanding, our analysis—as well as any other mediation analysis—would have to be complemented with the perspective of the primary parties.

This book raises pertinent questions of what a go-between actually does, and thus analytically examines the role of a mediator. Although we will make a critical assessment in the concluding section of this book, our emphasis throughout the book is not to question whether the "right" approach was used at particular junctures. It suffices here to determine how the different aspects of style actually played out. We will discuss how the particular profile of Eliasson's style contributed to the different outcomes, but we do not set out to explain factors behind the success or failure of international mediation. Rather, this book is a theory-generating, descriptive analysis trying to answer some of the how questions of international mediation.

We gratefully acknowledge the support of the Riksbankens Jubileumsfond, Uppsala University, and the European Union's 7th Framework Program on "Just and Durable Peace by Piece" (coordinated by Lund University), for generous funding. We have benefited from our institutional affiliations at the Department of Peace and Conflict Research, Uppsala University, Sweden; the Kroc Institute for International Peace Studies, University of Notre Dame, United States; and the National Centre for Peace and Conflict Studies, Otago University, New Zealand. We also acknowledge the excellent research assistance of Mathilda Lindgren of Uppsala University and Monica Lundkvist of the Swedish Ministry for Foreign Affairs.

In addition, let us note that in the spring of 2009, Jan Eliasson was a Senior Visiting Scholar at the United States Institute of Peace. The Institute's Jennings Randolph Fellowship program and the Institute's Center for Education and Training organized a workshop to discuss the first draft of this book while Jan Eliasson was in residence. The comments received were extremely valuable for us in completing this manuscript.

PETER WALLENSTEEN   ISAK SVENSSON
UPPSALA, SWEDEN   DUNEDIN, NEW ZEALAND

1

One Mediator, Six Experiences

International mediation often presents unexpected moments that surprise and confound even the most highly trained and experienced diplomats and statesmen. Ambassador Jan Eliasson, the world-renowned Swedish diplomat with a remarkable decades-long track record of third-party mediation in international armed conflicts, relates one such moment. In his capacity as personal representative of the UN secretary-general to Iraq and Iran, he traveled to Baghdad in 1989 to discuss the implementation of UN Security Council Resolution 598. He and his delegation were received by an expressionless Saddam Hussein, who sat stiffly, smoking a Cuban cigar that an Iraqi officer came up and lit whenever it needed more fire. At one point, the interpreter turned to Eliasson and asked who should make his "speech" first. Eliasson, who had not prepared a speech, replied that he only had some basic questions. Saddam immediately became irritated and asked, "What kind of questions?" The other Iraqis in the room—the foreign minister, the negotiators, and a general—all froze and paled.

This had clearly been the wrong response. According to Eliasson, words had been mistranslated. He had not been expected to give a speech. Rather, he had been expected to invite the president to give his statement. Saddam quickly continued in the same cold voice: "What is your most important question?" Eliasson told him it was whether Iraq could return to the internationally recognized border. Saddam did not answer. The other Iraqis seemed close to fainting. This clearly was not an appropriate question to ask the president. The meeting went on for two hours. Then Saddam suddenly turned to Eliasson and said in a stern voice, "I remember your first question!" The room again grew tense. The faces of the Iraqis again turned pale. Saddam then abruptly said, "Follow me!" The room fell completely silent. To many in the room images of Saddam's cruelty came to life in his mind. What was going to happen to the visitors? Eliasson had no idea what Saddam intended to do. To be on the safe side, he asked, "Can I bring my delegation?" Saddam nodded, and together they walked into a nearby chart room. Pointing to a huge map, Saddam explained to Eliasson that a withdrawal would be a great sacrifice and a great risk to Iraq and would make

Iraq more vulnerable to attack. In short, he could not accept full withdrawal, at least not then. In turn, like any good diplomat, Eliasson deftly moved the discussion to the idea of temporary buffer zones and other possibilities, without giving up on the principle of withdrawal.

This anecdote illustrates both the unexpected, often idiosyncratic nature of international mediation—how a single misinterpreted word risks derailing a process (or worse)—and the nature of conducting negotiations with famous (and infamous) personalities in very difficult situations involving war, human suffering, and material destruction. It also serves as an object lesson about the importance of the go-between as an individual. Any mediator has to relate to the situation at hand. It is important how well that third party understands his or her mandate and the issues under discussion, how that individual confronts moments of uncertainty, how well that individual responds to the cues of those with whom he or she is dealing, and, more generally, how that individual's particular style affects—and is affected by—the mediation process.

Research increasingly points to constructive roles for international mediation in preventing, managing, and resolving armed conflicts.[1] Indeed, mediation tends to reduce significantly the duration of conflicts, to increase the likelihood of negotiated settlement, and to facilitate the preventive transformation of crisis, among other things.[2] There is also a discussion of whether mediators tend to be involved in the

---

1.   Exactly how mediators might be effective is still debated. For instance, in a theoretical discussion on whether mediators might credibly transmit information between antagonists, facilitating agreement, Alastair Smith and Allan Stam conclude that no mediator is credible enough to solve the information asymmetries and outperform the effects of side payments. In practice, mediators are often biased toward peace or one of the parties and thus not credible, or they are biased toward war, which will inhibit them from revealing any information in the first place. Alastair Smith and Allan Stam, "Mediation and Peacekeeping in a Random Walk Model of Civil and Interstate War," *International Studies Review* 5, no. 4 (2003): 115–135.

2.   See, for instance, Patrick M. Regan and Aysegul Aydin, "Diplomacy and Other Forms of Intervention in Civil Wars," *Journal of Conflict Resolution* 50, no. 5 (2006): 748, which finds "dramatic" positive effects of mediation in shortening civil wars, both alone and in conjunction with structural intervention; and Michael J. Greig and Paul F. Diehl, "The Peacekeeping-Peacemaking Dilemma," *International Studies Quarterly* 49 (2005): 621–645, which looks at the relationships between peacekeeping and mediation in both intrastate and interstate wars. Though most aggregate studies on mediation focus on short-term outcomes, such as negotiated agreements, some attend to long-term effects of mediation in the form of durable settlements. See Jacob Bercovitch and Scott Sigmund Gartner, "Is There Method in the Madness of Mediation: Some Lessons for Mediators from Quantitative Studies of Mediation," *International Interactions* 32, no. 4 (2006): 329–354. For a study that contrasts short- and long-term outcomes of mediation, see Kyle Beardsley, "Agreement without Peace? International Mediation and Time Inconsistency Problems," *American Journal of Political Science* 52, no. 4 (2008): 723–740, which finds mediation to be effective only in the short term. The likelihood of negotiated settlement from mediation has been studied in civil wars in Isak Svensson, "Bargaining, Bias and Peace Brokers: How Rebels Commit to Peace," *Journal of Peace Research* 44, no. 2 (2007), and in ethnic civil wars in Jacob Bercovitch and Karl R. DeRouen, "Mediation in Ethnic Civil War," *Civil Wars* 7, no. 1 (2005): 98–116. For a study of prevention, see Magnus Öberg, Frida Möller, and Peter Wallensteen, "Early Conflict Prevention in Ethnic Crises, 1990–98, a New Dataset," *Conflict Management and Peace Science* 26, no. 1 (2009): 67–91, which shows how ethnic crisis can be successfully prevented from being escalated through facilitation and other diplomatic efforts—both coercive and noncoercive. For a study of sequencing of conflict resolution strategies, see Birger Heldt, "Sequencing of Preventive Diplomacy in Emerging Intrastate Conflicts" (presented at the 2008 National Conference in Peace and Conflict Research, University of Lund, Sweden, October 2–3, 2008), which offers trends

tougher or the least-demanding cases of conflict resolution.[3] In-depth case studies, comparative work, and statistical analysis present increasingly fruitful answers to questions such as when to intervene, how to judge the possibilities and constraints of different types of mediators, how to gauge the effectiveness of different strategies, how to manage elements that obstruct negotiations, and how to relate different initiatives.[4] But what of the question of the individual mediator's style?

of relatively ineffective mediation, emphasizing high frequencies of mediation events, yet few successful situations of deescalation.

3.   Michael Greig and Nicolas Rost find that third parties will intervene when bilateral negotiations are unlikely, important issues are at stake, or when a majority of the victims are civilians. More precisely, mediators are more sensitive to risks in intervening in intractable rather than intensive conflicts. Bercovitch and Gartner also find support for these trends. See Greig and Rost, "Which Tools Get Used? A Multidimensional Analysis of Conflict Management within Civil War" (presented at the Annual Meeting of the Midwest Political Science Association, Chicago, Illinois, April, 7–10, 2005), 32; and Bercovitch and Gartner, "Is There Method in the Madness of Mediation." Studying the threat of withdrawal from mediation, Isak Svensson suggests that democratic mediators can be less credible than nondemocratic mediators in threatening to withdraw from mediation. See Svensson, "Democracies, Disengagement and Deals: Exploring the Effect of Different Types of Mediators in Internal Armed Conflicts," in *Governance, Resources and Civil Conflicts*, ed. Kaare Strom and Magnus Öberg (London and New York: Routledge, 2007). Mohammed O. Maundi, I. William Zartman, Gilbert Khadiagala, and Kwaku Nuamah discover that threats or positive impact on the mediator's interests, high determination of the third party, as well as high confidence in the mediator's ability to achieve preferred outcomes, all make offers and acceptance of mediation more likely. Conversely, high stakes will make rejection of mediation more likely. See Maundi et al., *Getting In: Mediators' Entry into the Settlement of African Conflicts* (Washington, DC: United States Institute of Peace Press, 2006). See also Jacob Bercovitch and Gerald Schneider, "Who Mediates? The Political Economy of International Conflict Management," *Journal of Peace Research* 37, no. 2 (2000): 145–165; Michael J. Greig, "Stepping into the Fray: When Do Mediators Mediate?" *American Journal of Political Science* 49, no. 2 (2005): 249–266; and Michael J. Greig and Patrick M. Regan, "When Do They Say Yes? An Analysis of the Willingness to Offer and Accept Mediation in Civil Wars," *International Studies Quarterly* 52 (2008): 759–781.

4.   Few academics have devoted as much attention and care to the understanding of mediation timing as I. William Zartman. In brief, Zartman elaborates a framework for understanding conflict ripeness—when parties are mature for resolving their conflict—based on concepts such as "mutually hurting stalemate," "mutually enticing opportunities," and the existence of representative agents. See Zartman, *Ripe for Resolution: Conflict and Intervention in Africa* (New York: Oxford University Press, 1985), and Zartman, "The Timing of Peace Initiatives: Hurting Stalemates and Ripe Moments," *The Global Review of Ethnopolitics* 1, (2001): 8–18. Chester A. Crocker, Fen Osler Hampson, and Pamela Aall extend our understanding of timing, as not only based on phases and motivations of the parties in conflict, but also concerning the readiness of the mediator. In particular, the authors illustrate mediator readiness on operational and political, strategic and diplomatic, as well as relationship and cultural levels. Crocker, Hampson, and Aall, "Ready for Prime Time: The When, Who, and Why of International Mediation," *Negotiation Journal* 19, no. 2 (2003): 151–167. Amy L. Smith and David R. Smock also emphasize the importance of readiness when initiating mediation in terms of, for instance, determining appropriate mediation roles, building credibility, and having a clear mandate. Smith and Smock, *Managing a Mediation Process* (Washington, DC: United States Institute of Peace Press, 2008), 21–30. Concerned with the issue of when mediation will most likely produce a negotiated settlement, some studies support later (though not excessively late) intervention, because the parties need time to adjust their success estimates, incompatibilities risk becoming institutionalized, and mediation risks losing effect the longer a conflict continues (Regan and Aydin, "Diplomacy and Other Forms of Intervention in Civil Wars," 742, 753–754). Others, on the other hand, propose early engagement, because mediators become reluctant to intervene in longer conflicts due to "soured relationships" between the parties (Greig and Rost, "Which Tools Get Used?"). Other researchers contributing to the debate include Patrick M. Regan and Allan C. Stam and Michael J. Greig. See Regan and Stam, "In the Nick of Time: Conflict Management, Mediation Timing, and the Duration of Interstate Disputes," *International Studies Quarterly* 44, no. 2 (2000): 239–260, and Greig, "Moments of Opportunity: Recognizing Conditions of Ripeness for International Mediation between

This book explores the processes—the entry, strategies, cooperation, and termination—of international mediation through the study of Ambassador Jan Eliasson's international mediation experiences. It contends that international mediators vary in style and that a mediator's particular style is determined by the mediator's mandate. In particular, this study lays out four key dimensions of international mediation style: scope, method, mode, and focus. It suggests that these dimensions represent continua on which mediators can deal with their tasks in different ways. They will act differently depending on their scope (inclusive or exclusive), method (fostering or forcing), mode of accessibility (open or confidential), and focus on concepts of peace (wide or narrow).

The book investigates these different stylistic dimensions—the scope, method, mode, and focus—that international mediators can utilize and examines how Ambassador Jan Eliasson has approached his international mediation efforts. It reviews six specific cases that vary considerably in the types of conflict he faced (for a summary, see table 1.1).

First, Eliasson participated in two missions related to one seemingly "classical" interstate war: the Iran-Iraq conflict, which was primarily fought over territorial border issues, but included mutual hopes for regime change, ideological rivalries, religious dimensions, and ethnic tensions between Persian-dominated Iran and Arab-dominated Iraq. Eliasson's first mediation experience in this conflict was as a personal adviser to the late Swedish prime minister Olof Palme, in his capacity as personal representative of the United Nations secretary-general in 1980. The Palme mission visited the region five times between 1980 and 1982, trying to achieve both short-term confidence-building agreements and a longer-

Enduring Rivals," *Journal of Conflict Resolution* 45, no. 6 (2001): 691–718. The variety of mediators is not only a practical truth, but also a theoretical reality. The distinctions are numerous and discussion diverse. Mediators are differentiated along their character and features as IGOs, states, NGOs, or individual (see Saadia Touval, "Mediation and Foreign Policy," *International Studies Review* 5, no. 4 (2003): 91–95; I. William Zartman and Kristine Höglund, "Violence by the State: Official Spoilers and Their Allies," in *Violence and Reconstruction*, ed. John Darby, 11–31 [South Bend, IN: University of Notre Dame Press, 2006]; Diana Chigas, "Capacities and Limits of NGOs as Conflict Managers," in *Leashing the Dogs of War: Conflict Management in a Divided World*, ed. Chester A. Crocker, Fen Osler Hampson, and Pamela Aall, 553–582 [Washington, DC: United States Institute of Peace Press, 2007]; Paul F. Diehl, "New Roles for Regional Organizations," in *Leashing the Dogs of War: Conflict Management in a Divided World*, ed. Chester A. Crocker, Fen Osler Hampson, and Pamela Aall, 535–552 [Washington, DC: United States Institute of Peace Press, 2007]); as official or nonofficial, working in different "tracks" of peace processes (see Roger Fisher, "Negotiating Power-Getting and Using Influence," *American Behavioral Scientist* 27, no. 2 [1983]: 149–166; Ronald J. Fisher and Loraleigh Keashly, "The Potential Complementarity of Mediation and Consultation within a Contingency Model of Third Party Intervention," *Journal of Peace Research* 28, no. 1 [1991]: 29–42; Louis Kriesberg, "Formal and Quasi-Mediators in International Disputes: An Exploratory Analysis," *Journal of Peace Research* 28, no. 1 [1991]: 19–27; Paul Wehr and John Paul Lederach, "Mediating Conflict in Central America," *Journal of Peace Research* 28, no. 1 [1991]: 85–98; H. C. Kelman, "Interactive Problem Solving: An Approach to Conflict Resolution and Its Application in the Middle East," *PS: Political Science & Politics* 31, no. 2 [1998]: 190–198; Ronald J. Fisher, "Coordination between Track Two and Track One Diplomacy in Successful Cases of Prenegotiation," *International Negotiation* 11, no. 1 [2006]: 65–89; Susan Allen Nan and Andrea Strimling, "Coordination in Conflict Prevention, Conflict Resolution and Peacebuilding." *International Negotiation* 11, no. 1 [2006]: 1–6; Pamela Aall,

term settlement of the conflict. Palme remained special representative until his tragic death in 1986. We refer to this case as Iran-Iraq I.

Eliasson's second mediation experience (Iran-Iraq II, 1988–91) followed the cease-fire and UN Security Council Resolution 598, which was mutually accepted by the parties and called on them to meet in direct talks on their disagreements. Eliasson, as Sweden's ambassador to the United Nations, was appointed personal representative of the secretary-general in August 1988. The negotiations over implementation of Resolution 598 took place in Geneva and New York, but Eliasson was also involved in shuttle diplomacy between Baghdad and Tehran.

Second, Eliasson undertook two more novel types of diplomatic action that emerged in the early 1990s, conducting humanitarian diplomacy in Burma/Myanmar (1992) and Sudan (1992) to prevent humanitarian crises there from escalating. As a top international civil servant and under-secretary-general of the United Nations Department of Humanitarian Affairs (UNDHA), he was called to act in Burma/Myanmar in March 1992. His objective was to avoid a humanitarian refugee disaster, which had the possibility of turning into an unpredictable interstate dispute between Burma and Bangladesh. The source of contention was the status of the large ethnic group of Rohingya expelled from Northern Burma to Bangladesh.

In the same capacity, Eliasson became an intermediary in Sudan in the fall of 1992, with the mandate of securing the delivery of humanitarian aid to areas that were closed to the outside world because of the civil war. Civilians caught in the cross-fire between troops from the North and the South, in the areas of Juba and parts of Bahr el Ghazal region, faced starvation due to famine and the severe difficulties international aid organizations had in delivering food and assistance there because of the heavy fighting.

"The Power of Nonofficial Actors in Conflict Management," in *Leashing the Dogs of War: Conflict Management in a Divided World*, ed. Chester A. Crocker, Fen Osler Hampson, and Pamela Aall, 477–496 [Washington, DC: United States Institute of Peace Press, 2007]); as biased or neutral toward the parties or issues (Laurie Nathan, "When Push Comes to Shove: The Failure of International Mediation in African Civil Wars," *Track Two* 8, no. 2 [1999]; Bidisha Biswas, "The Challenges of Conflict Management, a Case Study of Sri Lanka," *Civil Wars* 8, no. 1 [2006]: 46–65; Svensson, "Bargaining, Bias and Peace Brokers"); and as more or less resourceful in terms of coercive power (I. W. Zartman, and Saadia Touval, "International Mediation: Conflict Resolution and Power Politics." *Journal of Social Issues* 41, no. 2 [1985]: 27–46, and Saadia Touval, "The Superpowers as Mediators," in *Mediation in International Relations*, eds. Jacob Bercovitch and J. Z. Rubin, 232–248 [New York: St. Martin's Press, 1992]) or organizational power (Gilbert M. Khadiagala and Terrence Lyons, eds., *Conflict Management and African Politics: Ripeness, Bargaining and Mediation* [New York: Routledge, 2008]), to mention a few. (For a more in-depth discussion, please refer to chapter 2 of this volume.) A popular categorization of mediation strategies comes from Zartman and Touval, "International Mediation." The authors conceptualize mediation strategies into three clusters according to their degree of intervention in the negotiation process: (1) facilitation, (2) formulation, and (3) manipulation. This distinction is increasingly being applied to statistical analysis on international conflicts (see Jacob Bercovitch, Theodore J. Anagnoson, and Donnette L. Wille, "Some Conceptual Issues and Empirical Trends in the Study of Successful Mediation in International Relations," *Journal of Peace Research* 28, no. 1 [1991]: 7–17; Jacob Bercovitch and Richard Wells,

Third, he participated in two missions in conflict situations described by many as "typical" of the post–Cold War: internal armed conflicts involving regional secession, ethnic issues, and the distribution of power inside a state. In 1994, upon leaving the United Nations and prior to becoming state secretary of Sweden's Ministry for Foreign Affairs, Eliasson was elected chairman of the Minsk Conference, a committee within the Organization for Security and Co-operation in Europe (OSCE) that was assigned to mediate in the Nagorno-Karabakh conflict—a state-formation conflict in Azerbaijan between an ethnic minority with aspirations for a state of its own and a government wanting to uphold the territorial integrity of its state. The conflict also had a strong interstate dimension: the Karabakh Armenians were actively supported by the neighboring state of Armenia. To some this made the conflict interstate in character, but still clearly distinct from a "classical" conflict, such as the Iran-Iraq War.

Eliasson's most recent experience of international mediation was in his role as special envoy of the UN secretary-general for Darfur (Sudan) 2007–8, following his roles as president of the UN General Assembly and Swedish foreign minister. Eliasson entered the position after a peace agreement in 2006 had failed to put an end to the conflict between the government in Khartoum and the various rebel factions fighting against the marginalization of the Darfur region. Thus, the mission was to revive a peace process dealing

"Evaluating Mediation Strategies: A Theoretical and Empirical Analysis," *Peace & Change* 18, no. 1 [1993]: 3–25; Jacob Bercovitch and Allison Houston, "The Study of International Mediation: Theoretical Issues and Empirical Evidence," in *Resolving International Conflicts: The Theory and Practise of Mediation*, ed. Jacob Bercovitch [Boulder and London: Lynne Rienner Publishers, 1996]); and negotiated agreements (see Jonathan Wilkenfeld, Kathleen J. Young, Victor Asal, and David M. Quinn, "Mediating International Crises—Cross-National and Experimental Perspectives," *Journal of Conflict Resolution* 47, no. 3 [2003]: 279–301; Kyle Beardsley, David M. Quinn, Bidisha Biswas, and Jonathan Wilkenfeld, "Mediation Style and Crisis Outcomes," *Journal of Conflict Resolution* 50, no. 1 [2006]: 58–86; David M.Quinn, Jonathan Wilkenfeld, Kathleen Smarick, and Victor Asal, "Power Play: Mediation in Symmetric and Asymmetric International Crises," *International Interactions* 32, no. 4 [2006]: 441–470). For instance, Bercovitch and Gartner find that intense mediation efforts—directive strategies—contribute to increased likelihood of a lasting settlement (Bercovitch and Gartner, "Is There Method in the Madness of Mediation," 833–834), supporting previous findings (Jacob Bercovitch and Allison Houston, "Influence of Mediator Characteristics and Behavior on the Success of Mediation in International Relations," *The International Journal of Conflict Management* 4, no. 4 [1993]: 297–321, and Bercovitch and DeRouen, "Mediation in Ethnic Civil War"). However, Beardsley et al. instead find that while directive strategies increase the likelihood of settling the conflict, facilitative strategies produce better long-term reduction of tension and more durable peace, as the parties learn more about the true distribution of capabilities (Beardsley et al., "Mediation Style and Crisis Outcomes, 81–82). Moreover, Daniel Kurran, James K. Sebenius, and Michael Watkins contrast mediators along dimensions of means of influence (forceful, persuasive, facilitative, etc.) when talking about strategies. Specifically, they study strategies for (1) creating coalitions, (2) understanding processes based on control or consensus, (3) dealing with issues from a substance or process-oriented approach, and (4) understanding timing in the process. Kurran, Sebenius, and Watkins, "Two Paths to Peace: Contrasting George Mitchell in Northern Ireland with Richard Holbrooke in Bosnia–Herzegovina," *Negotiation Journal* 20, no. 4 (2004): 513–537. The debate on so-called spoilers in peace processes has, since the tone-setting work of Stephen John Stedman (Stedman, "Spoiler Problems in Peace Processes," *International Security* 22, no. 2 [1997]: 5–53), inspired works on tactics for spoiler management (see Andrew Kydd and Barbara F. Walter, "Sabotaging the Peace: The Politics of Extremist Violence," *International Organization* 56, no. 2 [2002]: 263–296); the devious objectives of rebel leaders in armed

with issues of power inside the state of Sudan and relating to the country's ethnic dimensions.[5]

These cases of international mediation by a go-between also occur in different phases of conflict. As will be seen, international mediation can help bring parties to the negotiation table, facilitate their negotiations in order to reach an agreement, and make sure that agreements are implemented. Each step in this process is a daunting task, requiring sensibilities for the historical and cultural context in which mediation takes place. Eliasson has been involved in different mediation processes in all of these different conflict phases—prenegotiations, substantive negotiations to put an end to a conflict, and negotiations over the implementation of an agreement—and his insights in this regard serve as a particularly useful basis for discussing the general conditions for international mediation.

The entry into and the exit from a mediation assignment is an important element in determining what a mediator can do. This will be emphasized in this book, as much as it deals with the mediation process itself: what does the go-between actually do when he or she goes between the parties? Indeed, the study will identify some of the main features of Eliasson's mediation missions: the emphasis on diplomacy, personal relationships, and cultural understanding; the issue-based approach, the use of international principles in mediation; the inclusiveness of

conflicts (Oliver Richmond, "Devious Objectives and the Disputants' View of International Mediation: A Theoretical Framework," *Journal of Peace Research* 35, no. 6 [1998]: 707–722); and how to relate to and manage violence during peace negotiations (John Darby, *The Effects of Violence on Peace Processes* [Washington, DC: United States Institute of Peace Press, 2001]; Zartman and Höglund, "Violence by the State"; Kristine Höglund, *Peace Negotiations in the Shadow of Violence* [Leiden: Martinus Nijhoff Publishers, 2008]). Finally, mediation cooperation and coordination of peace initiatives, both before, after, and during conflict, has been attended to in Chester Crocker, Fen Osler Hampson, and Pamela Aall, eds., *Herding Cats: Multiparty Mediation in a Complex World* (Washington, DC: United States Institute of Peace Press, 1999); Chester Crocker, Fen Osler Hampson, and Pamela Aall, "Is More Better? The Pros and Cons of Multiparty Mediation," in *Turbulent Peace: The Challenges of Managing International Conflict*, ed. Chester Crocker, Fen Osler Hampson and Pamela Aall (Washington, DC: United States Institute of Peace Press, 2001); Diana Chigas, "Negotiating Intractable Conflicts: The Contribution of Unofficial Intermediaries," in *Grasping the Nettle: Analyzing Cases of Intractability*, ed. Chester Crocker, Fen Osler Hamspon, and Pamela Aall (Washington, DC: United States Institute of Peace, 2005); Isak Svensson and Mathilda Lindgren, "Peace from the Inside: Exploring the Role of the Insider-Partial Mediator" (presented at the ISA Annual Conference 2009, New York, February 2009); and Patrick M. Regan, Richard W. Frank, and Aysegul Aydin, "Diplomatic Interventions and Civil War: A New Dataset," *Journal of Peace Research* 46, no. 1 (2009): 135–146.

5. It should be noted that Eliasson was not far removed from mediation efforts in other periods of his career. For instance, from 1994 to 2000, he served as the state secretary for foreign affairs of Sweden, leading the successful Swedish bid for a seat on the Security Council in 1997–98. From 2000 to 2005, he was Sweden's ambassador to the United States, garnering U.S. support for Swedish conflict prevention in Macedonia in 2001, dealing with the crises following September 11, 2001, over Afghanistan and Iraq, and sometimes pitting the United States against the European Union. In 2005–6, Eliasson served as president of the UN General Assembly, which involved him in multilateral negotiations on the establishment of the new Peacebuilding Commission and the reformed Human Rights Council. Similarly, as Sweden's foreign minister, Eliasson had to deal with the rescue of Swedish nationals in the 2006 Lebanon War. This too involved considerable diplomacy, though in this case Sweden had its own interests to protect. Since this book's focus is on mediation in the context of armed conflicts and humanitarian crises, these experiences are not covered in this book.

Table 1.1 International Mediation Experiences of Jan Eliasson

Conflict	Year(s) of mediation	Capacity	Organization	Purpose of mediation	Type of conflict
Iran-Iraq I	1980–86	Personal adviser to Olof Palme, the SRSG to Iran-Iraq	UN, UNSG	End the conflict	Interstate armed conflict
Iran-Iraq II	1988–91	Personal representative of the secretary-general on Iran-Iraq	UN, UNSG	Implement Resolution 598 (1987)	Interstate armed conflict
Burma/ Myanmar-Bangladesh	1992	Under-secretary-general for humanitarian affairs	UN, UNDHA	Secure return of expelled Rohingya refugees	Humanitarian crisis
Sudan	1992	Under-secretary-general for humanitarian affairs	UN, UNDHA	Secure delivery of international aid to Southern Sudan	Humanitarian crisis
Azerbaijan (Nagorno-Karabakh)	1994	Chairman of the Minsk Group	OSCE, Minsk Group	End the conflict	State-formation conflict
Sudan (Darfur)	2007–8	Special envoy of the secretary-general for Darfur	UN, UNSG	Revitalize the political process	Internal armed conflict

actors, the division of labor among different international actors; the mobilization of the public; and the policy toward media, to name some of the themes.

We have been fortunate enough to discuss these mediation cases with Ambassador Eliasson. Excerpts from these interviews are presented in italics in the text. We have also had access to Mr. Eliasson's personal diaries from these mediation experiences. Such quotes have a reference to the date they are recorded in the diary. Interviews and diary entries are translated from Swedish by the authors.

Reaching agreement in these types of conflicts is, of course, extremely difficult. This underscores the delicacy of some of these situations. Still, there are important outcomes to report: there was an agreement not to attack civilian villages in the Iran-Iraq War in 1984; an agreement to exchange Iraqi and Iranian prisoners of war in August 1990; a full cease-fire in Nagorno-Karabakh in 1994; a bilateral agreement, reached in April 1992, whereby Rohingya refugees were allowed to resettle; and an agreement that allowed humanitarian aid to be delivered to the people facing starvation in the South of Sudan in 1992. Often outcomes do not just reflect the achievements of the mediator, but also the ambitions of the primary parties.

Our purpose is not to establish the outcomes, but to draw lessons for the process of peacemaking by examining how Eliasson has entered, prepared, pursued (also with other mediators), and finally ended his international mediation efforts. In all of these instances, Eliasson, as a go-between, has generated hopes and expectations, entered into the calculations of the primary parties, and thus, inevitably, had an impact on the course of the conflict. In any conflict, however, the mediator also faces other forces that remain focused on "winning," destroying the opposite side, or simply delaying agreements for hidden reasons. Thus, determining the impact of his mediation efforts will necessitate a larger undertaking than attempted here. Still, this book's contribution is significant in its attempt to record and analyze six separate cases of mediation, across which one factor is kept constant: the mediator. In the following chapters, we lay out the theoretical framework of mediation styles and the origins of the mandate in international mediation and then turn to actual experiences in mediation, before finally offering lessons for mediation theory and practice.

2
How Mediators Mediate: Styles of Mediation

Quite a number of international mediators have been involved in peacemaking processes around the world. Many more personalities will become involved in such activities in the coming years. This chapter outlines a typology of international mediation styles across the four basic dimensions—scope, method, mode, and focus—as a way of capturing significant mediation challenges. However, before describing this typology, we need to understand the conditions under which mediators mediate. Mediators cannot choose their style without considering the very situation in which they find themselves. Personal traits play a role, but we suggest that the styles of international mediators are also set by the particular mandate under which a mediator operates. The emphasis on the key importance of mandate and style are the two major contributions of this book, and they consequently require explanation.

Mandating Mediation

No mediator ends up by chance in a conflict. There is a history. We argue that the mandate of the mediators is central in explaining the styles used in international mediation. The mandate, furthermore, consists of two elements. The first deals with the origin of the mandate, the second with its operational implications—that is, what the mediator is actually mandated to do.

Who Sets the Mandate?

A crucial moment in the mediation experience of one of the authors was a meeting with skeptical guerrilla leaders on the island of Bougainville, Papua New Guinea. In an unwelcoming voice, with stern eyes focused on him and with a clenched fist, a man shouted: "Who is paying you?" The question was legitimate. In four words he was saying: you are from some other part of the planet, why do you appear here, what are you doing in "our" conflict? Suspicion abounds in any conflict. Treason, plots, betrayals, secret designs are part of any conflict, particularly one involving the lives of many people. It is hard for a primary party to understand why a foreigner would be concerned about a particular situation. The default understanding is clearly that the foreigner has some hidden, ulterior agenda. Such a straight question cannot be answered with the words, "I think you should not fight and I would like to help you and your opponent." In this case, the fact that the mission was undertaken on the initiative of the local branch of the national university was helpful.[1] But the money trail was key. The answer was simple: the Swedish International Development Authority (SIDA). That was sufficient. Swedish development aid had a positive, neutral, peaceable, and friendly image to it. The skeptic relaxed, his fist opened into a handshake. But, his question has a general value.[2]

This brings us to an issue that has been underestimated in the literature: the mandate given to the mediator by the mandating agency.[3] While the mandating agency can be an asset to the mediator, it may also restrict what the mediator can do,[4] because the mediator must navigate between the primary parties and the mandating agency. For someone coming with a government mandate, this is less problematic, as a government is authorizing or sending the mission. For example, Ambassador Richard Holbrooke, leading the Dayton negotiations in his capacity as U.S. assistant secretary of state, had to check with the U.S. leadership about what he could agree to. He could ask his president for support, but it would be the president, not Holbrooke, who decided what he should do.[5]

Thus, the origin of the mandate is of central concern. In a sense, it says who controls the mediation process and it shapes the way the primary parties view the third party. The mediator and the parties will be highly aware of the origin of the mediation mandate, which constitutes a significant dimension of the realities

---

1.   In situations where the costs for identification with a peace process are high for some of the primary parties in conflict, low-key actors such as academics—similar to the actors mediating in the informal workshops leading up to the Good Friday Agreement in the Northern Ireland peace process—with little direct connection to the parties, can be useful for creating spaces for communication. Aall, "The Power of Nonofficial Actors in Conflict Management," 484.

2.   For more on this academic mediation case in Bougainville, Papua New Guinea, see Wallensteen, "The Strengths and Limits of Academic Diplomacy: The Case of Bougainville," in Aggestam, K and B. Jamëk, eds., *Diplomacy in Theory and Practice, Essays in Honor of Christer Jönsson* (Liber: Malmö 2009), 258–81.

3.   We have been struck by the neglect to this aspect in much of the mediation literature. For instance, entries for "mandate" or similar terms are not found in I. William Zartman, *Negotiation and Conflict Management, Essays on Theory and Practice* (New York: Routledge, 2008); Jonathan Wilkenfeld, Kathleen J. Young, David M. Quinn, and Victor Asal, eds., *Mediating International Crises* (London: Routledge, 2005); Jacob Bercovitch and Scott Sigmund Gartner, eds., *International Conflict Mediation: New Approaches and Findings* (London: Routledge, 2009); or Jacob Bercovitch, Victor Kremenyuk, and I. William Zartman, eds., *The Sage Handbook of Conflict Resolution* (Los Angeles: Sage Publications, 2009).

4.   When entering a conflict, a mediator will have to be clear on its objectives and scope of action. States, IGOs, NGOs, and individuals will all have different organizational resources and different objectives, both reflected in their mandate. Whether the mediation is about maintaining the status quo, reenergizing a stalemated peace process, or resolving a conflict, the mediators will have to base their actions in their mandate, as "Strategies that exceed mandates are unlikely to find political support." Smith and Smock, *Managing a Mediation Process*, 24.

5.   See Holbrooke, *To End a War* (New York: Random House, 1998), 301.

of any mediator. As Chester A. Crocker, Fen Osler Hampson, and Pamela Aall starkly express:

> Without [a mandate], the mediator has no ground to stand on at home and can be blown off course or neutralized by the parties (or factions within the parties) and by domestic factions (perhaps in league with elements within the parties). . . . The mediator's mandate provides a bedrock of institutional support. . . . Equally vital, the mandate provides authority to the mediator and serves to remind all others that the mediator speaks for the organization, institution, state or group of states, which have provided it. . . . Without such backing, the contending parties will turn the mediation into a leaf swept down a stream.[6]

Few mediation researchers have expressed this point more succinctly. All mediators operate under a mandate. With the mandate given by an actor based externally to the parties, it is likely that the mediation mission can continue over a longer period of time. If the parties give the mandate, they retain a veto and can deny further entry to the situation if they are dissatisfied by what is accomplished.

There seems to be an important difference between those mediation missions that have a mandate from an external actor—to which the parties have to agree to, of course, but not necessarily control—and those that have their mandate straight from the fighting parties themselves.[7] The origin of mediations falls into these two categories. The distinction seems to capture different types of mediation and each category includes a rich variety of initiatives.

First, an external actor can give the mandate. This could be a major power, an international or regional organization, or some other body or group to which the country in question formally belongs or whose authority it has to respect. Yet, the parties are not without influence. Mediation requires the consent of the parties, even if they are not necessarily enthusiastic about the mediation initiative. Whereas their room for maneuver in regard to the whole mediation effort sometimes can be limited, they can object to particular individuals before they are appointed as official mediators. The parties will have to live with the externally appointed mediator, although they may develop techniques to make life difficult for mediation, if they are not happy with the objective of the mediation or the personalities. They can backpedal, procrastinate, and withdraw, as their cooperation is vital, but at the expense of appearing to be a "troublemaker" and jeopardizing long-term relationships.

Second, the mandate can be given by the parties themselves, through a more informal process, in which indirect channels of communication are established, resulting in an invitation to a third party to enter the situation. Such communication is likely to be secretive, easily deniable, and less specific; thus, when a more formal invitation is finally extended, the mandate may be less clear-cut. Indeed, much of the work of the mediator may continue under confidentiality and only when a

---

6. See Crocker, Hampson, and All, "Ready for Prime Time," 154.

7. This is what Maundi et al. refer to as "entry by proposition" versus "entry by invitation." Maundi et al., *Getting In*, 6.

result is achieved will the world know what has been going on. Mediators who build on a party-given mandate may be those most reluctant to explain or even attempt to use publicity for their purpose, as this may risk undermining the parties' confidence in their activity. Mediators in this category are likely to be the ones most unwilling to take credit or even inform the general audience of their work.

Some examples of such party-based arrangements are the involvement of Norway in the Palestinian question (what became known as the Oslo process) and in Sri Lanka; Australia and New Zealand in the conflicts in the South Pacific; neighboring countries in conflicts in Burundi, Rwanda, and the Democratic Republic of Congo; and a host of civil society and nongovernmental initiatives in conflicts in Mozambique, Papua New Guinea, and East Timor.

Let us note that an official mandate is not a necessary condition for a mediator's engagement. In particular, third-party mediation need not be officially sanctioned.[8] On the contrary, the rationale for such unofficial third-party intervention is that it is outside official mandates and, if it becomes publicly known, the political leadership can deny and, even, denounce such peace initiatives. Notable centers performing unofficial mediation include the Carter Center, led by former U.S. president Jimmy Carter, and the Conflict Management Initiative (CMI), led by former Finnish president Martti Ahtisaari. In addition, former presidents Nelson Mandela, Julius Nyerere, and Joaquim Chissano, and former UN secretary-general Kofi Annan are actively involved in "private" initiatives in African conflicts.

One type of mediator may be replaced by another. That was the case in Aceh, where the earlier mission of the Henri Dunant Center for Humanitarian Dialogue (HDC) was terminated by Indonesia, and a new one started by CMI, following the Indonesian elections in late 2004.[9] The unofficial track was restarted, with new actors, but still on a party-driven mandate. Many conflicts see such sequencing of actors. That is also the case for the externally mandated mediations, of course. The conflict dynamics (or lack thereof) can lead to changes in mediation, as well as to changes among the parties. Furthermore, there are often other, parallel efforts mandated by the parties or organizations. Thus, it will always be relevant to relate mediation efforts to one another. It adds to the complexities of mediation and affects the style chosen for a particular situation.

Thus, mandates can change. Mediators may initiate such changes, but it is the sending authorities, be they an international organization or the warring parties, that have the final say in what the mandate is all about.

---

8. See Smith and Smock, *Managing a Mediation Process*.

9. See Harriet Martin, *Kings of Peace, Pawns of War* (London: Continuum International, 2006); Timo Kivimäki and David Gorman, "Non-governmental actors in peace processes: the case of Aceh," in Third Parties and Conflict Prevention, eds., A. Mellbourn and Peter Wallensteen, 163–85 (Hedemura: Gidlunds Förlag, 2008).

What Does the Mandate Say?

The mandate of a mediator can vary depending on the objective of the third party's commitment. An important distinction needs to be made between primarily political and humanitarian mediation. In fact, the significance of humanitarian mediation has been disregarded in the international mediation literature.

Political mediation involves diplomatic negotiations between conflicting parties to find a way to solve an incompatibility or to develop a procedure for settling the conflict. This type of international mediation represents efforts to handle the core contentious issues at stake in serious conflict. Humanitarian mediation is the diplomatic negotiations between actors in an impending or acute humanitarian crisis. International mediation in humanitarian intervention does not aim at resolving underlying political issues but serves to manage a humanitarian situation. Of course it may be the result of war or armed conflict but can also have other origins.

The exact purpose of political mediation can vary, and the operational mandates can relate to different phases of a conflict. Thus, mandates can vary to include attempts, for instance, to initiate a political process, to actually conduct negotiations to find a peaceful end of a conflict, or to negotiate the implementation of an agreement. The what and who of the mandate are clearly linked. In armed conflict, even the request for mediation is a highly sensitive issue, since such a request by one party to a conflict can be interpreted as a sign of weakness by another party. Moreover, if the conflict deals with national issues of power and territory, governments will be particularly reluctant to accept "interference" into what they consider domestic affairs. It is thus logical that the international community often initiates political negotiations and enters a conflict from a level "above" the parties. On the other hand, in situations of humanitarian crises, there are organizations that can assess the consequences of continuous conflict and, thus, without losing credibility, may offer assistance, even including mediation. Furthermore, humanitarian issues may be less sensitive and can therefore become entry points for dealing with other, politically crucial issues.

In the following, we will attempt to compare Eliasson's political and humanitarian mediation efforts with respect to the various styles of mediation.

Styles of International Mediation

A mandate's origin and instructions set the outer framework for a mediation initiative. In this book the way the mediator chooses to act is referred to as the "style" of a particular mediator. Variations in mediation style may be hard to pin down. The literature traditionally refers, for instance, to "soft" and "hard" mediation, to "power-based" or "trust-oriented" approaches, or to a set of fixed categories of mediator strategies, such as "facilitation," "formulation," and "manipulation/ directive strategies." However, we find these notions too simple to describe the nuances of international mediation. The four stylistic dimensions we present in this section can be useful for identifying overarching approaches, where some mediation efforts may be narrow and targeted, and others wide and more comprehensive. Just as different types of mediators may use different styles, so too may an individual mediator use different styles when working in different settings.[10] We present known cases of mediation both to exemplify the four stylistic dimensions and to situate Jan Eliasson's style in the broader context of international mediation.

Scope: Inclusive or Exclusive

"Scope" refers to a stylistic dimension that closely relates to the mandate of international mediation and the boundaries of the mediator's engagement or, put differently, the parties to which the mediator targets his or her efforts. There is a difference, although not always clear-cut, between a more exclusive scope and more inclusive ones.

In the Norwegian-mediated process in Sri Lanka, President Chandrika Kumaratunga was kept outside the core negotiation framework. Prime Minister Ranil Wickremasinghe was in charge of the negotiations. The approach entailed certain risks, as the exclusion of Kumaratunga in the signing of a cease-fire in February 2002 led to further tensions within the governmental party. Coupled with lobbying by pro-Kumaratunga media, this fueled distrust toward the mediators.[11] In addition, on the Tamil side, only the Liberation Tigers of Tamil Eelam (LTTE) was included in the talks, whereas non-LTTE Tamil groups as well as civil society organizations were excluded.[12] Similarly, the mediation efforts of Sant'Egidio between the warring parties in Mozambique were initially quite exclusive, but gradually broadened. Only after the parties had agreed to an agenda and the process risked to be stalemated did U.S. diplomat Cameron Hume and his colleagues, in support of the efforts of Sant'Egidio, decide to broaden the process to include major powers and regional actors of relevance for the resolution.[13]

Betty Bigombe, who has been a lead national mediator in Uganda since 1988, had a more domestically inclusive style in her mission to assist in ending the civil war. At times the war engulfed as much as one-third of the country

---

10. It is also possible for a mediator to adopt different styles within one mediation. We are grateful to Bill Montross for suggesting this. However, we do not explore this here.

11. See Martin, *Kings of Peace, Pawns of War,* 18–19.

12. See Kristine Höglund and Isak Svensson, "Fallacy of the Peace Ownership Model: Exploring Norwegian Mediation in Sri Lanka," in *Liberal Peace in Question: Politics of State and Market Reforms in Sri Lanka,* eds. Kristian Stokke and Jayadeva Uyangoda (London: Anthem Press, 2010).

13. See Cameron R. Hume, *Ending Mozambique's War: The Role of Mediation and Good Offices* (Washington, DC: United States Institute of Peace Press, 1994).

and involved many conflict actors. Not only did Bigome talk to rebel groups, but she also visited the villages. In her meetings with parents, sisters, and brothers of the rebels, she could better understand the conflict and find a way to start the negotiations. During latter phases of talks in 2007, Bigombe even shuttled between Lord's Resistance Army (LRA) soldiers and the LRA leadership to facilitate a common understanding within the LRA, which was lacking at the time.[14]

The inclusiveness in scope not only relates to the parties to conflict, but also to the wider international context. For instance, Alvaro de Soto was inclusive in his approach in El Salvador, as he insisted on his right to consult with other actors (notably the United States, the Soviet Union, and Cuba) that might "usefully assist in our efforts" and constructed a Group of Friends to support the process.[15]

Method: Forcing or Fostering

"Method" refers to a stylistic dimension that involves how mediators try to influence the parties' perception of the mediation process. For instance, international mediators may vary in their preferred timing of engagement in a conflict and in their reliance on dynamics and deadlines, such as whether to push or cajole the parties or when to end a mediation effort. A more forceful method includes pressure, threats, and deadlines, while a more fostering method capitalizes on positive dynamics and creating momentum.[16]

With regard to timing and the mediation process, former U.S. senator George Mitchell represents one end of the spectrum. He applied a patient and permissive approach in his involvement in the Northern Ireland peace process, facilitating the largely procedural negotiations for almost a year and a half. This method was the result of both his personality—being a seasoned politician with a developed sense of patience—and his mandate, which was designed mainly to support cooperation between the parties.[17]

On the other end of the spectrum is UN mediator Alvaro de Soto, who in El Salvador used an agreed-upon deadline for each phase of negotiations—as a "psychological device to egg negotiations on" and keep the process "sufficiently intense."[18] Still, de Soto admits there are downsides to real deadlines. In this case, the end of Pérez de Cuéllar's term as UN secretary-general was coupled with

---

14. See the United States Institute of Peace video report of Betty Bigombe's trip to Uganda in early 2007, www.usip.org/in-the-field/in-the-field-uganda.

15. See Alvaro de Soto, "Ending Violent Conflict in El Salvador," in *Herding Cats: Multiparty Mediation in a Complex World*, eds. Chester A. Crocker, Fen Osler Hampson, and Pamela Aall, (Washington, DC: United States Institute of Peace Press, 1999), 365, 370–376.

16. For more on this, see Kurran, Sebenius, and Watkins, "Two Paths to Peace."

17. See ibid., 525–527.

18. See de Soto, "Ending Violent Conflict in El Salvador," 363.

warnings of a future decline in UN attention to El Salvador. This contributed to "galvanizing the negotiations,"[19] but it also resulted in a lack of commitment to an effective reintegration of combatants. The agreement became weak on aspects of implementation. However, de Soto asserts that "real deadlines—those that are not in the power of the mediator or the parties to move, such as constitutionally established terms—can and should be grasped and manipulated by a mediator to prod a negotiation along and pry concessions from recalcitrant parties. Let the mediator beware, however, of conjuring up deadlines not anchored in reality."[20]

Related to the timing question is also the question of whether the international go-between chooses to use a step-by-step approach or aim for a more comprehensive grasp of the process. An example of the comprehensive method can be found in former U.S. president Jimmy Carter's mediation between Sudan and Uganda. Carter prepared an eleven-point agenda in prenegotiations, together with the representatives of Sudan and Uganda, on how to end fighting between the governments and the LRA and the Sudan People's Liberation Army (SPLA), respectively. Before the final Nairobi talks with the heads of state, Carter went through all the points of the agreement, first with Sudan's leader Omar Bashir and then with Uganda's Yoweri Museveni. Lead mediator Joyce Neu recalls, "As Carter went back and forth between the two presidents in a method he first used at Camp David in 1978—the 'single document approach'—each head of state and his contact group made and reviewed modifications. By mid-afternoon on December 8, earlier than any of us had thought possible, we had an agreement. Kenyan president Daniel Arap Moi was quickly notified and a signing ceremony was held at State House with Carter and Moi as witnesses. Bashir and Museveni shook hands, and the Nairobi Agreement came into existence."[21]

A contrast to the comprehensive approach is the way the Norwegian mediators facilitated talks between officials representing the Palestine Liberation Organization (PLO) and the Israeli government during the Oslo peace process in 1993. In that case, the mediators and the parties separated the questions into smaller components and discussed each of them. In relation to this mediation experience, Jan Egeland emphasizes that "a third party should define realistic goals when embarking on conflict resolution. More often than not it is advisable to seek limited humanitarian or other confidence-building agreements on the way toward the very ambitious goal of making peace."[22]

---

19. See ibid., 379.

20. See ibid., 387.

21. See Joyce Neu, "Restoring Relations between Uganda and Sudan: The Carter Center Process," Protracted Conflict, Elusive Peace: Initiatives to End the Violence in Northern Uganda, *Accord* 11 (2002), www.c-r.org/our-work/accord/northern-uganda/carter-center.php.

22. See Jan Egeland, "The Oslo Accord: Multiparty Facilitation through the Norwegian Channel," in *Herding Cats: Herding Cats: Multiparty Mediation in a Complex World* (Washington, DC: United States Institute of Peace Press, 1999), 544.

Mode: Confidential or Open

"Mode" refers to a stylistic dimension that involves the issue of transparency and openness—that is, the degree to which the third-party assignment is conducted openly or secretly. Mediators are likely to vary in their approach to open mediation. Some will prefer to say as little as possible, whereas others actively engage the media.

Traditionally, go-betweens have shunned media.[23] Since mediators must often build on trust and persuasion, they may be unwilling to explain to the general public what they are doing. Swedish ambassador Gunnar Jarring, who served as UN mediator in the Middle East, was known for his complete silence toward the international press and went under the nickname of "super clam." Jan Eliasson recalls an anecdote that illustrates Jarring's mediation style:

> Once Gunnar Jarring, after arriving from a mediation mission in the Middle East, met the international press at the airport in New York. Unusual for him, he stopped in front of the press corps and made an announcement: "Ladies and gentlemen of the press, I want to say that I have no comments. Have a good day." The press secretary to the secretary-general at that time reported what he had said. The secretary-general replied: "Did he really go that far?"

Jarring's action illustrates the tradition of confidentiality and secrecy that have permeated international mediation efforts. A more recent example is Jamsheed Marker, the lead mediator in the negotiations over the status of East Timor, who said that he was taking more or less "Trappist vows" not to reveal the content of the confidential discussions between the parties.[24] Likewise, Lazaro Sumbeiywo refused all media contact when facilitating an agreement between the Sudan rebel group SPLA and the government of Sudan.[25]

Other go-betweens see the utility of media but still may have difficulty getting access to or even acceptance of the parties. For instance, James LeMoyne facilitated video-recorded negotiations between the Colombian government and guerrilla representatives. This evolved into what he as UN special adviser to Colombia refers to as a "soap opera."[26] Likewise, Mauretanian diplomat Ahmedou Ould-Abdallah in Burundi, as well as Norwegian mediators Erik Solheim and Vidar Helgesen in Sri Lanka, were all attentive to the needs of the media. They would—in situations of acute crisis, when the peace process might be at risk— urgently prepare official statements, often together with the parties, to submit

---

23. See Connie Peck, "The Role of Special Representatives of the Secretary-General in Conflict Prevention," in *Third Parties and Conflict Prevention*, ed. Peter Wallensteen and Anders Mellbourn, 223–234 (Hedemora: Gidlunds Förlag, 2008).

24. See ibid., 229, and Jamsheed Marker, *East Timor: A Memoir of the Negotiations for Independence* (Jefferson, North Carolina, and London: McFarland and Company Inc., 2003).

25. See Martin, *Kings of Peace, Pawns of War*, 170.

26. See Peck, "The Role of Special Representatives of the Secretary-General in Conflict Prevention," 229, as well as United Nations Secretary-General, "James LeMoyne Appointed Special Adviser on Colombia" (press release SG/A/823, November 1, 2002).

them to news media before rumors could spread and risk derailing fragile ne-gotiations. During the Berlin talks in 2003, Solheim and Helgesen assisted in drafting a joint statement expressing the parties' mutual concern about a recent violent incident in Sri Lanka.[27] After the sudden death of Burundian president Cyprien Ntaryamira, on April 6, 1994, Ould-Abdallah organized the first official television appearance with, among others, the speaker of the National Assembly, Sylvestre Ntibantunganya, to prevent the situation from escalating further.[28]

In an increasingly media-driven world, the ability of the go-between to explain what he/she is up to is likely to become more central. Many of the go-betweens are known to the public and, thus, try to use the public arena as a tool for influ-encing the parties and the international political environment. The outcome of a mediation effort, of course, concerns many more than those present in closed room, individuals reachable by phone or text message. If those not involved be-come suspicious about mediation efforts, persuasion may become more difficult, reducing the chances of agreement and implementation. The understanding of what goes on will affect the legitimacy of the outcome, and legitimacy is what provides the lubricant for a deal and its functioning.

However, this has to be balanced against exaggerated public expectations. The international go-between may say too much, or even express what is agreed or disagreed in ways that antagonize crucial groups in a delicate process. It is es-sential for a go-between to understand the role of the media as a basic vehicle for generating public trust in a process.

Focus: Narrow or Wide Peace

"Focus" refers to a stylistic dimension that relates to priorities and what the mediator concentrates on achieving through a mediation effort. Specifically, the go-betweens can vary their "focus" on peace or justice, or what could be labeled as a "narrow" or "wide" peace. Optimally, all international mediators seek a wide peace—that is, an end to the fighting, which also entails respect for human rights and the harmonization of outcomes with principles of international law. Peace and justice may reinforce each other. Sustainable peace is most likely to occur when injustices have been addressed. Yet, sometimes these two norma-tive goals can be in contradiction with each other.[29] Thus, the mediator will

---

27. See Martin, *Kings of Peace, Pawns of War*, 113–14.

28. See Ahmedou Ould-Abdallah, *Burundi on the Brink 1993–95: A UN Special Envoy Reflects on Preventive Diplomacy* (Washington, DC: United States Institute of Peace Press, 2000), 56–57.

29. For some time now, researchers have been discussing the imperatives of peace and the demands for justice in different types of settings, of which we are mostly concerned with the process of negotiating an end to social, and often violent, conflicts. The dimensions of peace and justice are commonly either con-trasted as mutually exclusive—peace today is achievable at the expense of justice for past atrocities—or seen as complementary and even reinforcing (I. William Zartman and Victor Kremenyuk, eds., *Peace versus Justice: Negotiating Forward-Looking or Backward-Looking Outcomes* (Lanham, MD: Rowman and Littlefield, 2005). Most, however, discuss a contradiction between the two. In the context of negotiations, Pauline H.

have to make a choice of whether to focus on narrow objectives concerning war-related issues, or wider objectives of, for instance, justice, freedom, and democracy.

The issue of justice appears in different forms in peace negotiations. There is the issue of correcting historical injustices and claims of aggression. In international law, this is described as jus ad bellum: each party is likely to view its cause as "just," but probably on different grounds. In a negotiation this may lead to a focus on the importance of who started the war. Having such a responsibility acknowledged can be significant for one actor, while having one's historical record of grievances acknowledged can be significant to another actor. Thus, unilaterally apologizing for historical grievance can serve as a confidence-building measure, but it is rare that such issues can be mediated between the parties. Previous research suggests that shifting the parties' attention from history to the future is an important prerequisite for a productive outcome.[30]

A different dimension is the conduct of war itself—that is, jus in bello, which here refers to the responsibility for atrocities and human rights violations during

---

Baker elaborates two types of peacemakers focusing on peace and justice, respectively. The "conflict managers" are inclusive, builders of trust and relationships, who stress reconciliation as a primary goal of peace and do not attribute blame on any of the parties. Conversely, so-called democratizers come in with a long-term perspective and a focus on institutions and laws, stressing justice as the objective of peace and seeing it as nonnegotiable (Baker, "Conflict Resolution versus Democratic Governance: Divergent Paths to Peace?" in *Turbulent Peace: The Challenges of Managing International Conflict*, ed. Chester Crocker, Fen Osler Hampson and Pamela Aall [Washington, DC: United States Institute of Peace, 2001] 759–760). When it comes to post-conflict reconciliation processes, peace and justice are instead conceptualized as being on equal footing, with other elements such as trust and forgiveness. See Dean G. Pruitt and Sung Hee Kim, *Social Conflict: Escalation, Stalemate, and Settlement*, 3rd ed. (Boston: McGraw-Hill, 2004), 218–224. For John Paul Lederach, justice can be understood as (1) energies for accountability of those responsible for atrocities of war, (2) compensation for the negative effects of conflict, and (3) equality and fairness with regard to meeting basic human needs. See Lederach, *Building Peace: Sustainable Reconciliation in Divided Societies* (Washington, DC: United States Institute of Peace Press, 1997); *The Journey toward Reconciliation* (Scottdale, PA: Herald Press, 1999); and *The Moral Imagination: The Art and Soul of Building Peace* (Oxford: Oxford University Press, 2005). Similarly, peace includes two processes, concerning the end of violence and the creation of a new common ground for building new relationships. Differentiating between two ways to compensate, Donald W. Shriver argues that restorative justice (in which relationships are repaired and forgiveness is encouraged) will be more conducive to reconciliation than so-called retributive justice (finding appropriate punishments). See Shriver, *An Ethic for Enemies: Forgiveness in Politics* (New York: Oxford University Press, 1995), and Shriver, "Where and When in Political Life Is Justice Served by Forgivenss?" in *Burying the Past: Making Peace and Doing Justice after Civil Conflict*, ed. Nigel Biggar (Washington, DC: United States Institute of Peace Press, 2003). For similar research, see also Priscilla Hayner, *Unspeakable Truth: Confronting State Terror and Atrocity* (New York: Routledge, 2001), and James Meernik, "Justice and Peace? How the International Criminal Tribunal Affects Societal Peace in Bosnia," *Journal of Peace Research* 43, no. 2 (2005): 271–289. In the context of negotiations, recent laboratory research has found evidence for compensating and possibly even mutually enforcing effects of peace and justice elements. In particular, Jean Poitras finds that cooperation between conflict parties can be achieved when a mediator actively mitigates parties' indifference toward the process and when parties are encouraged to take their share of the responsibility for the conflict. In other words, supporting justice might in fact facilitate peace in the form of cooperation at the negotiation table. See Jean Poitras, "A Study of the Emergence of Cooperation in Mediation," *Negotiation Journal* 21, no. 2 (2005): 281–300.

30. See I. William Zartman, "Negotiating Forward- and Backward-Looking Outcomes," in *Peace versus Justice: Negotiating Forward-Looking and Backward-Looking Outcomes*.

the conflict. This dimension may also have to be handled by the international mediator and constitute part of a final settlement (e.g., in terms of dealing with war crimes and the return of prisoners of war).

In addition, we want point to a third dimension that is not normally referred to in international law—namely, the significance of international principles and how they are used in the mediation process and its mediated outcome. This may be called jus in deliberatione—that is, that the deliberations are pursued in ways the parties find just and correct.

There are few examples of mediators dealing with justice and the responsibility for war during the war itself. Often such issues are dealt with as parts of peace treaties, where victors want to make clear the responsibility of the vanquished. It becomes an element in peace negotiations directly between the parties. Thus, the Versailles Treaty after World War I had a special clause that acknowledged Germany's guilt for the war. Similarly, the United States' peace treaty with Japan signed in San Francisco in 1950 included an admission of guilt by Japan for its actions in World War II. The issue of responsibility is closely connected to reparations and associated costs after a war. Thus, it is an issue of power between the parties, and mediators may often not be invited.

In mediation of internal armed conflicts, the responsibility for one-sided violence by governments or nonstate actors alike has often been avoided through the granting of amnesty, the expulsion of leaders from the country, and other actions that do not confront the underlying search for justice and demands for compensation. Mediators may have contributed to such solutions, in the belief that achieving a narrow peace is preferable to prolonging the war through the quest for a wider peace.

Mediators have also had different foci in terms of how they handle the role of war crimes and human rights violations during the peace process. For example, President Carter has been criticized for being too flexible with oppressive leaders, offering them deals for concessions and indirectly legitimizing them, such as during his political and humanitarian mediation efforts in Haiti 1994. However, in other situations, he has insisted on the principles of human rights.[31] In the prenegotiation talks between Presidents Bashir and Museveni of Sudan and Uganda, respectively, mediated by Neu and Carter, a contentious issue involved the Aboke girls—more than one hundred young girls from the St. Mary's College boarding school in Aboke who had been abducted by the LRA. In order to reach an agreement between the two governments on the issue, "Carter referred to Sudan's relationship with [Joseph] Kony and reports of slavery in Sudan as

---

31. On this, Baker questions, "One may ask whether the net effect of Carter's intervention was to tilt Haiti toward democracy and peace at the cost of justice or to simply buy time." Baker, "Conflict Resolution versus Democratic Governance," 757.

'indefensible.'"[32] In this case, Carter was tough on principle and insisted the parties come to an agreement on this issue as well.

Other mediators have tended to focus on reaching peace and ending the fighting. For instance, Martin Griffiths, director of the Center for Humanitarian Dialogue in Geneva, found himself in a situation where the parties in the Aceh peace process refused to include stipulations on human rights. Today, regretting having allowed this, as the agreement partially derailed due to lack of future protection of human rights, Griffiths asserts having had few options in light of the threat of escalated fighting.[33] In the final outcome of the Sant'Egidio mediation in the Mozambique peace process, there were few stipulations concerning truth or justice. The Northern Ireland peace process, mediated by George Mitchell, included de facto amnesty for almost all Irish Republican Army (IRA) and Protestant Loyalist killers and did not mention truth or recognition of victims.[34]

Here we would like to draw attention to the justice focus in the mediation process itself, jus in deliberatione.[35] The key principles for international mediators are, of course, the principles anchored in international law. Mediators, however, may vary in their reliance on principles: they may interpret the principles more strictly and apply them accordingly or they may use them in a more pragmatic or strategic manner.

Though peace and justice can appear to be contradictory and competing, this is—as the above cases reflect—the result of different time horizons or a focus on different dimensions. If the immediate ending of violence is at the forefront of a mediation effort, issues of justice may be pushed into the background. If, on the other hand, sustainable solutions are the primary focus, then go-betweens may create space for dealing with long-term issues of justice and reconciliation.

There is an evolution of international norms over time. Granting amnesty to perpetrators of violence was seen as acceptable earlier, but is now questioned. The concern for transitional justice in intrastate peace-building processes has increased. This has implications for the focus of international mediation. Today there are higher expectations for mediation efforts and outcomes to be clearly embedded in a human rights framework than was the case in the 1980s.

---

32. See Neu, "Restoring Relations between Uganda and Sudan."

33. See Martin, *Kings of Peace, Pawns of War.*

34. See Hume, *Ending Mozambique's War,* and the final peace agreements for Mozambique ("The General Peace Agreement for Mozambique") and Northern Ireland ("Northern Ireland Peace Agreement") signed in 1992 and 1998, respectively.

35. Another important aspect of justice is the "procedural justice," relating to how parties are treated during negotiations. For more on this, see, for instance, Cecilia Albin, "Peace versus Justice—and Beyond," *The Sage Handbook of Conflict Resolution,* ed. Bercovitch, Zartman, and Kremenyuk, 580–594.

Mandates and Style

The origins of a mandate and the specific goal it gives the mediator will affect the style of mediation in three particular ways.

First, the mandate stipulates what the mediator should do. It sets boundaries for the mediator's freedom of movement. It directly affects the style of the mediator. For instance, when mediation is mandated from the international setting, the style can generally be expected to be carried out in a public mode. Intervention through a mediator is a form of signaling from the international community to the conflicting parties. By contrast, when the mandate originates from within the conflicts and crises themselves, the international mediator may have more reasons to act in a confidential mode.

Second, the mandate is intimately related to the question of resources. Resources are necessary for the mediator to fulfill the mandate. The resources available to the mediator will be dependent on the mandate. Short interventions aimed at specific tasks can be expected to require more limited resources than full-fledged negotiations on basic political incompatibilities. This will affect the style of the mediator, although in a more indirect way. However, the mandating agency does not always supply the resources necessary for the go-between. There can be a discrepancy between mandates and resources.

Third, the mandate is affected by the phase of the conflict. Thus, the precise goal also has implications for the style. A mediator needs to attune the style of mediation to the situation on the ground and the relationships between the antagonists. If the purpose is to implement an agreement, then the parties that have accepted the agreement may determine the scope. If, instead, the purpose is to initiate a peace process, then the scope might be more inclusive. Similar reasoning can be applied to the question of the mediator's method. If the purpose were to invite the parties into a process of political dialogue, then a fostering style of mediation would be the primary choice. If the purpose were related to ending the fighting through negotiations, there could be more room for pressuring the parties through a forcing style, for instance, that used timing in a deliberate way.

Here we have pointed to some ways through which mandates shape the style of mediation. We will return to this general discussion in the concluding chapter. Before that, we will need to carry out a specific and empirical exploration. In the following chapters, we will analyze the experiences of Jan Eliasson in the five components of a mediation process: the entry of the international mediator, the diagnostics to prepare for mediation, the instruments used in negotiations, the ways of handling coordination and competition during the process, and the termination of a mediation effort.

This will give us an understanding of the complexities of mediation and assist in generating new ideas on mediation style and research.

3
Going In: The Diplomacy of Entry

The start of mediation is a success in itself. There is often considerable diplomatic work before a mediator can enter a particular situation. Accepting international mediation may be seen as a concession by one side. There may be considerable wrangling on what a mediator is allowed to do, the resources mediation will have, and who is going to be recruited for the assignment. Thus, not all conflicts have international mediators. From a peace perspective, the entry of a mediator on the scene is a hopeful sign that a war may soon be ended. However, obstruction by one party is enough to keep a mission from getting anywhere close to actually ending a war.

The way a mediator enters a conflict colors the perceptions of the mediation effort and shapes his or her scope of action. The mandate of mediation is crucial for understanding the style of mediation. Thus, we start with an empirical analysis of mediation mandates. This leads to an analysis of the reasons for parties to request mediation as well as for third parties to offer mediation.[1] This, in short, is the diplomacy of entering a mediation role. The issues are general, and we will illustrate them with Jan Eliasson's six missions.

Giving the Mandate

Mediation requires a mandate and may, consequently, be initiated and constructed in different ways. At the outset, it may be a request from the parties themselves, or stem from other actors in the conflict setting. It can also be an offer of mediation from concerned outside actors, such as an international organization. In such a case the mediation initiative comes "from above" or "from the outside"—that is, from the third-party actor who seeks to mediate.

The experiences of Jan Eliasson point to an important difference in this regard: his mediation efforts involve four instances where the purpose was to end

---

1. The acceptance of mediation has two dimensions: the third parties and the primary parties. In other words, the *offer* of mediation regards the supply side of international mediation, whereas the *request* of mediation concerns the demand side.

a war with an agreed-upon political arrangement (what we term political mediation) and two cases of humanitarian mediation to alleviate human suffering as a consequence of conflict. The latter clearly stemmed from international institutions that were worried about the conflicts' humanitarian implications. The political interventions were initiated by requests from the warring parties or other actors concerned with the conflict as such.

In the case of Burma/Myanmar, the call for international mediation came from one of the parties to an interstate dispute that followed a humanitarian crisis. Burma, renamed Myanmar in 1989 by the military regime, is a country where about two thirds of the population belongs to the Burman ethnic group. There are numerous ethnic minorities, primarily occupying border areas. This crisis concerned a group of some 250,000 ethnic Rohingya, whom the Burmese regime had decided to expel from northern Burma/Myanmar. The Rohingya are Muslims (as is the majority in Bangladesh), unlike the Buddhist majority of Burma. The Burmese authorities accused the Rohingya of being illegal immigrants who were taking jobs and land that belonged to Burmese. The Buddhist-dominated Burmese government also perceived the Muslim minority as a potential opposition group. In February 1992, Eliasson, at that time UN under-secretary-general for humanitarian affairs, received worrying news on the situation from two different directions. Not only was there an emerging refugee crisis in Bangladesh, but the situation also risked turning into an interstate crisis between Bangladesh and Burma. As Eliasson describes,

> In February 1992, I received a pointed message from the government of Bangladesh. It said that the Burmese regime had intentionally pushed out 250,000 people belonging to the ethnic Rohingya group. This was confirmed by reports from the UNHCR [United Nations High Commissioner for Refugees]. The Burmese regime claimed that these were illegal immigrants from Bangladesh, but only a miniscule part of this population had arrived in the last years. The situation was alarming and the interstate tensions between Bangladesh and Burma were rapidly increasing due to the refugee issue. The government of Bangladesh called for outside intervention, asking the UN to act as a mediator in the conflict.

The Bangladeshi government contested the claim that this group constituted a threat. It also stated that the group's homeland was in Burma/Myanmar. As the Rohingya people were placed in refugee camps in Bangladesh, they became a burden for the country and, thus, the government requested third-party mediation to assist the civilians to return to their homes. Eliasson further recounts:

> To me this was a clear-cut case of humanitarian concern. As Sweden's permanent representative at the United Nations, I had developed good contacts with the Bangladeshi and Burmese UN ambassadors in New York, which I now used to get a first access to the parties. Before I eventually went off to Bangladesh, I met with the representatives from both sides at the UN headquarters in New York. This opened the doors to the intervention. It was also easier since it was a humanitarian mission.

Eliasson's other humanitarian mediation began when the Norwegian Church Aid, a Norwegian humanitarian nongovernmental organization (NGO) with local presence in Southern Sudan, issued an appeal to the United Nations in 1992. It pointed out that more than 200,000 civilians were stuck in inaccessible areas due to the fighting between the government in Khartoum and the Sudan People's Liberation Movement/Army (SPLM/A) in Southern Sudan. This large-scale armed conflict started in 1983 (and continued until the Comprehensive Peace Agreement in 2005), with the SPLM/A being based in the south. Under John Garang's leadership, the SPLM/A fought for regime change and territorial autonomy. At the time, the situation was alarming. Since humanitarian aid could not be brought to areas where these civilians were located, they were threatened with mass starvation. The Norwegian Church Aid requested third-party intervention to negotiate a cease-fire in order to allow humanitarian aid to get to the people in need. Eliasson, as an under-secretary general for the department of humanitarian affairs, was asked to mediate:

> The UN had a history in Sudan, since the civil war had made the humanitarian situation severe. Yet, the warning signal came not from the UN, but from the NGO community, which had presence on the ground in South Sudan. The rebel group SPLA welcomed UN action because it gave them international legitimacy and would help "their" people. The problem was to get the necessary agreement of the Sudanese government. My access was through the Sudanese UN ambassador in New York. I stressed the explicit humanitarian goal, which helped to get the acceptance for the UN to intervene.

In these two cases we can see that the initiative came from the local situation. There were first-hand observations. Clearly, there had been no meaningful direct talks on the Rohingya refugee issue, thus Bangladesh's turning to the United Nations became a natural course. Similarly, the aid organization in Sudan saw no alternative but to go to the United Nations, as the primary parties obviously were too involved in warfare to listen to a humanitarian organization. In both cases Eliasson saw the need to act and initiated a series of measures of humanitarian diplomacy, primarily designed to ease the situation for the victims. In the Bangladesh-Burma/Myanmar case, his mediation led to the first high-level visit from Burma/Myanmar to Bangladesh, in April 1992. More was to follow.

These two experiences are different from Eliasson's other missions, which are instead examples of political mediation. The Palme mission during the Iran-Iraq War was initiated and mandated by the United Nations. On November 11, 1980, Secretary-General Kurt Waldheim announced that he was sending former Swedish prime minister Olof Palme—at the time, Sweden's Social Democrat opposition leader—to the region as his personal representative. Following a period of increased tensions between Iran and Iraq, Iraq under President Saddam Hussein had attacked Iran in September 1980, demanding a renegotiation of the 1975 bilateral border agreement. Iran had just gone through the revolution that eliminated the pro-West authoritarian regime under the Shah. It was replaced by a mass-based Islamic political movement, led by Ayatollah Khomeini. The new regime may also have been seen by Iraq as a threat, as it was based on the Shia Islam, to which the majority of Iraqis belong.

Palme's assignment was to "facilitate authoritative communication" through meetings with the leaderships in Tehran and Baghdad. The initiative came from the secretary-general, even though his decision was anchored in the Security Council. Six days earlier, the Security Council had welcomed the fact that Waldheim was considering sending a representative to the region "in order to facilitate authoritative communication with and between the governments concerned so that negotiations for peace could proceed on an urgent basis."[2] Although the wording was the same, the fact that it was the secretary-general and not the Security Council that sent Palme was important to Iran. Iran saw the Security Council as biased against Iran. Palme's mandate was to lay the ground for peace negotiations between the two sides. Palme was the leader and Eliasson was his close confidant. The team also consisted of UN staff members Diego Cordovez, Iqbal Riza, and others.

In 1988, warfare between Iran and Iraq ended by both sides accepting UN Security Council Resolution 598, which stipulated a process for terminating the conflict. Eliasson was then appointed personal representative, partly as an "homage á Palme," partly as he "knew the file" on the Iran-Iraq war.[3] His team included UN personnel, notably Giandomenico Picco, Paul Kavanagh, and Swedish diplomat Anders Lidén.

In the Nagorno-Karabakh conflict, it was not the United Nations but a regional interstate organization that mandated Eliasson's mediation efforts: the Conference for Security and Co-operation in Europe (CSCE), which in 1994 transformed into the Organization for Security and Co-operation in Europe. Although the conflict concerned a territory inside newly independent Azerbaijan, it had a strong interstate component. One of the primary parties to the conflict was the Karabakh Armenian minority, which was fighting for independence of an area that was primarily populated by Armenians. The other primary party was the Azeri government, which disputed the Armenian claims of independence and wanted to uphold the territorial integrity of the country. The conflict had historical roots, but had been suppressed during the time of the Soviet Union. After the Soviet collapse, the conflict escalated to war. Armenia supported the aspirations of the Karabakh Armenians, and after initial military difficulties, Karabakh Armenian forces, no doubt supported by Armenia, gained the upper hand in 1992–93. Azerbaijan regarded the conflict as involving foreign occupation by Armenia and considered it to be an interstate conflict.

---

2. See the letter of UN secretary-general Kurt Waldheim to the Security Council on November 11, 1980, in which he states the mandate and objective of the Palme mediation mission. "Letter Dated 11 November 1980 from the Secretary-General Addressed to the President of the Security Council," UN Security Council document S/14251, November 11, 1980.

3. From interviews with Picco and Kavanagh.

In 1992, Armenia and Azerbaijan became members of CSCE. Hence, the CSCE experienced an armed conflict between two of its members and therefore decided at its meeting in March 1992 to organize an international conference for a solution to the conflict—the Minsk Conference, named after the capital of Belarus, where it was to be convened. To this day, it has still not been held. Instead, a working group, known as the Minsk Group, was formed to do the groundwork for the conference. Eleven CSCE countries originally participated in the group and the chair of the group became a key actor in the mediation efforts.[4] When Sweden was elected president of the CSCE at the end of 1993, Swedish delegates, led by Jan Eliasson, took over the presidency of the Minsk Group and the Minsk Conference:

> *In November 1993, I announced that I was ending my position at the United Nations in February. I needed some time off and was planning for a sabbatical year, as a visiting professor in Uppsala. At that time I received the request to take up the chairmanship of the so-called Minsk Group, which was leading the mediation attempts in Nagorno-Karabakh. At first, I was skeptical—I do not believe that you can mediate in committees—but was later convinced, partly due to the possibility of also using the academic milieu in the mediation efforts.*

Eliasson's most recent mediation mission, the one in Darfur, is an example of a cooperative effort between a regional organization, the African Union (AU), and the United Nations. The conflict started in 2003 in the marginalized region of Darfur in western Sudan. Two rebel movements took up arms demanding change of the political system in Sudan. The conflict, and the actions by the government-aligned militia Jinjaweed, created one of the worst humanitarian disasters in recent years.

The basis for the mediation mandate was worked out in May 2006 during a joint meeting with the permanent members of the UN Security Council, the Sudanese government, other African countries, and the African Union.[5] An example of how one mediation initiative builds on previous efforts,[6] the Darfur Mission had a mandate to reenergize efforts for a political solution and build on what the African Union had done in the preceding years.[7]

---

4. On the mediation of the OSCE in Nagorno-Karabakh, see Rexane Dehdashti, "Nagorno-Karabakh: A Case Study of OSCE Conflict Settlement," in *The OSCE in the Maintenance of Peace and Security: Conflict Prevention, Crisis Management and the Peaceful Settlement of Disputes*, ed. Michael Boothe, Natalino Ronzitti, and Allan Rosas, 459–478 (The Hague, London, Boston: Kluwer Law International, 1997); Jan Eliasson, and Mathias Mossberg, "Nagorno-Karabach: Den Glömda Konflikten," *Internationella Studier* no. 2 (1998): 2–11; Richard K. Betts, "The Delusion of Impartial Intervention," in *Managing Global Chaos: Sources of and Responses to International Conflict*, ed. Chester Crocker, Fen Osler Hampson, and Pamela Aall (Washington, DC: United States Institute of Peace Press, 1996); and Svante E. Cornell, *The Nagorno-Karabakh Conflict* (Uppsala: Department of East European Studies, Uppsala University, 1999).

5. See the United Nations and African Union, "High Level Consultation on the Situation in Darfur, Conclusions," May 16, 2006.

6. On the matter of cumulative effects of international mediation, see Regan and Stam, "In the Nick of Time."

7. See the United Nations, Secretary-General, "Terms of Reference, Special Envoy of the Secretary-General for Darfur," January 29, 2007.

The distinction between a mediation request and a mediation offer is increasingly blurred. Mediation assignments may originate one way or the other. In reality, there seems to be a dialogue between the would-be third party and the primary parties. For a multilateral organization, there is always the option of independent action: it may appoint a special envoy at its own discretion. For such an envoy to be effective, however, a minimum level of acceptance by the primary parties is needed. Thus, we need to turn to the parties and analyze why they might endorse outside mediation.

Requesting Mediation

Acceptance by the belligerents is a key defining characteristic of mediation, since mediation in principle always is voluntary.[8] Third parties may exert some influence over the parties in order to get their acceptance. Belligerents may accept other mediators or accept mediation at times or under circumstances that they might not have preferred. Yet, by the end of the day, they will always have the possibility of ultimately blocking or accepting mediation in general. This also applies to the choice of a particular mediator.[9] There are, in effect, three main reasons for primary parties to request mediation.

The first reason for favoring mediation is the unacceptable cost associated with continued conflict.[10] When parties believe they can make progress on the battlefield, or think that the issues at stake are too high for any compromise, they are less likely to accept a third party. By contrast, when they believe that the way to their own victory and the defeat of their opponent will be long and bloody, or that there is great uncertainty whether they ever will reach this preferred outcome, they might be ready to accept a go-between. Also, the party that is weak

---

8.   There is literature on mediation selection where these issues are discussed. See John B. Stephens, "Acceptance of Mediation Initiatives: A Preliminary Framework," in *New Approaches to International Mediation*, ed. C.R. Mitchell and K. Webb (New York: Greenwood Press, 1988); Saadia Touval, "Gaining Entry to Mediation in Communal Strife," in *The Internationalization of Communal Strife*, ed. Manus I. Midlarsky (London and New York: Routledge, 1993); Greig, "Stepping into the Fray"; Kyle Beardsley, "Politics by Means Other than War: Understanding International Mediation" (dissertation, University of California–San Diego, 2006); and Greig and Regan, "When Do They Say Yes?"

9.   On mutual acceptance as a key characteristic of mediation, see, for instance, Saadia Touval and I.W. Zartman, "International Mediation in the Post-Cold War Era," in *Turbulent Peace: The Challenges of Managing International Conflict*, ed. Chester Crocker, Fen Osler Hampson, and Pamela Aall, 427–443 (Washington, DC: United States Institute of Peace Press, 2001); and Jacob Bercovitch, "Introduction: Putting Mediation in Context," in *Studies in International Mediation: Essays in Honor of Jeffrey Z. Rubin*, ed. Jacob Bercovitch (New York: Palgrave Macmillan, 2002).

10.   An aspect of this factor is the mutually hurting stalemate, as a condition for accepting mediation; see I. William Zartman, "Dynamics and Constraints in Negotiations in Internal Conflicts," in *Elusive Peace: Negotiating an End to Civil Wars*, ed. I. William Zartman, 3–29 (Washington, DC: Brookings Institution, 1995), and Zartman, "The Timing of Peace Initiatives." Greig finds that elapsed time of enduring interstate rivalries, as an indication of stalemate of conflicts, increases the likelihood of rivals to request mediation, but has no significant effect on the likelihood of a third-party offer of mediation. Greig, "Stepping into the Fray."

may be in greater need of international mediation to improve its position. For instance, we can see that Iran clearly was more positive to international mediators than Iraq, as long as they came from the secretary-general rather than the Security Council.

A second reason for accepting third-party efforts has to do with the primary parties' inability to deal with the conflict. In situations of internal armed conflict, international mediation is particularly sensitive since it may infringe on national sovereignty. In general, parties in internal armed conflict will not request third-party mediation if they can deal with the conflict with their own resources. In particular, governments will be reluctant to accept third-party involvement in conflicts with nonstate actors.[11] The go-between will have to be sensitive to this. The public profile of the international mediator may increase image costs for the government associated with mediation. Also, the multilateral setting may function to "internationalize" the conflict by drawing attention to the conflict situation. For the rebel side, this may be an advantage and even support its desire for recognition. For the government side, however, this may be particularly sensitive. Hence, the go-between will be accepted into situations where the parties (primarily the government) think that they do not have an alternative to accepting mediation, because their own efforts to settle the conflict have clearly failed.

A third factor has to do with trust. A trustworthy and respectful relationship is an important factor for the belligerents' acceptance of the go-between. A third party who is not respected by them will have little chance of successfully resolving a conflict through mediation. The United Nations had problems mediating in the Iran-Iraq War as it had lost credibility in the eyes of the Iranian side. To Iran, the Security Council had failed to condemn the Iraq military intervention (as aggression). The distinction between the Security Council and the secretary-general was necessary for Iranian acceptance of UN mediation in 1980. The Palme mission stressed this distinction.[12] This in fact goes back to the so-called Peking formula, first applied by Dag Hammarskjöld when meeting the Chinese leadership in Peking in 1955. At that time the People's Republic of China was not a member of the United Nations and particularly not of the Security Council. Thus, it was skeptical about the organization. It could, however, relate to the secretary-general, who had his own independent position within the UN system.

---

11. On the problem that external mediation may confer legitimacy or a degree of recognition to the rebels, see C.R. Mitchell, "External Peace-Making Initiatives and Intra-National Conflict," in *The Internationalization of Communal Strife*, ed. Manus I. Midlarsky, 274–296 (London and New York: Routledge, 1993), and Touval, "Gaining Entry to Mediation in Communal Strife." This also implies that it can be in the interests of the rebel side to seek third-party mediation, whereas it will be in the interest of the government side to reject it. See Touval, "Gaining Entry to Mediation in Communal Strife," 266.

12. More on the importance of upholding the distinction between the Security Council and the secretary-general, see Giandomenico Picco, "The U.N. and the Use of Force: Leave the Secretary-General Out of It," *Foreign Affairs* 73, no. 5 (1994): 14–18.

Eliasson further points to the early actions of the mediation team in overcoming Iranian perceptions:

> *In Iran-Iraq, we gained the confidence of the Iranians by establishing the principle of nonacquisition of territory by force. This was risky but fair.*

In fact, the Palme mission spent considerable time establishing the principles for a solution, making sure they would be in line with international law. Other principles concerned nonintervention in internal affairs, as Iraq claimed that Iran was exporting revolution and fomenting unrest in Iraq. Principles of free navigation also featured in the mission's internal deliberations.

It is likely that the belligerents will relate to the person who is suggested for the mission. Palme was well regarded by both sides as a champion of third world causes, particularly by the revolutionaries in the newly established Islamic Republic of Iran. In Iraq, he was acceptable as an outstanding international personality. Thus, the two sides quickly agreed to this suggestion. In 1988, when Eliasson's name was brought forward, he could be seen as Palme's heir and thus was easily supported by the parties. Eliasson's international reputation was later enhanced by his position as UN under-secretary-general for humanitarian affairs. In a way, the Palme mission became formative and helped to create momentum for one particular mediator. It is likely to be a pattern for other international mediators.

In general, the primary parties are less likely to turn down an envoy coming from an organization of which they themselves are members or aspiring to belong to. Such an envoy provides recognition to a state or even to a nonstate actor. Also, international organizations build on particular normative and legal principles, which may appeal to the parties as a foundation for a settlement. However, there may be a difference in the willingness of the parties to accept mediation. The party that perceives itself to be in an inferior position militarily or politically may be more open to the idea of mediation.

Offering Mediation

Why would someone take on the task of mediation? To be involved in alleviating human suffering under difficult circumstances or interjecting oneself between fighting actors is obviously going to be demanding. For the international mediator, the acceptance and even the respect of the parties is a prerequisite for entry into a conflict. But this factor is not enough to explain why multilateral mediators choose to involve themselves.

Mediation does not occur in every conflict situation. Mediation tends to take place at particular moments in time. Yet, mediators are not by any means randomly distributed across conflict situations around the world. On the contrary, the allocation of willing mediators is highly asymmetrical. Some types of conflicts attract more mediators than others. There is a discussion in the literature whether international mediation is chosen for particularly difficult conflicts (the "hard" cases), or for situations where the belligerents are already willing to settle their conflict (the "easy" cases). International mediation can also be a function of other factors, such as the closeness of a conflict to the centers of the politically relevant actors, or the generated costs of a conflict in terms of refugees and risk of regional escalation.

The timing of mediation depends on many circumstances, but three factors stand out: (1) the interest of the mediator, (2) the cost of the conflict, and (3) the potential success of an effort, including third-party leverage.[13]

The first factor, the "interest" of the mediator, is not necessarily restricted to material interests; it could also refer to issues such as reputation (for the mediator or for the sending organization) and to aspirations that may serve to justify the organization. The mediation initiative demonstrates relevance and significance. Given that the different organizations have to prove themselves useful to their members, they have an incentive to engage in mediation efforts. This was a rationale behind the CSCE's Nagorno-Karabakh mission. The failure of the CSCE to be effective in the preceding armed conflict in Bosnia increased the pressure on the body to prove itself a valuable actor in European conflict resolution.[14] By the end of the Cold War, the CSCE (and later the OSCE) was searching for a distinct role as a European interstate body. The Nagorno-Karabakh intervention was a test case and was perceived as a way of demonstrating relevance. Sweden saw this as important and wanted to give the organization a role, notably vis-à-vis other interested actors, such as Russia.[15] Eliasson explains:

> To me it is obvious that OSCE needed to enhance its status in conflict resolution. The organization had done very little in the wars in the former Yugoslavia. Now it had the opportunity to show that it was a relevant actor in this field.

The second factor that explains the timing of a mediation initiative, the "costs of conflict," refers to the recognition that as costs and risks of a conflict mount, the pressure to take action increases. Refugee flows, civilian suffering, the cost for rebuilding destroyed societies, regional tensions, the risk of conflict diffusion and outside intervention—all these aspects create incentives for third parties to act. This is particularly true for organizations that have peace and interstate cooperation as their responsibility. The Darfur case illustrates this point. After a long period of silence and passivity, the public conscience

---

13. For a discussion of "mediation readiness," in terms of operational, strategic, and relationship building, see Crocker, Hampson, and Aall, "Ready for Prime Time."

14. From an interview with Jan Eliasson in Stockholm, 2008.

15. This has been confirmed in an interview with Mossberg. Sweden was indeed motivated by being able to contribute to strengthening the CSCE, which was at the time challenged by the unstable Balkans.

woke up with large-scale public campaigns for ending the suffering of the civilian population. The humanitarian costs of the conflict contributed to increased attention. When Eliasson explains why he was willing to accept mediating in the Darfur conflict, he points to the grave humanitarian situation:

> *I had stuck my neck out on the issue of Darfur in my speech as president of the UN General Assembly. I had publicly talked about the disgrace of the international community for neglecting the Darfur conflict. Then Kofi [Annan] called me in early December 2006 and said, "Jan, I know you are deeply engaged in Darfur." He knew which strings to pull. At that stage, I could not refuse to accept to act as a mediator, although I knew from the beginning that this probably was a "mission impossible."*

A third factor related to the timing of mediation, the likelihood of "success," refers to how mediators, before taking on a suggested assignment, will assess the chances of contributing positively to conflict dynamics, particularly given that a lack of success may be perceived as humiliating.[16] This judgment includes both a survey of the resources available as well as an initial assessment of the willingness of the parties to make an agreement.[17] Further, the go-between is likely to consider whether there are positive developments or trends in the conflict at the time of engagement. The support of the key actors in the multilateral system is thus significant. Eliasson describes this when speaking of a proposed follow-up Nagorno-Karabakh mission:

> *Later on, the Azeris approached me to explore the possibility for me to reenter as a mediator in the Nagorno-Karabakh conflict. Since that implied that I would open up a parallel process to the contemporary official negotiations led by Russia, the U.S., and France (the Minsk Group at the time), I did not think it was realistic.*

To this it should be noted that the resources for mediation are often limited. A multilateral mediator will be able to draw on the secretariat of the organization (be it the United Nations, OSCE, or African Union), but the material and staff resources are generally strained. In fact, in all of his political mediation efforts, Eliasson has had to rely on the additional support of the Swedish Ministry for Foreign Affairs. It was only in 2007 that a Mediation Support Office was set up within the United Nations. Seldom have the mediators had offices on the ground constantly monitoring developments. This, of course, is likely to be a consideration for the mediator when taking on the assignment.

---

16. There is a debate in previous research whether mediators intervene in the most difficult (see Regan and Stam, "In the Nick of Time," 240; Jacob Bercovitch and Richard Jackson, "Negotiation or Mediation? An Exploration of Factors Affecting the Choice of Conflict Management in International Conflict," *Negotiation Journal* 17, no. 1 [2001]: 59–77; Scott Sigmund Gartner, Molly M. Melin, and Jacob Bercovitch, "The Opposing Effects of Mediation on Conflict Settlement and Durability" [prepared for the American Political Science Association 2004 Annual Meeting, Chicago, Illinois, 2004]), or the least difficult conflict situations (see Betts, "The Delusion of Impartial Intervention"; Kyle Beardsley, "Not All Mediators Are Created Equal: Choosing Who Mediates" [prepared for the 2005 Annual Meeting of the American Political Science Association, Washington, DC, September 1–4, 2005]; Greig, "Stepping into the Fray").

17. See, for instance, Smith and Smock, *Managing a Mediation Process*.

The third parties' interests, their perceptions of the costs of conflict, and the chances of success can vary over the dynamics of the conflict. In general, mediators will offer to mediate when it is perceived to be in their interest, when the costs of conflicts are high, and when the potential mediators have the greatest possibility to influence the parties. However, these factors should be seen as balancing one another. For instance, the international mediator with a perceived low probability of success may still decide to intervene if the potential mediator believes that mediation will be good for him or her and the sending organization, such as by demonstrating international concern.

Style and the Diplomacy of Entry

Whether the international mediator enters the conflict by a mandate from the parties or from an international body affects the style of the mediator. There is an important difference between humanitarian and political mediation in this regard. In the case of Eliasson, humanitarian action often was initiated from an NGO or a government, while political mediation stemmed from international bodies. Eliasson's style has varied between an inclusive and a more exclusive scope depending on the mandate of the mission. The origins of the mandates for his political mediation efforts have been multilateral, deriving from the international system. Having a multilateral mandate also means that the mediation effort is anchored in the wider international community. Whereas some mediators may focus on the primary parties only, Eliasson has taken a broader, more multilayered approach that includes regional actors, great powers, and the wider civil society, some of them being significant secondary parties to the conflict.

To some extent, the public mode of his mediation is a continuation of the multilateral setting and aims at drawing the attention of the international community to the conflict. In this sense, a multilateral mandate has created room for a more inclusive scope. For Eliasson, it has been logical to address different levels since their mandates are derived from the international setting.

By contrast, the origins of the mandates for his humanitarian mediation efforts have come from the conflict parties or the conflict setting. In these cases, the scope of Eliasson's mediation efforts have been more exclusive, focusing primarily on the two parties in conflict, not bringing in wider sectors of the international or local communities.

Closely connected to the origin of the mandate is also the operational definition of the mandate: what specifically is a mediator mandated to do in a particular conflict? For Eliasson this had important ramifications for his style. For instance, humanitarian mediation in Sudan and Burma/Myanmar-Bangladesh had the focus of "wide" peace, including respect for human rights and international law, since it commonly aimed at lessening humanitarian suffering of civilians. On the other hand, the political mediation missions in Iran-Iraq, Nagorno-Karabakh, and Darfur were more directed to a "narrow peace,"—to end the violent phase of the conflict without necessarily at that stage addressing human rights issues or the application of newer principles of international law.

It is also interesting to note that the general mandate and the purpose of mediation often does leave it to the mediator to choose the methods for his or her mediation. For instance, the mandate seldom specifies whether there should be a comprehensive or step-by-step approach. Nor does it say whether the mediator is expected to be fostering or forcing in his or her approach to the parties. Mandates give a lot of choice to the mediator. Let us now see how this space can be used.

4

Going About:
The Diagnostics of Diplomacy

O nce international mediators enter the scene of crises and conflicts, they need to prepare. The mediator will need to diagnose the situation to get a proper picture of what is possible. This is not simply a matter of practical preparation but also a way to set the stage for direct negotiations. It lays the groundwork and prepares both the parties and the mediator for the continuation of the process. It is imperative for the mediator to study the parties, their interests, and the issues and to assess whether there is a real possibility to advance toward a negotiated settlement. It might also be possible to use the entry moment itself to make progress toward peace.

Assessing the Initial Situation

Once a mediator has decided to intervene in a conflict and been accepted by the parties, a first need is to assess the possibility of opening direct and productive negotiations. Much of what the mediator does, as we will explain shortly, is to lay the ground for negotiations. Elements such as prenegotiations, shuttle diplomacy, and internal analysis of the parties' demands are all efforts to build a foundation for fruitful and direct negotiations. Therefore, the mediator needs to know the right time to initiate—or at least try to initiate—negotiations.

In international mediation, the issue of timing is of central importance: at what point are the parties ready to discuss solutions or processes for managing conflict? Eliasson emphasizes this very strongly:

> In my view, timing is absolutely crucial and central to the art of mediation. It is about the momentum toward a settlement and when to take steps toward peace. The mediator needs to take the temperature of the situation. Are the parties receptive? Is the environment conducive to a settlement? Are the internal relationships within the parties ripe for resolution? Are their allies on board? These are critical questions for any mediator and need to be seriously taken into account in order to determine when to take different steps.

There is a useful concept in the mediation literature—ripeness—which captures the notion that there are certain points or phases when the parties are open for "real" negotiations. What constitutes a ripe moment for conflict resolution is debated.[1] It is common to point to three basic elements. First, there must be a mutually hurting stalemate, a situation where the parties are locked in a painful and costly situation from which they cannot escape with unilateral strategies. The mutually hurting stalemate is about the perception of the parties: they realize that they cannot escape the situation without talking to the other side; thus, they will be willing to seek options beyond the battlefield. Second, there must be a perception of a "way out," or a "mutually enticing opportunity."[2] And third, valid spokespersons must be available on each side—that is, persons with whom the conflicting parties can talk.[3]

Expanding on these three basic elements, we submit that a conflict is ripe for negotiation (and for a peace agreement) when there is also readiness on three different levels—that is, among the primary parties, regional actors, and the international community.[4] Addressing these different levels is natural for the go-between, who is not merely focused on the conflicting parties themselves. Hence, for international mediation to have a chance to succeed in serious political negotiations, these levels have to be ripe simultaneously. Such an assessment can be made at the outset of the mission. Let us illustrate this from Eliasson's cases.

The Primary Parties (Governments and Nonstate Actors)

The primary parties form the basic level that needs to be ripe for negotiations to start—in particular, their internal cohesion. It applies also to intrastate conflicts. The requirement for a meaningful settlement process to be initiated is that there is political will on the government side. This depends on the cost and benefit calculus of the government. When the battle costs are rising and the possibilities for advancement utilizing military means are decreasing, governments

---

1. Several researchers have contributed to the "ripeness" discussion. See Richard Haass, "Ripeness and the Settlement of International Disputes," *Survival* 30 (1988): 232–251; Marieke Kleiboer, "Ripeness of Conflict: A Fruitful Notion?" *Journal of Peace Research* 31, no. 1 (1994): 109–116; Zartman, "Dynamics and Constraints in Negotiations in Internal Conflicts"; I.W. Zartman, "Ripeness: The Hurting Stalemate and Beyond," in *International Conflict Resolution after the Cold War*, ed. Daniel Druckman and Paul C. Stern, 225–250 (Washington, DC: National Academy Press, 2000); Khadiagala and Lyons, *Conflict Management and African Politics*.

2. On mutually enticing opportunities, see Thomas Ohlson, "Power Politics and Peace Policies: Intra-State Conflict Resolution in Southern Africa" (Department of Peace and Conflict Research, Uppsala University, Sweden, 1998), and I.W. Zartman, "MEOs and Durable Settlements: A Theoretical and Empirical Evaluation of the Reasons for Durability of Peaceful Settlements in Civil Wars" (paper presented at the annual meeting of the American Political Science Association, Chicago, IL, September 2, 2004).

3. Zartman has changed his definition (2000) and does not include this element any longer in his definition of ripeness (Zartman 2003). See Zartman, "Ripeness: The Hurting Stalemate and Beyond," and Zartman, "The Timing of Peace Initiatives."

4. Note that Stedman includes patrons—they need to perceive the mutually hurting stalemate. See John Stephen Stedman, "Conflict and Conflict Resolution in Africa: A Conceptual Framework," in *Conflict Resolution in Africa*, ed. I.W. Zartman and Francis M. Deng (Washington, DC: Brookings Institution, 1991).

are more inclined to try the negotiation option. Hence, the political will of the government is dependent on the dynamics on the battlefield.

One important aspect of building momentum is to identify and instill a sense of urgency into the conflict resolution process.[5] The cease-fire agreement in Nagorno-Karabakh in 1994 was reached through Russian mediation, with the Swedish CSCE team providing some of the footwork.[6] This agreement was basically made possible because the cost from the battlefield was unbearable for the Azeri side.[7] Azerbaijan experienced substantial battle losses in the spring of 1994, enabling the peace initiative. This illustrates a dilemma for the go-be-tweens. On the one hand, there is a humanitarian imperative to rapidly end the fighting. On the other hand, substantial political negotiations on the core issues of the status of Nagorno-Karabakh might have been more successful if they had taken place within the context of high-intensity fighting and deadlock. The cease-fire took away one of the incentives for the parties to resolve the conflict. The conflict froze—that is, the fighting stopped—but the basic incompatibility remained unresolved. In the months following the cease-fire agreement, Elias-son and his team tried to generate new political movement and to persuade them to develop strong "links" between the different steps of the process. This turned out to be difficult.

The political will of the government is also contingent upon its internal co-hesion. When strong internal factions do not question moves toward accommo-dation, the possibilities for negotiations increase. Thus, the intraparty situation may affect the political willingness to seek a negotiated peace.

In Darfur, some government actors in Khartoum thought for a long time that a military solution was possible. Even though the government said publicly that it believed in a political solution, several governmental and military factions put their faith in a military outcome, and thus the government accepted the UN-AU mediation team without enthusiasm. One of the main reasons for this was a perceived increased international consensus on the need to settle the conflict. During that period, Khartoum was not able to effectively play the different ac-tors in the international community against one another.

Such internal divisions were not a problem with respect to Azerbaijan. At the time Eliasson undertook his assignment, the government showed a desire to seek a negotiated solution. President Heydar Aliyev held a firm grip on power.

---

5. For more on timing in conflict resolution processes, see Zartman, *Ripe for Resolution: Conflict and Intervention in Africa*; Zartman, "Ripeness: The Hurting Stalemate and Beyond"; Zartman, "The Timing of Peace Initiatives: Hurting Stalemates and Ripe Moments"; and I. William Zartman and Guy Olivier Faure, eds., *Escalation and Negotiation in International Conflicts* (Cambridge: Cambridge University Press, 2005).

6. Details on the Nagorno-Karabakh conflicts come from interviews with Mossberg, as well as the writ-ings of Cornell, *The Nagorno-Karabakh Conflict*, and Elizabeth Fuller, "The Karabakh Mediation Process: Grachev versus the OSCE?" *RFE/RL Research Report* 3, no. 23 (1994): 13–17.

7. See Moorad Mooradian and Daniel Druckman, "Hurting Stalemate or Mediation? The Conflict over Nagorno-Karabakh, 1990–95," *Journal of Peace Research* 36, no. 6 (1999): 709–727.

Hence, there was little room for internal divisions. Eliasson summarizes the situation as one where both sides were willing to negotiate:

> *When I assessed the situation in 1994, the Nagorno-Karabakh leaders had achieved their goals to win territory and clear the territory of the Azeri population. They were basically satisfied with the situation on the ground. At the same time, the Azeri government realized that it did not have the capacity to win militarily. Both sides were therefore ready for negotiations on a cease-fire.*

A similarly difficult and contentious issue is who will represent the nonstate actors fighting against the government.[8] The problem is that the rebel side is not always unified and does not necessarily have representatives with clear authority. In conflicts with ethnic components, this can be further complicated by traditional connections or rivalries.

In Nagorno-Karabakh, the nonstate actor—the Karabakh Armenians—was coherent and disciplined. This enabled it to agree and adhere to the cease-fire agreement reached in 1994. However, getting to the cease-fire was a long process. Many conflicts never reach the first stage of starting negotiations. In fact, both in Darfur and in Nagorno-Karabakh, Eliasson was involved in shuttle diplomacy but never got the chance to lead direct negotiations between the parties. For the go-between, there is a great achievement just to get the parties to the table. As Eliasson recalls from his experience in the Iran-Iraq conflict,

> *In August 1988, when we sat down for negotiations, I had a tremendous sense of "FINALLY!" When you get them to the table—then you have won a half victory. We had been working for this since November 1980.*

Regional Actors

The regional context forms the second level that needs to be ripe for negotiations to start. Internal armed conflicts commonly have important regional linkages.[9] In many internal conflicts, internal actors have close connections to governments of an outside state. Furthermore, interstate conflicts do not occur in a vacuum, the neighborhoods are affected by and affect the dynamics of the conflict. Conflicts breed on other conflicts and interstate tensions. The primary parties need their neighbors for arms deliveries and secure trade routes, for building their own international prestige and reputation, and for possible political support. Primary parties need secondary parties. Therefore, protracted conflicts will not be fruitfully negotiated unless there is a movement also on the regional level.

In Sudan, the regional context is particularly problematic. The historical legacy of colonization, not least the borders of the 1884–85 Berlin conference, means that the region's borders do not reflect ethnic lines. Chad and Libya are both

---

8. This is related to what Zartman calls the "valid spokesperson." Zartman, "Dynamics and Constraints in Negotiations in Internal Conflicts," 10.

9. See Lotta Harbom and Peter Wallensteen, "Armed Conflict and Its International Dimensions, 1946–2004," *Journal of Peace Research* 42, no. 5 (2005): 623–635.

important regional actors for a settlement to work. Several of the tribes that are in Darfur also live in Chad. Eliasson explains:

> *I have repeatedly said that there could be no solution to the Darfur conflict in Sudan unless there is also a normalization of the relationship between Chad and Sudan. Intrastate and interstate tensions breed on each other.*

In the Nagorno-Karabakh case, one of the main mediators—the Russian Federation—was also the most influential and important neighbor. Hence, the regional context was problematic: Russia could obstruct any multilateral political negotiation process. Although the CSCE/OSCE tried actively to develop a comprehensive negotiation process, the Russians were keen on having their own negotiation track. Eliasson explains:

> *When I, as representative of Sweden in the Minsk Group, took over the mediation efforts in Nagorno-Karabakh, there was an emphasis on the importance of including Russia in the mediation efforts. There could be no sustainable solution without the Russians on board. However, the Russians tried to monopolize the mediation efforts, and they were afraid of losing control over what they saw as their backyard.*

In addition, other regional actors were crucial to work with in order to pave the way for political talks, primarily Turkey and Iran. Armenia saw itself as a secondary actor, although Azerbaijan perceived Armenia as a primary actor. Armenia was essential in order to move forward. It was necessary to anchor the mediation efforts in Yerevan as well as Stepanakert in Nagorno-Karabakh.

In the Iran-Iraq War, the Arab world both actively and passively stood behind Iraq. Iran was perceived as the most expansive power in the region, intent on trying to export its revolution. Saudi Arabia, with a Shia minority, was frightened by such prospects. Thus, in the Iran-Iraq War, neighborhood actors played supporting roles but not third-party roles. Iran was isolated, which may have contributed to its intransigence. Although there was a risk that the conflict would spread, it was basically kept to the two main antagonists.[10] The Arab world supported the appointments of both Palme and Eliasson. At the outset, however, it seemed clear that the Arab world was not necessarily going to be helpful until Iran was weakened.

Thus, in all of Eliasson's political mediations, the regional context caused considerable concern.

The International Community

The third level that needs to be ripe for negotiations is the international community and, in particular, the UN Security Council. The international community must be united in its will to settle the conflict, and in basic agreement on what this settlement process should look like. For instance, there are limits to the United Nations if the Security Council is not in agreement with what to do.

---

10. In the final deliberation for the implementation of the cease-fire, Saudi Arabia actually played a significant role. Picco, "The U.N. and the Use of Force."

Perceived national interests of the five permanent member states (P5) may be at stake in some conflicts.

From the onset of the conflict in Sudan, this was problematic. To China, the conflict in Sudan was a matter for the Sudanese government, and the international community was not to interfere in Sudan's internal affairs. Russia shared that position. Although neither used its veto against peacekeeping efforts, both Russia and China did delay agreement in the Security Council on how to proceed. The Western powers regarded the conflict as humanitarian and highly international, not only as an internal Sudanese issue. Eliasson comments,

> *The lack of unity and political will in the Security Council was one of the major obstacles for a settlement at the outset of our mission to the conflict in Darfur. It was not until the Security Council agreed on Resolution 1769 in 2007 that the situation became ripe for serious negotiations to settle the conflict.*

In the Iran-Iraq War, the Security Council was united but biased toward Iraq; thus, it was not seen by Iran as credible for finding a settlement. As we have seen, this created problems for the mediator and reduced the chances for successful negotiations between the two countries. It was not until the council had passed a more balanced resolution (UNSCR 598) in 1987 that a foundation was formed for direct talks through the United Nations. The mediators had to distance themselves from the earlier Security Council resolutions, with Palme explaining to Iran that he was appointed by the secretary-general and not by the council, which in fact did not act until convened by Secretary-General Kurt Waldheim.[11] Waldheim and Palme could then build on Articles 99 and 100 in the UN Charter. Eliasson recalls,

> *One of the main obstacles to a solution to a conflict in Iran-Iraq was a lack of international political will—an international sense of urgency—in settling the conflict. I can still feel disappointment over the passive approach of the Security Council, not the least in light of Iraq's brutal use of chemical weapons—a shameful practice that members of our mediation team tried to bring to the world's attention.*

During the Nagorno-Karabakh conflict, the Security Council passed a number of resolutions, but left mediation in the hands of the CSCE/OSCE. Yet, in practice, there was an implicit tension between Russia and the United States, as this regional conflict was interwoven with global power politics and national interests. Hence, the United States, which backed the OSCE initiative, and Russia worked in different directions. For the United States, it was important that the mediation efforts led to an agreement that gave a role to the wider international community, whereas for Russia, it was important that a Russian presence be kept on the ground—even in the form of peacekeeping troops—to maintain its sphere of influence. As Eliasson summarizes,

---

11. See Javier Pérez de Cuéllar, *Pilgrimage for Peace: A Secretary-General's Memoir* (Basingstoke: MacMillan, 1997), 131–132.

To us in the mediation team, it was clear that the Russians could not accept the choreography of the Minsk Group: the OSCE was supposed to lead the mediation effort but cooperate with the Russian Federation, which was a key regional and international actor. Unfortunately, the Russian negotiators had not fully adapted their thinking to the fact that the Cold War was over and that we were living in a new era.

In the humanitarian crises that we have identified, international political considerations seemed to be less of a problem. Humanitarian issues are obviously not seen as equally intrusive and consequently not subject to the same political scrutiny as ongoing war efforts. Thus, Eliasson could act in Burma/Myanmar and Sudan without the political attention that was always present in the other situations. Even so, the regional context and positions taken within the international community do affect whether primary parties to a conflict begin a mediation process. Taken together, observing these levels of analysis may help the mediator to make the appropriate assessments.

Identifying the Issues

In armed conflicts, belligerents fight in order to attain certain goals. During the conflict, the parties tend to be attached to key demands, often formulated in general terms, such as "independence," "territorial integrity," "regime change," or "justice." When parties confront each other with incompatible demands, there can be little prospect for reaching a solution through negotiations. There seems to be no possible solutions that satisfy the opposing sides at the same time, particularly if their aspirations are defined in a zero-sum way.

The international mediator needs to deconstruct the different components of the central incompatibility, thus helping to identify the issues.[12] The benefit is threefold. First, it helps to detach the parties from their devotion to the incompatibility. During the conflict, many have sacrificed their life for "independence" or "protection of the motherland." For a leader to retreat from such ultimate goals is extremely difficult. Hence, shifting focus from visionary goals to more precise positions may open space for the negotiators without yielding on the final goal. Second, the mediator may help clarify misunderstandings of what the parties really mean with their demands. Third, as not all positions may be mutually exclusive—even if the basic incompatibility is—the mediator can help to identify a common ground where the parties' aspirations actually may be achieved.

---

12. This is a process known as *fractionation, fractionalization,* or *disaggregation.* Roger Fisher, "Fractioning Conflict," *International Conflict and Behavioural Science: The Craigville Papers,* ed. Roger Fisher (New York: Basic Books, 1964); Terrence P. Hopmann, *The Negotiation Process and the Resolution of International Conflict* (Columbia, SC: University of South Carolina Press, 1996); Sarah Rosenberg and Joshua N. Weiss, "Sequencing Strategies and Tactics," in *Beyond Intractability,* ed. Guy Burgess and Heidi Burgess (Conflict Research Consortium, University of Colorado, Boulder, September 2003); Pruitt and Kim, *Social Conflict.*

The most sensitive issue in the Nagorno-Karabakh conflict was the question of the definitive status of the region. At the time of mediation, Eliasson was also a visiting professor in the Department of Peace and Conflict Research at Uppsala University. An academic team was formed to complement the one working with Eliasson in the Ministry for Foreign Affairs. The status issue related to the question of autonomy. The academic team dealt extensively with this issue.[13] One of the members, Kjell-Åke Nordquist, developed an analytical matrix on varying forms of autonomy. Six categories of autonomy—security, fiscal, economic, political, cultural, and international—were identified on a vertical axis. In turn, the horizontal axis provided fields for three levels of autonomy (low, intermediate, and high). This matrix provided a range of options for the parties. For Eliasson, this gave an opportunity to move the negotiations forward. He recounts:

> *I told each of the parties that I actually was carrying two hats. One was as the mediator, the other as a visiting professor at a well-known university. Let me now put on my academic hat and give to you a table of possible autonomy arrangements. Tell me what you prefer!*

In this way, Eliasson tried to deal with the key issue of the status of the contested territory by asking the parties to specify more exactly what they wanted. What did they actually mean when they asked for "liberation" or "territorial integrity," respectively? Where in the matrix would they locate their demands? No response was ever given by the parties. Five years later, when Eliasson had left this case, he met with his former counterparts: Deputy Ministers of Foreign Affairs Vardan Oskanyan (Armenia) and Tofiq Zulfugarov (Azerbaijan), both now Ministers of Foreign Affairs. Oskanyan told Eliasson that the Armenian side had encountered great trouble in generating their answer. They had a whole team unsuccessfully trying to come up with a response. "You really gave us a lot of grief," Eliasson recalls him saying.

This shows that working with operative definitions of the key disagreement is difficult—it is likely to be hard to get the parties to define their positions in some detail. It is politically sensitive, since doing so risks revealing information about the positions of the parties—information that the other side can exploit to its benefit. The reluctance of the parties in the Nagorno-Karabakh conflict to respond may, thus, have stemmed from a fear of signaling weakness to the adversary. Each party's negotiating team has to be aware of the hawks on its own side as well as the designs of the other side.

In Darfur, the fragmentation of the opposition side created an imperative for the international go-betweens to search for that side's position on the basic issues before meaningful negotiations could be initiated. These movements, caught in the processes of fragmentation and internal power struggles, had difficulty

---

13. The team was led by Peter Wallensteen and consisted also of Erik Melander, both from the Department of Peace and Conflict Research at Uppsala University, and Klas-Göran Karlsson from Lund University, an authority on the modern history of the Caucasus.

communicating their real aspirations internally as well as toward their adversary. The issues as such were of less significance, but the internal and external power relationships proved increasingly vital. Issues such as denied rights, grievances, and injustices became interwoven with and increasingly overtaken by power aspirations.

In a conflict there is often likely to be a struggle over power among different factions and/or personalities within the opposing sides. This may serve to limit the space for agreement. For the mediator, focusing too heavily on the power concern of the parties may lead to agreements that do not include constructive solutions for the underlying issues. If the question of who should hold power stands at the forefront, less attention may be paid to crucially important issues for long-term relationships, such as security, reconciliation, justice, transparency, and pluralism. In Darfur, the rebel side was engaged in internal power disputes. There was a discernable trend toward factionalism, rivalry, and challenges to the leadership. Add factors of ethnicity, tribal connections within the region, and linkages to contending political parties in Khartoum, and the complexity the mediators faced becomes obvious.

In 2007, Jan Eliasson—together with AU representative Salim Ahmed Salim—worked specifically to get the opposition groups to focus on the substance of the political negotiations. Eliasson and Salim decided to attempt an issue-centered approach: they tried to get the parties to focus on identifying the issues that needed to be sorted out. At a meeting in Arusha, Tanzania, August 3–6, 2007, the team succeeded in getting seven of the eight most important movements to agree on a common platform for negotiations with the government side.[14] This agreement dealt with three issues of the conflict. First, power sharing concerned the need for enhanced representation for the Darfur region in Khartoum. It also included a demand that Darfur reunite into one region rather than the present three. Second, there was the issue of wealth sharing, which meant a demand for a fairer distribution of the income from oil production. This also raised the need for compensation for the 2003–5 genocide, when more than 100,000 people were killed. Third, there was security, which implied a disarmament of the government-supported militia Janjaweed, a halt to arms transfer to the Janjaweed, the initiation of a demobilization process for rebel soldiers, and compensation to those who demobilized. Eliasson explains:

> In August 2007, the AU mediator Salim and I decided to bring the different Darfurian movement leaders together. We changed the format of the negotiations, giving them more than half of the days to coordinate between themselves. Through this process they arrived at a common platform that could constitute a basis for the negotiations.

---

14. See "Security Council Press Statement on Darfur," UN Security Council document SC/9094 and AFR/1567, August 9, 2007; the European Union's press release on Darfur dated August 9, 2007; and "Conclusions of Darfur Rebels' Consultations in Arusha," *Sudan Tribune,* August 6, 2007.

Through this process, the mediation team found a surprisingly high degree of common agreement despite the intense rivalries among factions and personalities. This illustrates the importance for the mediator to shift the focus from goals and power to actual issues. Such a transformation can begin before the parties are ready to negotiate with each other. When the sides and their constituent units agree internally among themselves on their aspirations, the prospects for finding common ground increase. This may set the stage for later and substantial negotiations.

This issue-based approach has several advantages. It creates a basis for unity. If factionalism of one side depends on power concerns, then a return to the original issues that once sparked the insurgency may lead to greater cohesion in the movement. This is positive, since in-group tensions may lead to hostility and fighting between factions and add complexity to the negotiation process. An issue-based approach can also pave the way for negotiations with the other side. It will be very difficult to pursue political negotiations if one side is not unified.

We have also seen that the agenda itself can be an issue for the negotiations. This is not always so. At times, the agenda may be set by, for instance, the Security Council, as was the case in Iran-Iraq II. Still, even if the issues to be negotiated are given in the mandate, there may be room for the mediator to influence the priorities in the negotiation process. Sequential ordering can be a way for the mediator to enable smoother progress in mediation. Eliasson recalls:

> In Geneva [in 1988] the agenda was set: UN Resolution 598—this was our Bible, we just went through paragraph by paragraph. When we decided on the order of dealing with them, we ordered them in the order of difficulty—and started with the easiest. Questions relating to compensation and guilt were avoided, since this would have blocked the process.

Identifying the Actors

Issues are also tied to actors. A first question for an international go-between is to find out whom to talk to. In order to be able to initiate constructive mediation, there is a need for clarity of who the representatives of the belligerent sides are. For Jan Eliasson, the extent of this problem has varied across the mediation cases. In the two mediation efforts with Iran-Iraq, the internal division of the Iranian side was a constant obstacle for any advance of the talks. The Iraqi side used the fact that there were internal tensions among the Iranians, primarily between "fundamentalists" and "moderates," as an excuse for not entering serious negotiations. They would rhetorically ask Eliasson, "Who should we talk to?"

In the case of Nagorno-Karabakh, the definition of the dispute—whether it was an interstate or an intrastate conflict—was extremely sensitive, with detrimental consequences for both sides. The mediation efforts took the form of a trilateral process. However, the internal tensions and splits were most acute in the case of Darfur.

Power concerns will not disappear just because the international go-betweens help the parties to focus on the issues. Once Salim and Eliasson had finally worked out a platform of demands for a joint delegation, the opposition movements raised their chief concern: who should be the leader of the joint delegation? This illustrates that the power concerns cannot be wished away. They have to be dealt with at one point or another. At that point in the process, the UN-AU mediation team concluded that it was not in their mandate to decide who would be the authentic spokesperson—and who would not—for the opposition movements. Instead, the mediators decided to be inclusive in their invitation to the talks, which were to be held in Libya in the autumn of 2007. Eliasson recounts:

> Our inclusive approach to the negotiations in Darfur backfired. The tensions between the different factions were so high that inviting some of them led others to opt out. The major movements said they did not want to sit at the same table as those they saw as traitors and who had divided the movements. This was a dilemma: we as mediators were not in a position to prioritize among different factions. I ask myself whether I was right to use the inclusive approach. It was a tough call. Our successor tried a different approach, only inviting the main movements. That did not work either. Some of the splinter movements were strong enough to prevent any progress.

Thus, the effort to be inclusive and not impose its choice of the most valid spokespersons among the many rebel factions still resulted in a setback for the team: key actors decided not to come. They could not accept having their representatives sit side-by-side with what they saw as splinter groups. Thus, they preferred not to attend the negotiations. This in turn reduced the legitimacy of the talks, because they were not fully representative. The effort to be inclusive came at a cost of reduced legitimacy for negotiations. For the mediation team, it required establishing separate channels with the different factions and unrepresented organizations.

Using the Entry

At the entry phase, the mediator may be able, theoretically, to exercise leverage over the parties, which could possibly be used to move the parties' positions. The acceptance by the mediator to mediate may be an important opportunity for pressing the parties to make concessions. For instance, in late 1980, Eliasson and Palme discussed the possibility of using the announcement of Palme as the special representative of the secretary-general to also get the parties to make changes in their demands. However, this remained a discussion only; in practice, there are no examples of Eliasson pressing parties in this way.

Certain conditions must hold in order for this entry moment to be useful as a bargaining asset for the mediator vis-à-vis the parties. It is important that the parties really want a particular mediator and, thus, are open to third-party mediation in general. Otherwise, the parties have no interest other than to reject such demands from the mediator. In reality, the mediator has little chance to pressure the parties. Also, if there are other comparable mediators available, the belligerents can choose the least demanding one. They can start "forum shopping." Furthermore, to have leverage, the would-be mediator must demonstrate reluctance to take on the assignment. Mediators who are too eager to involve themselves cannot credibly set conditions for their involvement. They will not be in a position to demand such concessions. There may, in fact, be a difference between the mediator who has to be cajoled into the assignment and the narcissistic one who does not require much persuasion. However, in most cases—and that includes Eliasson—mediators take on the task from a sense of duty. This means that they will not raise such demands, but will be more concerned about available resources and possible results of negotiations.[15]

The Palme mission met these conditions. Palme was a well-known and respected personality, not the least in the third world. He was acceptable to both sides, as well as to the United Nations. In fact, this mission was the only one of the ongoing mediation interventions that was taken seriously by the Iranian regime. This also implied that Saddam Hussein and the Iraqi regime regarded it as the most important effort. Moreover, the Palme mission was unique. There were several mediation attempts by other intergovernmental organizations, but this was the first time that the United Nations offered to mediate in this conflict. Also, Palme was not primarily a mediator. As leader of the opposition party in Sweden, his main obligations were naturally to the domestic political scene in Sweden. Thus, he was not prepared to risk his reputation by being too eager to mediate without results. At the same time, he could demonstrate a commitment to achieving results. There was a delicate balance between dedication and reluctance in this case.

A mediator can turn the entry into a momentum for a negotiated settlement. A new mediator can raise the expectations among the parties or the general public that a political solution to an armed conflict is at hand. The mediator can use the entry for creating a "self-fulfilling prophecy"—that is, positive expectations of peace that at the same time increase the possibility that these expectations will materialize.

---

15. According to some researchers, war-averse mediators will be less credible in carrying and transmitting information between adversaries. See, for instance, Smith and Stam, "Mediation and Peacekeeping in a Random Walk Model of Civil and Interstate War"; Andrew Kydd, "Which Side Are You On? Bias, Credibility, and Mediation," *American Journal of Political Science* 47, no. 4 (2003): 597–611; Robert W. Rauchhaus, "Asymmetric Information, Mediation, and Conflict Management," *World Politics* 58, no. 2 (2006): 207–241. In a similar vein, Chester A. Crocker, Fen Osler Hampson, and Pamela Aall claim that mediators who are primarily involved for boosting their own status or image will be less successful in resolving the conflict. Crocker, Hampson, and Aall, *Taming Intractable Conflict: Mediation in the Hardest Cases* (Washington, DC: United States Institute of Peace Press, 2004), 41–42.

In Darfur, the entry of Eliasson as the special envoy of the secretary-general was used to reinvigorate and reenergize the political negotiation process. When Eliasson became mediator in 2007, the parties to the conflict in Darfur had already been at the negotiation table. The Darfur Peace Agreement had been concluded in May 2006, but only one of the rebel organizations, Sudan Liberation Movement/Minni Minawi faction (SLM/MM), became a signatory to it. The agreement failed to put an end to the fighting. At the Addis Ababa high-level meeting on November 16, 2006, the United Nations and the African Union therefore decided that "new momentum was needed."[16] The new idea was that the United Nations would work in tandem with the representative of the African Union, the Tanzanian statesman and diplomat Salim Ahmed Salim. By involving two respected and capable mediators, there was a hope of creating something new in the process. In other cases, a novel opportunity was created before the mediator appeared. For instance, when Eliasson became personal representative for the Iran-Iraq War in 1988, this was after the parties had agreed to a cease-fire and to tripartite talks. As the talks quickly bogged down in sterile conversations, the Eliasson team had to invent new elements to create momentum.

The entry provides a chance for new developments in a conflict, but it is likely to be short-lived and highly dependent on the calculations of the parties. The choice of mediation and mediator, however, may signal that there is an interest among the parties for new ideas and, thus, for meeting some conditions for resolution. However, not all parties agree to mediation from an interest in mediation or even in settlement. The individual mediators certainly are motivated by an ambition to achieve a change in the conflict, but the parties may instead seek recognition, confirmation, or other benefits. For the mediator, it is important to assess to what extent time is ripe for real negotiations, at this moment or in the near future.

It can be important to create a sense of momentum in the entry phase to promote the perception that now is the time to take necessary action. It is a way of raising positive expectations and giving the parties an increased sense of responsibility for the progression of the talks, a point Eliasson illustrates:

> When I start the negotiations I usually have a sort of "sermon." I talk about the expectations and that confidence-building among nations also is about confidence-building among the people. And that our failure would influence the people we represent. I stress the responsibility that the negotiators have.

Style and the Diagnostics of Mediation

In the preparatory phase, Eliasson has worked with the international community, regional actors, and the primary parties in order to assess the possibilities for further progress. Except for his 1988–91 mission in the Iran-Iraq conflict, wars

---

16. See "Statement by Special Envoy of the Secretary-General for Darfur, Jan Eliasson, to the United Nations Security Council, 6 March 2007," UN Security Council, March 6, 2007.

were ongoing in all cases. In all his political mediation efforts, there was basic international agreement on the necessity of the missions. Thus, the major powers provided pro forma support. In reality, their backing could be questioned already at the outset. The regional actors were also supportive on the formal level, but more narrow considerations pointed them in other directions. And in each case, the primary parties accepted the mediators, though for different reasons. Iraq had the upper hand, both in 1980 and in 1988. It was not going to accept a "bad" compromise from its point of view. Both Palme and Eliasson realized that, but—as we shall see—worked constructively nevertheless. Armenia was the strong party in the 1994 conflict, as was the Sudanese government in 2007–8. Such a position does not make the superior party inclined to believe there is a hurting stalemate, which can reduce its interest in a political settlement. Finally, there were internal divisions among at least one actor in each of the conflicts. In some cases, there appeared to be a united, superior actor on one side (Iraq, Armenia, the Sudanese government) and a divided, weaker opponent on the other (Iran, Azerbaijan, and the Darfur rebels). Such imbalances may have worked against the chances of a successful mediation from the beginning. Nevertheless, a number of efforts were undertaken and they bore some fruit.

We can also see that the different mandates have affected Eliasson's style in the preparatory phase. The mandate can create different dynamics in the mediation process. When the initiative comes from the parties or the conflict situation, the mediator does not have to justify his or her role, function, and usefulness for the parties. In such a situation, the mediator can use a more forcing approach. On the other hand, if the initiative comes from the international community, there is a need to get the process accepted by the parties, because some may be more interested than others. Here the mediator may instead have to use a more fostering method to create momentum toward a settlement.

In all instances the missions were accepted by the parties, but Eliasson sometimes had to act on his own to make that clear. In the humanitarian missions, we can see that Eliasson entered with considerable goodwill and was able to generate momentum toward a solution. These cases fairly quickly turned into processes of accommodation and settlement. Not unexpectedly, the four political cases are much more problematic.

A core problem of a conflict resolution process is that the primary parties are often uncertain about the motives of their opponents for taking part in mediation. There can be reasons for suspicion. The actors may have a hidden agenda that has less to do with a desire for a solution than other aspirations. It becomes important for the international mediator to be sensitive to the true intentions of the actors. There may be devious objectives.[17]

In other words, it is not necessarily so that the arrival of a mediator will signify a dramatic change in the conflict. It seems quite clear that neither Iran nor Iraq were willing to accept a peace settlement so long as no major concessions had been made (for Iran this was Iraq's withdrawal of forces, for Iraq changes in the Algiers border agreement). For Iraq, negotiations were a way to further isolate Iran by demonstrating international support for Iraq. For Iran, mediation was a way to break out of its isolation by demonstrating a willingness to talk. Similarly, Azerbaijan may have hoped for more from the mediation than Armenia, as would the rebels in Sudan more than the government. In general, the superior party wants the mediation only to give to it what it believes it has earned on the battlefield. The losing side may, however, see mediation as a way of informing the world of and generating sympathy for its cause, possibly even getting some concessions in the process.

At the moment of entry, the go-between is likely to be exposed to strikingly different expectations from the opposing sides. Consequently, political mediation is not only a matter of finding practical solutions but also one of managing relationships with parties that often find themselves in asymmetrical situations. However, humanitarian mediation may instead involve interests that are not formalized and do not constitute an immediate part of a political struggle. In fact, inviting mediation into humanitarian situations may be a way of avoiding being drawn into a political contest. Thus, it may be possible for a go-between to deal more effectively with humanitarian concerns.

In the initial stage, the mandate gives the mediator considerable leeway. This means the mediator can be—indeed, will have to be—open-minded about the scope: who should be included; and what method should be used? Only after having had first encounters with the parties will it be possible to devise the appropriate approach (comprehensive or gradual moves toward peace, fostering or forcing methods, and so forth). The same applies to the mode: will the parties be receptive to influences from the public? And indeed to the focus: should the mediator aim for a narrow or broader understanding of the peace to be achieved?

With this in mind, we can now turn to the craft of mediated negotiations: what does the mediator actually do when going between the parties? Chapters 5 and 6 will shed some light on these questions.

---

17. This is the term used by Richmond in his analysis of the objectives in the Cyprus conflict; see Oliver Richmond, "Devious Objectives and the Disputants' View of International Mediation: A Theoretical Framework," *Journal of Peace Research* 35, no. 6 (1998): 707–722.

5

Going On:
The Instruments of Mediation

O
n the basis of an elaborate diagnosis of the conflict, a mediator can pursue efforts to arrive at an agreement between the parties on the issues where they are prepared to agree. There are many tools available to the international mediator. In this chapter, we will describe the mediation process and how Jan Eliasson used varying strategies to move negotiations forward. The mediator may assist in creating confidence, establishing principles for talks and solutions, formulating proposals, and keeping the parties committed to the process. Together this contributes to a sense of momentum. As shown by Eliasson's experiences, the go-betweens have been flexible on how and when to use such instruments—and when to invent new ones.

Creating Confidence

Building trust between the parties and the mediator is a key activity for international mediators. This can be done in different ways and with different emphases. At the start of negotiations, as well as during talks, it is important to create a good climate and constructive atmosphere. Jan Eliasson has seen it as essential to create a sympathetic relationship between the mediator and the parties. In the longer run, this will also result in confidence between the antagonists themselves. According to Eliasson,

> As a mediator I want to create a climate where the parties feel comfortable. Often they are nervous and much is at stake for their personal and political future. Trust is necessary in the negotiations in order to make the parties ready to face the risks of peace. It is about how to accept compromise after so much suffering.

It is hard to describe the personality of Jan Eliasson without making reference to his charisma. Eliasson is positive, personable, and generous. He generates warmth. These traits are important in Eliasson's efforts to create an environment conducive for fruitful negotiations. As Eliasson emphasizes,

> Personal relationships boil down to trust and sympathy and must come from the heart. It is really to dare to be yourself. I always try to find a way to make such personal connections.

Important in this regard is the cultural sensitivity of the mediator. This does not necessarily mean that the mediator needs to come from the same culture as the main parties. It does, however, suggest that the mediator needs to carefully study the cultural context in which he or she operates. Above all else, it is essential for the international go-between to show a keen interest in the cultural values of the two sides. A basis for trust is to know culture, religion, tradition, and history. The mediator, by demonstrating interest in the cultures of the parties, can better connect with them. In fact, the Palme mission was the first of the international mediation missions that seriously tried to anchor the religious leadership in Iran within the Iran-Iraq I peace negotiations. Other mediators, notably the PLO, Bangladesh's Zia ul-Haq (representing the Organization of the Islamic Conference, or OIC), and the Cuban foreign minister (representing the Non-Aligned Movement, or NAM) met only with moderates within the Iranian regime, which resulted in negative reactions from the religious leadership toward the mediators.[1]

Trust building is not only relevant to the relationship between the mediators and the parties, but also for relations between the parties themselves. In the negotiations over the implementation of Security Council 598 in Geneva in 1988, Eliasson and Pérez de Cuéllar were frustrated by the parties' mutual reluctance to address each other directly. They only talked to the UN representatives. The mediators decided to organize the setting of the negotiation room in such a way as to stimulate them to talk to each other. Eliasson recalls:

> We set up a coffee table at the top of the negotiation triangle. We postponed the coffee break until the participants were really craving for coffee. When it was brought into the room we could say, "Why don't we have coffee together?" At the coffee table, the parties had to talk to each other.

Yet, creating a good climate is not necessarily linked to immediate advances in the process. One of the members of Jan Eliasson's team, Paul Kavanagh, drew the following conclusion on the shared coffee-drinking sessions: "They did not move the negotiations measurably forward, whatever their effect on the atmosphere might have been."[2] One may say, however, that the existence of such informal connections may be useful in later stages, and then open opportunities for straightforward communication.

Another approach of trust building has to do with creating confidence between the parties in relation to the process itself. Important in this regard is establishing principles for the process.

> One of the guiding principles of the process in the Iran-Iraq negotiations in 1988 was, what I called, a "verbal cease-fire." I told the negotiators, you have to start building confidence between yourselves. You should establish a verbal cease-fire, because if you stir up the sentiments of your own people, you will not be able to sell them any agreement that we reach.

---

1. See "Palmes Fredstaktik," *Expressen*, January 19, 1981.
2. Kavanagh, interview.

A good sense of humor can be an important asset for a go-between as an ingredient, even in difficult situations, for establishing personal contact with the negotiators. Humor can sometimes open the process, create more trust, and pave the way to constructive breakthroughs. However, there is a need for a caveat here: using humor can be risky, as much of what is considered entertaining is culturally bound. Eliasson recalls how he used humor to connect to the leadership of the Burmese junta when he was making his humanitarian mediation in the Rohingya case (1992):

> When I met with General Khin Nyunt in Rangoon and was asked about my official title, I presented myself as a "general." This created uneasiness in his staff. . . . Then I said, "I am a general—an under-secretary-general," and they all broke into laughter. Later in the negotiations, I said to Khin Nyunt, "Between us generals… shouldn't we make a deal?" And so we did!

Eliasson demonstrates the utility of an informal and accessible approach and the benefit of informal discussions. Eliasson tried this with the parties during the Iran-Iraq negotiations in 1988. The first opponents to talk to one other at the coffee table in Geneva were Ismat T. Kittani, vice foreign minister in Iraq, and M. Javad Zarif, who at the time was an interpreter but later became UN ambassador for Iran. Seeing the two of them starting to talk, Eliasson tried to capitalize on this as an initial trust-building effort. Referring to a subsequent event in Geneva, Eliasson recalls,

> I invited the parties, Sirious Nasseri, UN ambassador from Iran, and Ismat Kittani, vice foreign minister in Iraq, to a "confidential" breakfast with me. This was the first time substantial issues were addressed and this became very important for the rest of the process.

This breakfast occurred on October 11, 1988, in Geneva, on the last day of the negotiations.[3] Eliasson deliberately maintained a low profile. After explaining the purpose of the exercise, he only took notes from the discussions. Although the atmosphere was much more constructive during these talks and Eliasson in his diary describes this event as "historic," there was no immediate or substantial difference in the positions of the parties. But a direct channel had been created.

Informal discussions can be beneficial for the mediation process. Yet, during Iran-Iraq II, the Iranians were reluctant to engage informally and, in fact, told the mediators, "do not press too hard on informality."[4] The weaker side in an asymmetrical relationship may be reluctant to establish informal contacts before key concerns have been addressed. The issue of normalization of relations and recognition of equality was problematic for the Iranians, partly because some of its territory was occupied by Iraq.

---

3. Lidén, interview.
4. According to Lidén, Zarif made this statement to Picco on February 10, 1989. Ibid.

Sometimes talks are hindered by deliberate obstructions, notably, by raising unrealistic demands, threatening the other side, or using harsh rhetoric. Interestingly, Eliasson deals gently with such situations:

> *I never blame one side or the other side in front of the other side. I stop the discussion and go aside with the person that has obstructed the process, and say with a sad voice that I am very disappointed.*

Thus, the informal approach becomes a way of keeping the confidence of the parties and still being able to talk straight with them. Even so, international mediation has to build on some hard notions. Chief among these are the principles on which peace can be built.

Establishing Principles

An important approach for a go-between is to work from internationally established and respected legal and humanitarian principles. Although a mediator may be neutral toward the parties and their positions—not necessarily always a prerequisite for a mediator—Eliasson believes that mediators should not be neutral on the basic principles on which the negotiations are pursued.[5] Instead, mediators need to be firmly anchored in a set of principles. When the principles stem from the same basis as the mandate of the intervention, he believes, they actually help the mediator to maintain integrity, for instance, if and when the parties try to turn the mediator into a scapegoat.

In Iran-Iraq I, the mediation team had particular problems with their image as neutral mediators. The Security Council had a history of being biased against Iran. Let us recall that Iraq crossed the border and invaded Iran on September 22, 1980, and Security Council Resolution 479 was adopted a week later on September 28, after Iraq had already made significant territorial gains in Iran. The resolution called for an immediate cease-fire, but did not call for troop withdrawal to the previous lines before such a cease-fire, as would be the standard procedure. This was seen by Iran as a biased and unjustified position by the Council and, in Iran's view, in contradiction to the UN Charter and its article on the territorial integrity of the member states (Article 2.4).[6] Hence, by calling for a cease-fire without withdrawal, the Iranian side naturally considered the resolution unacceptable, and this threatened to make the Palme and Eliasson mediation efforts biased against Iran.[7] Eliasson recollects on Iran-Iraq I:

---

5. See, for instance, Kydd, "Which Side Are You On?" and Svensson, "Bargaining, Bias and Peace Brokers."

6. Lidén, interview, and Kavanagh, interview.

7. For more on the role of the UN in the Iraq-Iran War, see R.P.H. King, "The United Nations and the Iran-Iraq War, 1980–1986," in *The United Nations and the Iran-Iraq War*, ed. Ford Foundation (New York: Ford Foundation, 1987); Aage Eknes, *From Scandal to Success: The United Nations and the Iran-Iraq War 1980–1988* (Oslo: NUPI, Norsk Utenrikspolitisk Institutt, 1989), 183; and Hume, *Ending Mozambique's War.*

We tried to increase credibility by building our efforts on international principles. Using the UN Charter, we specified three basic principles for any solution to the conflict: (1) no acquisition of territory by force; (2) no interference in the internal affairs of other countries; and (3) freedom of navigation in the waters of the Gulf region.

The Palme mission pursued the negotiations with these principles in mind and made this public on January 19, 1981.[8] By being specific and open on the basis for its involvement, Palme's mediation also discretely distanced itself from the Security Council. It almost implied that the Council had failed to live up to its own principles in handling the conflict.[9] The new secretary-general in 1982, Javier Pérez de Cuéllar, also supported this separation between the actions of the UN Security Council and those of the secretary-general and his special envoys and representatives.[10] This was clearly appreciated in Iran and also helped him in his work to free the Western hostages in Lebanon, as his special envoy Giandomenico Picco reports.[11]

By being faithful to established principles, the Palme mission gained acceptance. The attribution of responsibility for the war continued to remain central for Iran throughout the war and in its immediate aftermath. Iraq attempted to develop a legal position for its actions by pointing to alleged incursions by Iran that had made it necessary for Iraq to attack Iran—that is, what could be construed as a legitimate claim of self-defense. But this was neither vigorously pursued nor documented by Iraq, not even at the stage when the secretary-general later had to determine responsibility for the outbreak of war.[12]

In the Darfur case, Eliasson and Salim built their mission on the principle of territorial integrity. Although the insurrection was territorially based in the Darfur region, the armed opposition groups primarily aspired to end political and economic marginalization and gain increased security within Sudan, rather than secession. For the mediators, it was important to stick to this stance and use it as a basis for their involvement. The territorial integrity of Sudan was therefore the

---

8. See "Press Release of the Special Representative of the Secretary-General, Olof Palme, to the Iran-Iraq War," press release, UN Security Council, January 19, 1981.

9. Dedring summarizes: "Whereas initially in 1980 Iran refused totally to associate itself in any form or shape with the institution and the role of the Council, explaining its anger by reference to biased Council decisions taken after the war had started, and only dealt with Secretary-General Perez de Cuéllar, following Waldheim's personal fiasco over the grave crisis arising from the illegal detention of US diplomats in post-Shah Tehran, the change of the international situation in the mid-1980s, largely owing to the previously mentioned rise to power of Gorbachev in the Soviet Union, must be estimated to have been decisive in breaking the ice over the Iran-Iraq war and restoring to its full authority and active involvement the Council as a factor in the search for peace. Nothing explicit on the matter in Waldheim's memoirs elaborate further." Juergen Dedring, *The United Nations Security Council in the 1990s: Resurgence and Renewal* (New York: State University of New York Press, 2008), 13.

10. See Pérez de Cuéllar, *Pilgrimage for Peace.*

11. This is an important point returned to repeatedly in Giandomenico Picco's memoirs. Picco, *Man without a Gun: One Diplomat's Secret Struggle to Free the Hostages, Fight Terrorism, and End a War* (New York, Toronto: Random House, 1999). There is more on this in chapter 6 of this volume.

12. See ibid., 183. See also chapter 6 of this volume.

point of departure for their mediation. Eliasson illustrates how it could also be used to reassure the Sudanese government, which was highly sensitive to secessionist demands:

> *We told the government members in Khartoum that if they were not more cooperative they risked contributing to a development in Darfur similar to South Sudan: escalating demands for secession and separation. In this way we tried to use the fact that the rebels did not [yet] demand secession as an argument for the government to promptly find a political solution to the conflict.*

Working with principles gives the international mediator a strong foundation for his or her mission. It is also consonant with the organization that mandates the mission. Principles such as territorial integrity and noninterference are central to interstate organizations. However, there are also instances where such international legal principles clash. In Nagorno-Karabakh, there was tension between the principles of territorial integrity and the right to self-determination. The principle of self-determination was particularly influential in the League of Nations and was used during the decolonization era of the United Nations. Thus, it had a strong international resonance. Clearly, neither the Karabakh Armenians nor Armenia wanted to agree to anything that would exclude the possibility of secession, whereas the Azeri government was equally strong on protecting its territorial integrity. Mediation efforts based on one or the other of these principles would mean taking a stand on the ultimate solution to the conflict. Eliasson therefore emphasized both principles simultaneously in the negotiations with the parties:

> *"Autonomy" was too little for the Karabakh Armenians to accept, whereas "independence" was unacceptable for the Azeris. Thus, we tried to elaborate on the possibility of a solution based on something I called "autonomy-plus/independence-minus." This was an effort to combine the contradictory international principles of territorial integrity and the right to self-determination.*

Interestingly, in the humanitarian mediation cases, legal principles such as those discussed here played little role. Humanitarian concerns seem to be based on principles that are less controversial and seen as less intrusive to the parties. Thus, Eliasson's mediation in such cases could rely entirely on his and the United Nation's credibility as a humanitarian organization. In some cases, however, Eliasson could also use this as an argument for ending a war. He would emphasize that the continuation of warfare only achieved more humanitarian suffering.

Formulating Proposals

The go-between may try to suggest proposals to settle the conflict. One of the fundamental choices for a mediator in designing a peace process is whether to aim for a complete solution directly, or for a process with agreements on more limited issues. The second approach would begin with, for instance, procedural and confidence-building measures, in the hope of this gradually leading to a fuller agreement. This is the distinction between a comprehensive and a step-by-step (or gradual) mediation strategy.

In Iran-Iraq I, the Palme mission tried both approaches. The mediators found the level of suspicion and hostility between the parties too high for a cease-fire without dealing with the sensitive question of the status of, in particular, the Shatt al-Arab waterway. Iraq feared that Iran aspired to export its Islamic revolution, which put the Iraqi leadership in a dangerous position, since Iraq was a secular state dominated by Sunnis (although the Shia were in the majority). The Palme mission, thus, opted for a step-by-step process, beginning with the commercial vessels trapped in the Shatt al-Arab. From this, it was hoped that other issues would open for settlement.

In order to get the ships out, the parties had to agree to the question of how they should be flagged and how the operation would be organized. It was also likely to be expensive. Iran wanted to pay half the sum, since this was seen as an indication of its sovereignty, and make the point that it owned its side of the waterway. Iraq, however, could not accept anything but paying for the whole operation, to make clear that the operation was on its territory. Hence, the parties' positions on this financial issue mirrored their positions on the larger territorial conflict and on interstate relations. Both sides wanted to state a point and the mediators were not able to find a formula that integrated both demands. Eliasson recalls:

> We worked very hard in the initial stage of the mediation process in Iran-Iraq on getting an agreement with the parties to enable the 72 ships to get out of the Shatt al-Arab, and we were deeply disappointed when the initiative failed. Ironically, the stumbling block for an agreement was the question of who should pay for the whole operation: this is the only time I have experienced a failure in negotiations because both sides insisted on paying.

Another attempt in the step-by-step approach was to make the parties stop attacking civilian targets. Both parties made an agreement, although not between themselves but with the United Nations, that they would not attack civilian border villages. A deal was reached on June 11, 1984.[13] When that agreement seemed to hold, the mediators returned with new confidence-building measures in order to decrease the level of mistrust between the parties. The hope was that this would pave the way for substantial negotiations on core issues. A next step was to produce an understanding to end attacks on the sea-lanes in the Gulf. The mediators were able to secure the traffic out of the Strait of Hormuz. Certainly their arguments were helped by the self-interests of the parties. This

---

13. See "Letter Dated 14 June 1984 from the Secretary-General Addressed to the President of the Security Council," UN Security Council document S/16627, June 14, 1984; "Message Dated 11 June 1984 from the Secretary-General Addressed to the President of the Islamic Republic of Iran," UN Security Council document S/16614, June 12, 1984; and "Message Dated 11 June 1984 from the Secretary-General Addressed to the President of the Republic of Iraq," UN Security Council document S/16615, June 12, 1984.

arrangement was, of course, particularly appreciated by the United States, Saudi Arabia, and Kuwait, all dependent on the transport of oil through the Gulf.

Parallel to this the Iran-Iraq I mediators worked on a proposal for a comprehensive solution to the conflict. It was deemed to be too sensitive to suggest complete package solutions. The mediators instead specified the relevant principles for a solution, in the form of an informal document, a so-called non-paper, to the parties. A proposal was put forward in June 1981. It contained three basic elements: (1) principles, (2) cessation of hostilities and withdrawal of forces, and (3) comprehensive settlement. As to the comprehensive settlement, the proposal suggested that direct negotiations under the auspices of the special representative of the secretary-general should be initiated the day after Iraqi forces had been withdrawn from Iranian territory. That meant after the full withdrawal had been confirmed, thus upholding the principle of territorial integrity of the member states.

Moreover, the mediators recommended the formation of a "Commission on Conciliation" in order to make a proposal for an amicable settlement of the Shatt al-Arab issue. The commission would consist of five members—two selected by each party—and a chairman selected by the four members. The commission was expected to reach its decision by majority vote. The recommendations from the commission would constitute the basis for direct negotiations between Iran and Iraq, again with mediation by the special representative of the secretary-general. Thus, the comprehensive settlement approach focused on how to get a solution to the basic issue, rather than on finding common ground for secondary issues. It was not, it should be noted, a comprehensive solution in itself. The proposal did not propose the ultimate solution, but instead envisioned a way of dealing with basic incompatibilities, a peace process of sorts.

In fact, the cleavage of a step-wise ending of the war and a comprehensive procedure was to haunt the negotiations to the final agreement on the implementation of the cease-fire in 1988. Consistently, Iran refused to open direct negotiations with Iraq unless Iraq was named as the aggressor. Only then could a cease-fire be initiated and direct talks started. For a long time, Iraq wanted a cease-fire, but not one that could be easily breached. Various semantic innovations were advanced, notably the cease-fire as an "irreversible first step."[14] In the final phase it came down to when different steps were to take place: when will the cease-fire be declared, when does the process of defining the responsibility for the onset of the war begin, and when do the direct negotiations start?

The cease-fire document to which the two states agreed in 1988 was short and came as a letter from the secretary-general, stating, inter alia, that "the governments have agreed to direct talks . . . under my auspices immediately after the establishment of the cease-fire . . . to reach a common understanding of

---

14. See Picco, *Man without a Gun*, 80.

the provisions of the Security Council Resolution 598 and the procedures and timing for their implementation." The agreed-upon end date was August 20, 1988.[15] Determining responsibility was, of course, one of the provisions in the resolution. In a remarkable way, the comprehensive and step-by-step processes merged into one document, where all the steps started at the same time. It was this document Jan Eliasson was entrusted with in the following years for the implementation talks on behalf of the secretary-general.

In some situations a gradual procedure will not be possible since every step will be locked by the overriding disagreement on the basic incompatibility. In Nagorno-Karabakh the status issue was at the center of the whole conflict. The mediators were confronted, therefore, with a dilemma in regard to the approach of the process. A step-by-step procedure was difficult to apply, since the parties were not ready to accept different steps if the parameters for solving the basic status issue were not determined. For instance, the third parties' efforts to try to regulate the Lachin corridor failed due to their concern about implications for the issue of the status of Karabakh itself. A step-by-step approach could not bridge the mistrust between the parties. Their rigid and incompatible positions made negotiations difficult. Before meaningful steps could be taken, there was a need for an agreed-upon vision of a comprehensive solution. However, agreeing to end the fighting was possible, as this did not seem to prejudice the final status.

It is interesting that the humanitarian issues also involve questions of gradual versus comprehensive approaches. In the case of the Rohingya refugees, Eliasson actually found himself in a discussion of how many refugees would be allowed to return to Burma/Myanmar. Would it be possible to compromise on a lower number, in order to hope for a possibility to negotiate for a higher number later on? Or should one immediately go for an inflated number in order to reach the total amount of refugees as part of a settlement? Such a negotiation may involve difficult moral choices. Eliasson says this could very well be handled in a correct way:

> *I said to General Khin Nyunt: "Shall we say 50,000?" This was not a random number. With the UNHCR person in my team we had assessed this to be a reasonable number. We realized that it would be necessary to document the identity of the returnees. Fifty thousand would be a good start and a beginning of a process of full repatriation. It was acceptable to the Burmese leadership.*

Using the Media

One important tool that the go-between can use is media. Indeed, the importance of the media has grown dramatically over the years. The media is now an extremely important channel for information as well as an arena for projecting a perspective. International press coverage was generally limited during the Iran-Iraq I and II mediations. It was more important during the Nagorno-Karabakh

---

15. See Picco, *Man without a Gun*, 94–95.

negotiations and, in particular, the Darfur mediation. An active media strategy and a capacity to handle media contacts are probably of utmost importance for today's mediators. For a go-between there is a delicate balance between upholding secrecy for building trustful relationships with the parties on the one hand, and creating public momentum or criticizing the parties for dragging their feet on the other.

Jan Eliasson, in the later missions, tried to use the media in order to get a peace process going. The inspiration seems to come from the Palme mission, which decided to actively use Palme's contacts with the international press. In an interview with Bernard Nossiter in the *International Herald Tribune,* Palme said about the parties contesting the Shatt al-Arab, that "they are doomed to run this river jointly."[16] Palme's purpose was to expose the untenable position of Iraq on the matter of the Shatt al-Arab. The statement was widely discussed in the region. Eliasson explains its background:

> *Taking the Iraqis by their words and declarations—that they were not aspiring to acquire territory—the logical conclusion we came to was that they should therefore be ready to use Shatt al-Arab together with the Iranians. Mr. Palme chose to use the word "run" [this river jointly] because the word had no legal connotations, but indicated a pragmatic solution.*

The media is important for at least two reasons. First, it can be a way to demonstrate that the mediator has the latest news information. Well-controlled leaks or public statements can affect the dynamics in ways conducive for a mediation mission. Indeed, what gets considerable coverage, coupled with official and public reactions, impact on the agenda itself. Second, media coverage can help to raise expectations about the possibilities of peace among the parties, the public, and outside actors.[17] As Eliasson explains, the media is an important arena for the mediator:

> *Public diplomacy is important for the mediator. I do not like it when the parties set the agendas. It is important for the mediator to define the issue and what objective he is aiming for. Otherwise there is no one who can counter the parties' versions.*

The mediator may issue public statements in which expectations on the parties are raised and their cooperation is encouraged or, sometimes, even requested. Studying official statements by Eliasson during his mediation efforts reveals this is a recurring theme. As the newly appointed special representative of the secretary-general for Iran and Iraq in September 1988, Eliasson asserted

---

16. Olof Palme, interview with Bernard Nossiter, *New York Times*, February 25, 1981.

17. On how a mediator should relate to the agenda of negotiations, and the issue of "ownership" in mediation processes, see, for instance, Crocker, Hampson, and Aall, who write: " The negotiating agenda is determined by the issues of the dispute, but not necessarily by all the issues in the dispute. It must cover those issues that are politically essential to the viability of the settlement, but if a settlement is also to cover relevant but nonessential items, the peace process may bog down. . . . The challenge for the mediator is carefully to calculate how much the settlement can bear before attempting to secure critical concessions from the parties. In the end, however, the parties' own political requirements will govern the settlement's content." Crocker, Hampson, and Aall, *Taming Intractable Conflict*, 155–156.

at different press conferences how the responsibility for keeping momentum lay with the parties.[18] Similarly, when assisting the governments of Bangladesh and Burma/Myanmar to jointly solve the Rohingya refugee crisis in 1992, Eliasson publicly affirmed the importance of the parties' commitment, letting the press know that he encouraged the parties to be pragmatic and generous on the issue.[19] In Darfur, Eliasson again used the media to raise expectations:[20]

> We will hope that the movements now will increase their work and crystallize their positions to prepare themselves for the talks. We know this is a difficult process, but we hope they realize that there are great expectations from the people of Darfur and Sudan and also from the international community for them to agree soon to a common negotiation team and issues.

This pressure can be coupled with statements on the need to move quickly, where the media again may be used to help the mediators. Eliasson says on his and Salim's approach:

> By talking to the media we wanted to show the parties that the process was moving forward and that they had better get on board.

Mediators talk of this as the "departing train" strategy: give the parties a feeling that they have to get on the train (toward a settlement) before it increases speed and leaves them behind.

Still, the media may also complicate matters. During Iran-Iraq I, Iran wanted to apply its new policy of "people diplomacy," based on its revolutionary ideology. Journalist Agneta Ramberg, who was in Tehran for the Swedish Broadcasting Corporation, picked up Iran's plans to have the government-controlled Iranian News Agency (IRNA) publish the entire transcript of a recent meeting with the international mediators. She asked the mediation team about this.[21] Publishing the negotiations was not in Eliasson's and his colleagues' interest:

> We had talked with the Iranians about our confidential communications with Saddam Hussein. Many of the issues were, of course, extremely sensitive. When we got to know that they [the Iranians] were planning to publish the entire transcript, that is, not only their own positions but also detailed information from the Iraqi side, we said that this was totally unacceptable.

At this particular moment, Eliasson and Iqbal Riza were able to change the minds of the Iranians. In their view, the mediation efforts would have been severely damaged if information had been published. Confidentiality remains central to the work of the mediator, but the media needs to be taken seriously. Eliasson has developed a particular awareness of the power of communication.

---

18. See articles by Randall Palmer: "U.N. Envoy Expects to Inch Towards Gulf Settlement at Geneva," *Reuters*, September 4, 1988, and "Gulf Talks Adjourn after Failure to Make Progress," *Reuters*, November 11, 1988.

19. See Inter Press Services Global Information, "Burma: Purge of Muslims Intensifies," *Inter Press Service Global Information*, April 9, 1992.

20. See Mohamed Osman, "Envoys Urge Darfur Rebel Groups to Work Hard to Hold Direct Talks Next Month," *Associated Press Newswire*, November 14, 2007.

21. Agneta Ramberg, telephone interview.

Dealing with Justice

The standard formulation for a solution to a conflict is that it should be "just and fair." Issues of justice are likely to be important aspects of any conflict, often in very concrete ways. However, "justice" incorporates many aspects. The ones that more directly affect mediation concern the parties' perception of justice and their behavior during the war. Eliasson's experiences give a number of examples of this and how the go-between can handle such issues.

In Iran-Iraq I, justice was central to the Iranian side. Iran felt that it had been unfairly attacked in September 1980, that it was a victim of aggression, that Iraq should be defined as the "aggressor," and that Saddam Hussein be brought to trial as a war criminal. As Iran's prime minister made clear to the UN Security Council: "We wish to declare that a fair end to this war can be found only if the aggressor is vanquished and punished. That is our final position."[22]

There was even a demand for compensation.[23] In essence, Iran's position was that peace required a regime change in Iraq. This was seen as a primary issue, preceding any other, including a cease-fire. For a third party to deal with this was extremely complicated. A go-between can hardly pursue such a demand directly to one of the belligerents who also, of course, would be able to point to injustices, such as interference in internal affairs or noncompliance with previous agreements. Eliasson explains:

> It will not be useful to start the process by discussing the question of the outbreak of the war, since this will lead to extremely difficult questions, such as issues of compensation after the war, etc. Therefore, as a mediator, I prefer to put off the larger issues of justice until there is a cease-fire.

This works, however, only if the demand is of little significance to a belligerent. In the Iran-Iraq War this was not the case. The Iranian side continued to insist on the issue of aggression. It may have had to do with a traditional understanding of its role in the world, as well as a concern for "justice" as such. The feeling of being martyrs permeated the new revolutionary regime whose leading personalities had been persecuted by the previous regime and even by Iraq. Thus, any settlement had to deal with the start of the war. It was a reason why all diplomacy had to be indirect. The Palme mission could not make the parties meet. To Iran this would have meant legitimizing the aggressor.

The solving formula in the Security Council cease-fire Resolution 598 from July 1987 is that the Council "requests the Secretary-General to explore, in consultation with Iran and Iraq, the question of entrusting an impartial body with inquiring into the responsibility for the conflict and to report to the Council as soon as possible." In essence, the question is dealt with at the same time as the

---

22. See the speech of Mohammad Ali Rajai to the Security Council, UN Security Council document S/PV.2251, October 17, 1980.

23. See *Pilgrimage for Peace*, 135.

cease-fire. Iraq has not been defeated, nor has Iran. A concession from Iran was to accept that a new process could be initiated, but it was to come after the war. The secretary-general's report on the origin of the war was presented to the Council in December 1991 and the UN secretary-general could then make a public statement that Iraq was, in fact, the aggressor. At the same time, he made clear that this issue should not be pursued further, eleven years after the start of the conflict. The report said nothing on issues of compensation. Iraq placed much of its air force in Iran during the Kuwait War, presumably to save them from U.S. air strikes. When the war was over, Iraq demanded to have the planes back. Iran kept them, as it was said at the time, "as compensation."[24]

The mediator may try to put off such issues or find other, more limited, matters that can be handled in the hope that this will create a momentum that eventually also arrives at the justice issue. In Iran-Iraq I the third parties concentrated pragmatically on questions of the ships locked in Shatt al-Arab. Basic issues of justice have emerged in other conflicts. Eliasson recalls:

> *I came to Baku and understood that Azerbaijan's government was extremely upset at the start of the war over Nagorno-Karabakh because the other side was not internationally condemned. To them it was obvious that Karabakh Armenians had initiated the war with strong support of Armenia. The Azeris gave me a long lecture of history, which underscored their concerns.*

In a way, Azerbaijan saw itself in a position comparable to that of Iran, as the victims of aggression. However, the issue was not pursued with the same vigor by Azerbaijan. Azerbaijan also failed to generate international condemnation of Armenian actions and no process to establish guilt was created.

Eliasson's effort in Darfur was influenced by the international accusations that the Sudanese government not only committed war crimes in the region but also pursued genocide against local populations. In the summer of 2008, the International Criminal Court (ICC) began an investigation. In March 2009, it issued an indictment against Sudan's incumbent president, Omar Hassan al-Bashir. He responded by expelling international humanitarian assistance workers from Darfur. This was a situation Eliasson did not have to face, but which was gradually brewing already during the UN-AU mission. The least one can say is that the indictment complicates the relationship between international mediators and Sudan.

A related issue is justice in the conduct of war. Are the parties following international norms and agreements? An ambition of the Palme mission was to work out an agreement on not targeting the civilian population. This was seen as a way of reducing violence, adhering to international norms on warfare, and creating more confidence between the parties. Although some limited agreements were produced, these were not lasting.

---

24. Though never publicly agreed on, Iran did keep some of the Iraqi planes based on its territory during the Gulf War. Trita Parsi, *Treacherous Alliance: The Secret Dealings of Israel, Iran, and the United States* (New Haven, CT: Yale University Press, 2007).

The introduction of new weapons would threaten to break norms of conduct as well as escalate the conflict. Eliasson is still agonizing over Iraq's use of chemical weapons against Iran and on Iraq's Kurdish population. The first reports on this came in 1982, and in 1986, the Security Council condemned the use of such weapons, although without mentioning Iraq.[25] Eliasson reflects:

> *I have often asked myself: should we as mediators have spoken out more clearly against the use of the chemical weapons? Saddam was extremely sensitive to these issues. If we had done so, our mission would have been in serious trouble. Iraq had started a campaign against my colleague Iqbal Riza who had investigated the use of chemical weapons. Still, I wonder if we discretely could have mobilized the Security Council. And could that have prevented other attacks, for instance, on Halabja in 1988? Saddam was never punished for any of these actions, using weapons banned in international law! This still haunts me.*

Formally, the conduct of war and the use of weapons were not part of the mediator's mission.[26] They were for others to pursue. However, the atrocities made it harder to deal with the representatives of a regime, particularly when it denied what was happening. Was it actually a trustworthy party to deal with? Mediating between two nondemocratic regimes is bound to present a number of moral dilemmas to the go-between.

In the Nagorno-Karabakh case a similar issue emerged, but now Eliasson had developed a way of dealing with it. Possibly this also reflected his experiences as an under-secretary-general for humanitarian affairs. Eliasson recalls:

> *The scorched-earth tactic [used by the Armenian side] was not internationally condemned although it led to 800,000 IDPs [internally displaced persons] within Azerbaijan. I expressed my disagreement with this tactic from a humanitarian perspective. I noticed that this question was a weak point to the Karabakh leaders. They wanted to create a buffer zone, but they did not perceive my concern as biased.*

By visiting the camps in Azerbaijan, he emphasized the humanitarian message. There were also opposing complaints, notably about indiscriminate bombings from the Azeri side, that he also raised with the parties. This means that a mediator who adheres explicitly to international conventions and treaties would have a stronger position. The parties could, of course, threaten to withdraw, which is what Eliasson feared in Iran-Iraq I (but not in Nagorno-Karabakh). If the parties adhere to the same system of norms, it might be more possible to take the moral high ground. Taking up moral issues with the warring parties in the South Caucasus may have been more acceptable, as these were new states, still finding their places in the international community. Eliasson summarizes his conclusion from this experience:

---

25. See Shahram Chubin and Charles Tripp, *Iran and Iraq at War* (London: I.B. Tauris, 1988), 59.

26. Riza's role and that of the other academics, doctors, and professionals involved in the investigative UN missions to the region were separate from the mediation process, though both were under the leadership of the secretary-general.

As a mediator, you need to establish yourself as a moral authority. When you witness atrocities as a human being, if you do not express yourself, you are not establishing trust. You can express yourself from a human compassionate perspective, without being seen as partial.

It may be more possible for a mediator to express his or her views on the conduct of the war than on the incompatibility itself. The parties may accept or even expect a mediator coming from an international organization to raise such issues. However, the way the UN secretary-general dealt with Iraq's issue of chemical weapons may reflect a strategy. By having Iqbal Riza handle the issue at the UN headquarters, the mediation mission was protected or insulated from the problem. Thus, the secretary-general could act on both fronts at the same time.

The dilemma for the international mediator is to keep the confidence of the parties and at the same time react to atrocities and human rights violations by the same parties. The humanitarian action in Sudan illustrates another facet of the problem. Eliasson was criticized for not condemning the abuses of the government of Sudan when it was forcefully relocating hundreds of thousands in Southern Sudan. His confidential approach toward the parties was said to have resulted in "failed quiet diplomacy."[27] In fact, something was achieved, but this illustrates that the dilemma is similar whether we are talking about humanitarian or political mediation.

Keeping Them at the Table

Bringing the parties to the table is an achievement in itself. The mediator then has to keep them there. There are several ways in which the parties may leave. A most dramatic moment is when the parties use the threat of withdrawal from the peace process in order to enhance their bargaining position. This is a way for the belligerents to elicit concessions from the other side. For the mediator it is difficult to know if this is tactical or actually means they will leave. It could mean a restart of the war.

The mediator has to take certain measures in order to keep the parties in the process and avoid a breakdown of mediation. Different counterstrategies can be employed. The first one is to keep the process moving, keeping up the momentum and avoiding possible excuses for the breakdown of the talks. Clearly, Eliasson emphasizes keeping the momentum of the negotiation process. Sometimes the go-between can even try to wear down the parties by keeping them at the table for long hours:

In the Iran-Iraq negotiations [September 1988], there was a fear that the parties would go back to war. If we had lost them in Geneva, there was a real risk of a return to war. These negotiations were really exhausting, we had to have an agenda and had to keep them busy, since a day of doing nothing could be potentially catastrophic—they would have flown off.

27. See the report by Human Rights Watch (HRW), "Human Rights Watch World Report 1993—Sudan," 1994, 5.

A second mediator countermeasure is to examine the credibility of the threat. This can be done concretely by investigating whether the parties are actually preparing to leave the negotiation venue or not. Eliasson faced threats of withdrawal by the negotiating parties several times during the intense Iran-Iraq II negotiations in Geneva in 1988. Eliasson recalls:

> *During the negotiations in Geneva in September 1988, the parties regularly threatened to withdraw from the negotiations. However, we had secretly arranged a control post at the airport in order to see whether the parties were actually preparing to leave. Our post could report to us whether a plane was made ready, or if other preparations were being done. This was a way for us to see through their negotiation tactics.*

A third way is to increase the perceived value of the mediation track and thereby get the parties to stay or return to the negotiation table. There is room for persuasion. The mediator can emphasize the chance of getting an agreement, or the benefits of such a deal. The mediator can also underline the international engagement in the peace process and remind the parties that the world is watching.

In Darfur, Eliasson and Salim had difficulties getting all parties to the table, and also keeping them there. The fear of fractionalization and losses on the battlefield may have made the parties reluctant to keep on negotiating. At the same time, costs of the conflict may stimulate parties to negotiate. Thus, keeping the parties at the table involves a complex trade-off between what can be achieved through talks and what is going on in the armed struggle.

Humanitarian issues avoid some of these problems. It is likely to be more difficult to end talks on humanitarian relief once they have started and while the problems remain unresolved. It may tarnish the image of the parties, both internally and externally. Thus, the dynamics of the political cases of mediation differ from those of humanitarian diplomacy.

Reframing the Issues

Reflecting on his experiences, Eliasson often emphasizes that words are the main tools of the diplomat. Therefore, it is crucial for international mediators to have a deep understanding of language. A good repertoire of synonyms in the diplomatic toolbox is essential for mediation.

By reformulating contentious concepts or words the international mediator can open more possibilities for the parties to find common ground on which agreements can be reached. Changes in wording can be critical. The reformulation of issues can also help to save face for the belligerents. When parties are stuck in their incompatible positions, they need assistance to move toward more conciliatory relationships.

An example of this is the negotiations in Nagorno-Karabakh in May 1994. The parties discussed how an agreement would be monitored and compliance observed. During the discussions, the concept of a "separation force" was used. However, since the issue of status was so politically sensitive, this concept had contentious political connotations. It could mean a separation between equal parties, for instance. At this stage, Eliasson suggested the concept of "security contingent" instead, in order to increase the likelihood of getting the parties' acceptance.

Reframing the issues also affects the distinction between humanitarian and political mediation. In Southern Sudan, Eliasson had been negotiating with the parties, asking for a local cease-fire, and discussing matters related to a cease-fire, such as signatories, monitoring, etc. Yet, these all carried political connotations. Only after a change in wordings from a political vocabulary to a more humanitarian one could a basis for an agreement be built. Eliasson recalls:

> After three weeks of fruitless negotiations, we had a brainstorming session. One of my assistants suggested to me that we should ask for something more "humanitarian." First we came up with the idea of a "zone of tranquility," but this was not chosen. Later we decided on "humanitarian corridors." This concept created a completely new situation in the negotiations.

The concept of "humanitarian corridors" was less politically charged compared to "cease-fire," which was a more legal term implying some degree of recognition of the other side. Hence, a stricter adherence to the mandate of humanitarian mediation effort led to a substantial breakthrough.

Style and the Instruments of Mediation

This chapter has described some of the instruments available in Eliasson's toolbox that could be applied in order to advance the process toward peace. Let us look at how the use of these instruments reveals more about his mediation style.

First, there is the scope of his mediation efforts. Here we can observe a change over time toward increased levels of inclusiveness. This may reflect a change in the global environment, an increased level of fractionalization: there are more groups involved in societal issues in the post–Cold War world. The disciplining nature of the old superpower dichotomy, which forced parties into joint fronts, has been replaced with "private initiatives." Thus, more actors must be involved in mediation. But there is also a concern for nongovernmental organizations and their role in the postagreement phase. Eliasson has left the traditional diplomacy of Iran-Iraq I and II for a more open and inclusive approach, trying to bring more actors to the table.

Second, there is the choice of methods. Clearly the parties' perception of the process is crucial. Eliasson avoids threats and tries to find ways to make parties avoid threatening or complicating stances. So far, we find him to prefer a fostering approach, emphasizing the need for momentum and achievements, even small ones, to generate dynamics toward peace. Timing is a matter of generating interest in possible proposals and preparing the ground for real initiatives at the right moment in time.

Third, Eliasson's mode of operation has changed over time. In Iran-Iraq I and II, there is largely a reliance on confidential mediation, and the media is used more for information dissemination. Gradually, this changes and it is particularly obvious that the Darfur case is one where public mediation is important. There are statements trying deliberately to press the parties, emphasizing the urgency of a settlement. This may reflect real changes in the world. The media has become more present and significant. Mediation has also become a better known activity. However, it may also reflect the complexity of the issue. As mentioned above, the Darfur conflict involves a large number of actors in a large country with many borders and outside interests. The media allows a way to communicate to a wider audience. The mediator has to adapt to this particular situation.

In terms of focus, Eliasson concentrates on the narrow issues of peace. In Iran-Iraq I, the ambition was to end the war, and changing the conduct of the war was a matter of generating first steps in a mediation process. Iran-Iraq II was closely guided by the UN resolution, which again did not give Eliasson a wide mandate that included justice issues. In both cases, however, there were issues concerning the use of chemical weapons and on the responsibility for the war. Some of those issues were dealt with outside the Eliasson mission. The same applies to the issue of war crimes in Darfur, which was a concern for the International Criminal Court, not for the mediators. The mediator's mandates had clear restrictions throughout the six cases. However, Eliasson could raise humanitarian concerns in the Nagorno-Karabakh and Darfur cases, visiting camps and talking to leaders, for instance. Although he did not have a humanitarian mandate, such matters could still be discussed without jeopardizing the main mission. In the humanitarian cases, discussion of politics, was generally restricted.

Many of the strategies that have been used by Eliasson are really about laying the groundwork for something that the primary parties themselves would actually need to build. This preparation includes identifying issues and parties, coming up with proposals, creating momentum (for instance, through the media), addressing issues of justice, and so forth. These are all parts of a process that constitute a basis for decisive actions by the parties to make peace. Thus, in some sense, much of what the international mediator does is to work on the basis for the parties to end their conflict and make an agreement—a decision that they may, or may not, take.

The instruments that the go-between uses during the process are not used in isolation. There are many others with an interest in the conflict and they take their own measures. Eliasson has encountered many challenges and possibilities in relating to other international actors. In fact, the special traits of an international go-between is precisely his or her multilateral mandate and systemic outlook on the conflicts. This makes it necessary to explore the cooperation (or lack thereof) between the go-between and other international mediators as well as other third parties of various types. When do they go together toward peace?

6

Going Together:
The Context of Mediation

An official mediator is seldom alone. Conflicts attract many interests. Some will act as facilitators for a solution, others as spoilers. Thus, the international mediator must go not only between the conflicting parties but also between such additional actors. Indeed, in many cases, there can be competing mediation efforts not coordinated with the lead mediation mission. Not everybody wants to go together with the others in a cooperative spirit. There are even those working against mediation, actively advising primary parties to continue to fight or to wait for a better deal. Some mediators are engaged before others enter the scene. Together this forms the mediation environment. The context of mediation is the object of this chapter. Here we also analyze relations between the Eliasson missions and other mediation efforts. We also discuss how different mediation efforts have been sequenced. Important themes in this chapter are related to how international support for mediation is created, how coordination is achieved, how international attention to a conflict can be created, and how norms can be established. We also discuss what implications the multitude of actors has for the design of the mediation process. We end with a discussion about the complications that arise when some third parties insert themselves into a conflict situation as mediator.

Coping with Other Conciliators

Ongoing mediation efforts have to build on previous efforts. No mission is likely to be the last. Even if there are agreements, they have to be implemented, and that task is often entrusted to others, not the "original" peacemakers. There is a sequence of mediation activities that the incumbent mediator will have to bring together. At any moment, ongoing efforts build on what predecessors have done.

A survey of Eliasson's six cases reveals that there are generally other actors in the picture (see table 6.1). If there is a trend, it may suggest that the number of missions is increasing. This raises the issue of which effort is the lead mission. It may invite the primary parties to go forum shopping: going to the one where

Table 6.1 Going Together: Other Mediation Efforts in Eliasson's Six Cases

Conflict	Previous efforts	Parallel efforts	Successive efforts
Iran-Iraq I		Algeria OIC NAM The Arab League The Gulf Coopera- tion Council (GCC) Other UNSG mis- sions	Eliasson mission Other UNSG missions
Iran-Iraq II	Palme mission UNSC cease-fire resolution	Other UNSG Missions	Implementation missions
Burma/Myanmar- Bangladesh			UNHCR Other implementation missions
Sudan			United States
Azerbaijan (Nagorno-Karabakh)	Iran Kazakhstan Russia CSCE through Italy and the United States Russia and Turkey	Russia	Russia OSCE through Finland
Sudan (Darfur)	UNSG mission of Jan Pronk (2004–6)	Eritrea Libya Arab League	UN-AU Bassolé mission

they may hope for a better deal. They may develop a way of playing mediators against one another. Also, the sheer number of peace-promoting actors means that a particular mediator needs to find ways to insert him- or herself into conflicts where other actors may prefer to be alone or relegate the international mediator to the margins.

It may also be that the same organization has several different missions in the same situation, but with different mandates. This results in a need for intraorganizational coordination. Furthermore, some missions have been composed as multinational teams, notably the CSCE mission in Nagorno-Karabakh, or bridge several organizations, as was the case in the Darfur mediation. Modern mediation certainly involves issues of coordination and competition.

The humanitarian mediation may be different. There may be fewer official mediators in such cases and even more commitment to implementation, with different governmental and nongovernmental organizations present with the necessary mediation expertise.

As table 6.1 demonstrates, political mediation cases often involve a host of other actors or mediators, unlike humanitarian missions. Further, with political mediation cases in particular, there are often preceding efforts to which the mediator has to relate. (For example, of course there was a history to Iran-Iraq I. With the Algiers Accord having been negotiated with Algeria as a third party, naturally Algeria wanted to be relevant in the new war, though with little success.) Thus, we now look at how the Eliasson missions were able to mobilize international support, maintain a leading position, generate attention, and thus keep itself at the center of mediation. The use of international norms is an important dimension in this, though in one case, Eliasson faced severe competition from one, highly motivated "third party" in particular, Russia, which we will highlight. Following this, these experiences can be related to the mandate and the styles of mediation.

Forging Global Support

An important task for mediators is to garner support for their efforts. Although most of Eliasson's missions had the support of the United Nations, UN backing cannot be taken for granted. A decision in the United Nations has to be converted into active support for the mission itself. Thus, meeting relevant leaders is an important element in any mediator's strategy, both on a global and regional level. (For data on Eliasson's travel in the four cases of political mediation, based on the chronologies in the appendix, see table 6.2).

In three cases, Iran-Iraq I, Nagorno-Karabakh, and Darfur, there was intensive travel diplomacy or, in effect, shuttle diplomacy. The Iran-Iraq II negotiations, however, were conducted more in the style of conference diplomacy. Most action was concentrated in the conference venues, shifting between Geneva and New York. Still, there were three trips by the Eliasson team to the region, in January 1989, October 1989, and September 1991. In the three other cases, visits to the region were highly significant, but there are interesting differences. The Palme-led visits went entirely to the two belligerents, thus demonstrating that the focus was on a narrow shuttle diplomacy involving just the primary parties. Meetings with other actors were held in New York, for instance. The Nagorno-Karabakh peace diplomacy involved a larger set of capitals in Europe—Moscow, Vienna, and Prague—as well as the key locations in the Caucasus itself, Ankara and Tehran. In the case of Darfur, the Eliasson and Salim travels included regional capitals—for instance, Khartoum, Juba, Accra, Cairo, Njamena, Tripoli, and Asmara—apart from frequent visits to New York and Addis Ababa (for the African Union) and one tour to Paris. The ambition was to be as inclusive as possible, even if it meant exhausting, cross-continent travel. Other actors could be approached in New York.

Table 6.2 Eliasson's Travels: The Four Cases for Ending a War

Conflict	Year	Total unique flights	Flights to or within the conflict zone	Proportion of flights to or within the conflict zone (%)
Iran-Iraq I	1980	6	2	33
	1981	13	6	46
	1982	2	2	100
	1983	-	-	-
	1984	-	-	-
	1986	-	-	-
	1987	-	-	-
	Total	21	10	48
Iran-Iraq II	1988	3	0	0
	1989	24	8	33
	1990	3	0	0
	1991	4	0	0
	Total	34	8	25
Azerbaijan (Nagorno-Karabakh)	1994	42	22	52
	1995	8	5	62
	Total	50	27	54
Sudan (Darfur)	2007	37	18	49
	2008	9	4	44
	Total	46	22	48

Note: Each visit Eliasson made to a conflict zone often comprised several flights, such as when he conducted travel or shuttle diplomacy.

Such travel was also important for an understanding of the effects of war. During his shuttle diplomacy to the Caucasus in 1994, Eliasson reflected on this in his diary:[1]

> *This is almost unbelievable. Here I am in a rundown guesthouse with windows demolished by the recent bombings in tiny, mountainous Nagorno-Karabakh, which finds itself in the middle of a bloody war over its own existence and future. I have almost never felt the unique power and mechanisms of hatred and violence as clearly.*

Mediator travel is clearly increasing over time. The conflicts in the post–Cold War period involve more parties and have more regional dimensions. This makes it imperative for the mediator to connect to as many actors as possible, and the vast and unavoidable travel points to the need for stronger teams. For instance, Salim and Eliasson divided necessary travel among themselves in the Darfur case. In Nagorno-Karabakh, the Swedish representative, Mathias Mossberg, did a considerable share of the traveling. That certainly made the efforts less strenuous on the individual, and speaks in favor of mediator teams rather than lone mediating stars.

To Eliasson, meeting the regional actors face-to-face has a particular value. It is a way of keeping them informed. It is a preventive strategy. If actors are not

---

1. Jan Eliasson, diary entry dated March 3–4, 1994.

updated on what goes on, from the most reliable first-hand source, they may turn into spoilers of the process. In fact, Eliasson did not hesitate to talk to actors who were often avoided or neglected by others. This includes Eritrea and a Sudanese leader exiled in Paris, for instance. Similarly, in Nagorno-Karabakh, it was important to have continuous contact with Moscow, which not only could veto an agreement but also had the power to entirely change the military equation in and around the battlefield.

Eliasson's travel itinerary reflects several forms of diplomacy. The narrow shuttle diplomacy used in the Iran-Iraq War was connected to constant briefings in New York. The wider form of peace diplomacy in Nagorno-Karabakh involved political centers in Europe that were both engaged in the issue and had possible connections to the parties. In Darfur it was important to have a way to reach actors with access to Sudanese opposition groups, notably Eritrea and Libya. Juba in Southern Sudan was a place to connect to some armed groups in Darfur. Thus, there was an element of indirect diplomacy in Eliasson's approach, not just direct negotiations. Preventing the rise of regional spoilers was an additional consideration, generating ideas for the solution was another, and anchoring a possible outcome a third. Travel can accomplish a number of tasks.

Forging regional and global support for mediation is always necessary. Even in the age of electronic communication, personal meetings remain as important—or even more important—as before. One may only ask if this travel was enough. There were some actors that were not visited, and thus they may have had less understanding of the results the mediators were trying to achieve.

Leading International Mediation

As we have said, ongoing conflicts draw the attention or interest of outside actors. Sometimes they will send in their own envoys and take their own actions. Coordination of mediation is an issue. Who is to lead the international effort? Forging international support is one element in this, but there are additional considerations.

Coordination of the mediation effort was central in Darfur. It was formalized in a dual chairmanship of the mediation efforts, dividing the leadership between the United Nations' Eliasson and the African Union's Salim. This created a situation where the international community approached the primary parties in a more or less unified "front," presumably giving the mediators some leverage. Having the support of both the United Nations and the leading African organization should have made that clear. The international attention toward Darfur meant that there was no lack of resources, unlike the other cases. Eliasson recalls:

In Darfur, we had a lot of resources, so that was not the problem. There was a feeling of guilt that made the Americans and others to provide resources. We had a joint mediation support team, operated together by the UN and AU, with a well-staffed office in Khartoum.

This could have potentially resulted in tensions between the two organizations, but the relations between Eliasson and Salim may have prevented that from turning into an operational problem. It is interesting to note that the Eliasson-Salim combination was replaced with a one man UN-AU mediation mission, former foreign minister Djibril Yipènè Bassolé from Burkina Faso. Based in Sudan, he had the advantage of being closer to the scene of battle, though he was perhaps disadvantaged by being far from international centers.

Another challenge was that the official mediators were not alone on the scene. Several neighbors had their own agendas, notably Chad, Egypt, Libya, and Eritrea. With the exception of Eritrea, their views could be channeled through the African Union, but they also had their own direct relations to different primary parties. International mediation might complicate their designs. Thus, it is important for the mediator to constantly report back to the mandating organization to have its reassurance and to assert his or her leading role.

Similarly, there were parallel efforts during the Iran-Iraq War, when a host of organizations and actors saw the war as threatening to their own ideas, be they nonaligned cooperation, Islamic unity, revolutionary movements, or regional interests. However, Palme established himself as the lead mediator. In fact, he did not try to compete with the others. Rather, he let them try to mediate first and then came onto the scene. Many other efforts became one-time events, whereas the UN team had persistence. When Eliasson chaired the Iran-Iraq implementation negotiations, there was no challenge to his UN role. It was, as far as we know, the only direct channel between the parties. It may, in fact, have served to create a direct link between them that was later used for bilateral understandings.[2] Similarly, when acting in his capacity as under-secretary-general for humanitarian affairs, Eliasson was alone on the scene. The Darfur experience is somewhat different, even indicative of a new age of conflict management: today there are likely to be more actors engaged in both promoting and containing conflict.[3]

Still, we note that a mission mandate by the United Nations carries an advantage. It has strong international standing, legally as well as politically. Obviously, the multilateral go-between has no direct leverage over the parties. Indeed, the UN Charter does not give the UN secretariat the tangible resources of a state or a private corporation. All funding is derived from the member states and any peace operation has to be negotiated with the same member states for committing soldiers, experts, services, logistics, and even money. The same is

---

2. This is the topic of a follow-up article by the authors.

3. See Lotta Harbom, Erik Melander, and Peter Wallensteen, "Dyadic Dimensions of Armed Conflict, 1946–2007," *Journal of Peace Research* 45, no. 5 (2008): 697–710.

true for most international organizations. The most significant resource is the secretariat's space for maneuver, which is based on Article 99 of the Charter: "The Secretary-General may bring to the attention of the Security Council any matter which in his opinion may threaten the maintenance of international peace and security."

We have seen how a special envoy can legally act beyond what the Security Council has stated. In Iran-Iraq I, this was the only way the United Nations could make itself relevant in ending the war. But it begs the question, what power is available to assert such a lead role? Most mediators would not even talk of "power," least not Eliasson, who explains:

> As a mediator, I would not threaten the parties with punishment. The mediator has to find ways for the international community to reward moderation. Moves toward peace must give benefit to the parties.

There are examples of bringing in the international community to reward concessions or agreements. Such positive actions or incentives actually have a limited record of success. In the negotiations on freeing the ships stranded in the Shatt al-Arab, technical international contributions were necessary, but the parties insisted on paying. The Gulf Cooperation Council's (GCC) offer to Iran of a large fund of money for reconstruction in exchange for a cease-fire was resented.[4] Iran was not in the war for money but for justice. The offer in essence ended the GCC role in mediation.[5] Today, it may be the European Union that has taken up the role of suggesting development assistance in return for peace. However, in the Darfur issue, this was not a proposal entertained by the mediators, even though, for instance, drilling for water under the deserts of Darfur would be an obvious benefit of peace requiring international capacity. Eliasson says:

> It is important for the population to note a visible peace dividend immediately after a war. In Darfur, we had parallel negotiations with the humanitarian organizations to encourage their work and to show to the population that peace is a better idea than war.

However, Eliasson is the first to recognize that this would involve a commitment from the international or regional community rather than the mediator. It would require its own round of negotiations as well as a process of implementation that may run into other obstacles. A third party is an outsider, a temporary one at that, and can offer few rewards to bring about an agreement. He or she is involved with finding formulas for future relations, not much else. However, the UN mediator may have a stronger position in actually generating sympathy for a particular situation and, thus, be more interesting for the actors to listen to. There is a potential reward in giving the UN mediator the lead role.

---

4.   This is specified in Fred H. Lawson, "Using Positive Sanctions to End International Conflicts: Iran and the Arab Gulf Countries," *Journal of Peace Research* 20, no. 4 (1983): 312, 314.

5.   Ibid.

Indeed, Eliasson at times has called on the international community to support mediation efforts, for instance, through humanitarian assistance. This is a tangible way in which a postaccord period can be made beneficial for the parties and the population at large. But it is also connected to the settlement of the conflict. On the situation in Darfur 2007, Eliasson said to the media:

> This is an enormous operation of 1 billion dollars a year with 13,000 humanitarian workers. But what they are actually doing is putting bandages over infected wounds. We would like, and the world community would also like, to use this money for health clinics, for education for children, for irrigation projects, for the development of this region.

By focusing on the humanitarian needs and appealing to the world community, the mediator is putting pressure on the government to be more forthcoming, both in assistance and in the negotiations.

Within such an approach, we would not expect the threat of punishment or sanctions to be part of either the third-party instruments or the instruments for asserting the UN mediator as the leader. Eliasson is very clear on this when he points to the negative utility of threats from the international community. He did not encourage the use of sanctions in Darfur and did not seem to be concerned about the lack of them. On May 16, 2007, Eliasson is reported to have said that the delay in imposing new sanctions on Sudan had given him "diplomatic space." Many mediators would probably agree with Eliasson on this score. But he also adds:

> *It may be helpful if there are some drums in the distance. This may make the parties listen to my message more carefully.*

The "drums in the distance" may be the threat of sanctions by the Security Council or by leading member states. An example is Darfur, where there were strong demands for general and targeted sanctions on Sudan, notably on arms deliveries to the parties and on Sudan's oil exports. Eliasson commented that the "parties certainly hear the drums in the background."[6] The drumming was generated by concerned organizations, but had an impact on government policies, particularly in Western states. Targeted UN sanctions were also introduced, initially against four individuals.[7] Later, the International Criminal Court decided to indict Sudanese president Omar Bashir. However, there is no evidence that this encouraged negotiations. On the contrary, the sound of the drums may now have silenced later mediation efforts.

There are also examples of a go-between having some leverage on the parties and thus being the actor the parties prefer. A fascinating case is how the agreement ending the Iran-Iraq War provided the negotiators, the Secretary-General, and his envoy Gianni Picco, with leverage on Iran in the hostage negotiations.

---

6. On how the delaying of sanctions was helpful in the mediation effort, see "US Delay on Sudan Sanctions Was Help—UN Envoy," *Sudan Tribune*, May 17, 2007.

7. See "UN Sanctions on Darfur Suspects," *BBC News*, April 26, 2006.

A number of American and West European citizens were held by Lebanese groups, many in the Bekaa Valley of Lebanon. Iran was seen to have influence on the situation. By linking this to the war, the secretary-general saw a way to get Iran's assistance on the issue. Iran was very keen on having an official and formally sanctioned statement on who was responsible for the war. This was an item in Security Council Resolution 598. It entrusted the secretary-general with the task of settling the issue. In 1991, he appointed three university professors to scrutinize the problem. This was actually an initiative parallel to Eliasson's mandate for implementation. It was, however, a separate paragraph in the resolution. Iran continuously and eagerly pressed for the report. By delaying the process until Iran was firmly involved in solving the hostage issue, the United Nations could actually push the Iranians to be more forthcoming. Picco records how he and the secretary-general cooperated with Iran during this period. "It was the only leverage on the Iranians that he and I had as individuals, irrespective of what governments might do. I would never recommend that the secretary-general give this up for anything less than a full resolution of the hostage problem. The report was really all that mattered now to the Iranians, and the hostages became only a means to an end in obtaining it."[8]

In other words, the Security Council, by giving a certain mandate to the secretary-general, may give some leverage to a multilateral go-between. It seems that Pérez de Cuéllar and his envoy Picco made the most of this possibility. His choice to have Picco's mission outside Eliasson's mandate, even though Picco was part of the Eliasson team, is interesting. It created uncertainty for Eliasson, as it was not always clear what Picco was doing and what implications it carried for Eliasson's mission. There were also moral objections to the way hostages were, in effect, traded for concessions on a completely different issue, which carried its own moral value. In principle, hostages should not be taken and not be freed through concessions. Many mediators may not share the enthusiasm for linkage politics. To some extent, the different teams appointed by the secretary-general did not always go together. In this case, it may have been a deliberate choice to separate the two tasks. Eliasson recalled in his diary during a later visit to Tehran:[9]

> My most recent visit took place three years ago in mid-September, together with Secretary-General Pérez de Cuéllar. His main objective was to free the hostages captured in Lebanon. . . . Even today, I still have difficulties in accepting "the deal"—the guilt of Iraq . . . in return for assistance in the Bekaa Valley.

On the whole, the UN mediator will not have direct leverage on the parties. By constantly informing key members in the region and in the Security Council, however, the go-between may be able to generate interest and support for his or her mission. At particular junctures, this may provide critical

---

8. See Picco, *Man without a Gun*, 184.
9. Jan Eliasson, diary entry dated September 20, 1994.

access through other governments. Studying Eliasson's itinerary, we see that much time is spent on informing significant actors. We conclude that it may sometimes be done with an expectation that they exert pressure on a closely allied actor. The ending of the Iran-Iraq War involved the enlistment of Saudi Arabia as an actor between the UN team and Iraq in getting Iraq's final approval of the cease-fire in August 1988.[10] Thus, the United Nations can generate resources and find ways to assert itself. There are ways of making the UN mission the leading mediation effort.

Generating Global Attention

The multilateral mediator may have an additional strength: the envoy is likely to have more credibility with the media and the general audience. Thus, he or she can bring international attention to an issue, which in turn may result in other actors joining to support the mediator's efforts. Eliasson is keenly aware of this, perhaps more than many other multilateral mediators:

> *In the Darfur conflict I told the recalcitrant parties: "I will convey this information to the Security Council," which implied that international media would get the story. I think they perceived a sort of a threat, but they could not blame me—this was my responsibility to those that gave me my mandate. In reporting back I would give my own version and they realized I had high credibility. Similarly, in the Nagorno-Karabakh conflict, I reported to the whole membership of the OSCE. The representatives from Armenia and Azerbaijan were often very nervous about that.*

Access to the media can be used to spread the third party's version and contribute to generating support. The more public interest there is in a given conflict, the more valuable media access becomes. In the Darfur case, for example, there was global interest as it related to issues of genocide (with the Rwanda genocide fresh on everyone's mind), human rights (in a nondemocratic regime), and novel issues, such as climate change (the dry conditions of Darfur being a possible example of what is to come for some areas). We may add that the composition of the mission, which had two envoys, may have helped to generate interest in Europe and Africa. Media attention appears lower for the mediation efforts since the pair left the scene.

However, several of Eliasson's cases involved a much more narrow perspective. Mediation in Iran-Iraq as well as in Nagorno-Karabakh was based on shuttle diplomacy, where the primary parties and their allies were furnished with information but not the general public. Thus, the public statements demonstrated that the mediators were active, without detailing what they were actually doing. Eliasson's statement to the assembled media in September 1988 on the Iran-Iraq cease-fire implementation is typical of this approach:

---

10. The endgame is described by Picco, *Man without a Gun*, 93ff. See also Pérez de Cuéllar, *Pilgrimage for Peace*, and Hume, *Ending Mozambique's War*.

> We are having discussions on the format of the talks, whether we are to meet with the parties separately or together.[11]

The statement only addressed the formalities. At other occasions, Eliasson would simply comment on changes in staff.[12] Thus, the open approach to the media was secondary to informing the parties themselves. The use of the media has been geared more toward pushing the parties than for getting the world to move together. Mediation coordination is more likely to be conveyed through closed meetings, for instance, in the Security Council and in relevant regional organs.

Using International Norms

With international involvement follows that solutions have to be consonant with international principles. This is necessary for regional and global support. The United Nations and African Union are likely to worry about settlements that break established norms and rules, unless they also want to change such rules. Thus, the international mediators may have to bring established principles into play to get international support and avoid unnecessary criticism. These may be traditional norms, notably the territorial integrity of states (e.g., not accepting changes of borders by force, which applies to both Iran-Iraq situations and to Nagorno-Karabakh) and national self-determination (an issue in Nagorno-Karabakh, potentially one in Darfur), as well as newer ones concerning the prevention of genocide, the responsibility to protect civilians, the pursuit of war crimes, and the application of human rights.

We can observe the evolution of such norms during Eliasson's three decades of mediation. This can be seen in matters relating to justice. In fact, such norms may be more intrusive from a government's point of view today, while at the same time becoming more important from a people's perspective. Mediation has to follow modern trends.

At the same time, the task of mediation is to end a war. When beginning the peace conference in Sirte, Libya, in 2007, for example, Eliasson's views did not coincide with those of the host, Libya's leader Muammar Al-Gaddafi. Agence France-Presse reported that Al-Gaddafi said: "It is not in the interests of the international community to intervene in an affair in which one of the parties does not want a solution," and there were "other issues more grave than Darfur" that did not attract similar attention.[13] However, Eliasson said that the Darfur problem was

---

11. See Claude Regin, "UN Mediator Tries to Break Deadlock in Gulf Peace Talks," *Reuters*, September 3, 1988.

12. See "CSCE and Russian Envoys Visit Baku and Yerevan; Settlement "Never Been So Close," *BBC Monitoring Service*, May 7, 1994.

13. See "Libya Slams Rebels over Internationalization of Darfur Crisis," *Sudan Tribune*, April 29, 2007.

> not just dangerous for Sudan, but also for the region and the whole world. . . . This confer-
> ence could be a chance to accelerate a solution to this problem and reinforce peace in the
> region.

Al-Gaddafi espoused the classical norms of state sovereignty and, in effect, preferred a settlement to the Palestinian issue prior to the Darfur one. For Eliasson, however, Darfur carried significance for the world, presumably because it underlined basic norms beyond those of state sovereignty. In doing so, Eliasson also made clear that the responsibility for ending the conflict was not just that of the sovereign state but also the international community. Eliasson's broader normative perspective pointed to the need for greater international inclusion in the peace process.

In Iran-Iraq I, the world initially did not support Iran's position on territorial integrity. No doubt this reflected a general reluctance to accept the new regime in Iran. Its revolutionary aims and illegal actions (including the occupation of the U.S. embassy in Tehran) made it an outlaw, although most observers probably would agree that Iran had a point on the issue of territorial integrity and on the start of the war. Indeed, the final report on the responsibility for the war was accepted internationally, confirming just that. The Western world ended up contradicting itself placing greater importance on the regime's character than on traditional legal norms. The revelations that the U.S. supplied weapons to Iraq, and that it had clandestine deals with Iran (the Iran-Contra affair), made the normative inconsistency even more obvious. It may have made it more difficult for the mediators to find a shared framework for a settlement. It also meant that for a long time there was only lukewarm international support for ending the war.

This situation paralleled the Nagorno-Karabakh case, with Russia in the role of the power that was willing to freeze the conflict while one country occupied territory that legally belonged to another. Again, the norms of territorial integrity and the inviolability of borders had to yield to other considerations.

In such situations, mediators will have difficulty mobilizing international support even for maintaining principles that normally are taken for granted. Although the responsibility rests with those particular states, the mediators may have to fend off the blame.

Designing International Negotiations

The international mediator needs to decide on the appropriate format for the negotiations. This is one more way in which the multilateral go-between can assert his or her role to find a format that the parties support and thus distinguish his or her effort from others. We find three major forms of mediated negotiations. First, there are international conferences, where the parties meet officially with their delegations. Second, the go-between can try to establish direct (sometimes informal) mediated negotiations outside the negotiation room. Third, the negotiator can conduct shuttle diplomacy between the centers of the antagonists, moving between capitals.

International conferences can be useful in order to clarify the positions of the parties. When the representatives met in New York in October 1988, the delegations from Iran and Iraq consisted of nineteen and six members, respectively. The Iranian delegation was quite diverse, with members of the Parliament as part of the delegation. Yet, with this format, the space for making concessions was limited. No one wanted to appear weak in front of the opposing side. One reason Iran's regime sent such a large delegation could, in fact, have been to prevent its delegates from making concessions. The Iranians held firm to their position that there should be no substantial negotiations until Iraq withdrew from Iranian territory. During these negotiations there was no direct dialogue between the Iranian and Iraqi sides. Each delegation merely read prepared statements.[14]

Eliasson and his team delivered the opening as well as closing statements. In addition, they wrote reports for the Security Council. These reports were instruments the go-between could use to pressure the parties. For instance, after one of the sessions had ended, the Iranian delegation stayed in New York in order to influence the secretary-general's report to the Security Council.[15]

During the negotiations, Eliasson often tried to discuss with the parties directly, away from the negotiation table. He recalls:

> During the negotiations [in Geneva] I invited them to meet me directly in my office. When the parties met at the negotiation table—they did not state their motives in front of the other side—they were very cautious and did not want to show any sign of weakness. But when the parties talked to me directly, they were more open and raised their suspicions about the other side, or said to me that "this is my red line"—indicating what they were ready, or not ready, to accept.

It is possible that such on-the-side negotiations are more common than what is documented. In this way, international conferences can be a way to establish informal connections. This is also the way the UN system functions. The plenary meetings of the annual General Assembly, for instance, give a number of opportunities for separate and direct contacts at top levels.

In principle, international conferences can be important in building global attention and support for mediation. However, the four political cases do not suggest that such formats are easily created. There was no regional peace conference ending the Iran-Iraq War, only the bilateral one under UN auspices. The Minsk Conference was seen as the ultimate forum for the solution of the Nagorno-Karabakh conflict. As we have seen, it was never convened, even though OSCE developed elaborate documents on the content of a future comprehensive settlement. In Darfur, Eliasson and Salim brought parties together to Sirte, Libya, as a follow-up to

---

14. Lidén, interview.

15. Ibid.

the previous peace conference in Abuja, Nigeria. The mediators invited more than twenty-five observers from civil society, including from human rights organizations and women's movements. However, none of these fora saw full participation of all actors and, consequently, no lasting and full agreements resulted from them. In general, it seems that peace agreements have only in exceptional circumstances been negotiated in larger international conferences.

It has been more common that mediators engage in shuttle diplomacy. Eliasson's approach has been to not let substantial negotiations take place at a distance. Neither should negotiations be held only with the representatives of the parties. Rather, it is important to have direct contact with key decision makers in the conflict. According to Eliasson, shuttle diplomacy and direct interactions in a conflict region are very important, including, of course, with those who hold power. For example, in 1988, following negotiations in Geneva with representatives from Iran and Iraq, Eliasson—together with his Swedish diplomatic adviser, Anders Lidén—initiated a process of shuttle diplomacy between Baghdad and Tehran. This approach did not immediately solve implementation disputes but was more fruitful in the long run and in making new connections.

A similar situation arose in Nagorno-Karabakh. Eliasson began his efforts at CSCE in Vienna, but wanted to anchor his mission both in Moscow and in Ankara—as these were key external actors with influence on the conflict. Eliasson explains:

> *When I took on the position as mediator in the Nagorno-Karabakh conflict, I thought it would be crucial for me to visit the region. In fact, it is an important part of a confidence-building process. It shows respect—and it was met with appreciation from the parties.*

Although shuttle diplomacy was also important in Iran-Iraq I, it led to the conclusion that the parties were not willing to pursue a peaceful solution. The Palme mission seems not to have taken on the idea of traveling in the region to enlist support. Instead, it brought the issue back to the United Nations. The intensive travel that was a hallmark of Eliasson in the Nagorno-Karabakh and Darfur cases had no antecedent in Iran-Iraq I. In short, shuttle diplomacy today focuses not only on the primary parties (and the mandating organization) but also on key regional actors and crucial allies. The design of international negotiations has evolved into more complex formats that necessitate engaging others in the process.

Inserting International Mediation

So far, we have mostly discussed the possibilities for cooperation among mediation efforts. However, in some instances, different mediation efforts could suffer from competition. The case of Nagorno-Karabakh is illustrative. In this case, Eliasson and his team had to insert themselves as international mediators in the face of Russian efforts to sideline and marginalize them.

The case of Nagorno-Karabakh drew considerable mediation efforts from neighboring countries. The Security Council had already called for a cease-fire in 1992. In the spring of 1992, the CSCE, the regional European security organization, decided to organize a peace conference in Minsk and to prepare for the monitoring of a cease-fire. The first task was given to Italy, and the other to Sweden. A Swedish diplomat, Mathias Mossberg, was appointed personal representative for the chairman-in-office of the CSCE. When Sweden took over the presidency of the CSCE in 1993, a main issue was Nagorno-Karabakh.

As we discussed in chapter 3, at the end of 1993, Eliasson was appointed chairman of the so-called Minsk Group, a group of countries formed within the CSCE to restore regional peace. All previous mediation attempts—by Iran, Turkey, and Russia—had their biases and vested interests. Iran was concerned about a possible influx of refugees, and Turkey had troubled relations with Armenia and saw Azerbaijan as a "Turkic" state. These mediators were not acceptable to the parties as the sole go-between. Being a regional power with a strong ability to influence the parties through its military, economic, and political power, Russia was inevitably a main actor. Furthermore, in the early 1990s, the region did not appear to be of particular concern to the United States. The United States gave priority to constructive relations with Russia and the nonproliferation of nuclear weapons. It was obvious to Sweden, however, that without Russia on board, any solution to the conflict would not be durable. This "realistic" approach had already been formulated in 1993 by Mossberg.

The CSCE had been criticized for lacking efficiency and relevance, mostly arranging meetings far away from the region. It pursued a comprehensive approach, outlining detailed documents for a final and complete settlement. Mossberg embarked on vigorous shuttle diplomacy, building on direct contacts with the primary parties. Eliasson continued this strategy and gained credence for a role for the international community in the conflict, although this strategy may have reduced the role of the Western powers.[16] It did not directly contradict Russia, but neither did it yield to Russia's interests. The hope was that by having Russia in the mission it would be possible also to influence Russia's approach.[17] This approach also meant turning mediation into a step-by-step strategy, where a permanent cease-fire became a primary goal, coupled to the deployment of international peacekeepers. Above all, cooperating with Russia would make the international mediators relevant also to this power.

---

16. "The implication of this was that the US was downgraded and could no longer counter-balance Russian influence." John J. Maresca, "The International Community and the Conflict over Nagorno-Karabakh," in *Opportunities Missed, Opportunities Seized: Preventive Diplomacy in the Post–Cold War World*, ed. Bruce Jentleson, 68–89 (Lanham, MD; Rowman and Littlefield for the Carneige Commission on Preventing Deadly Conflict, 2000).

17. By the end of 1994, Russia formally became co-chair of the process.

Eliasson and his team tried at great length to shape a genuine bipartisan mediation process with the Russian Federation.[18] They saw that Russia had a decisive role to play, not the least in exerting leverage on the parties to agree to a cease-fire. Cooperation was also important for OSCE in creating a role for the organization. This was particularly true in the questions of troop withdrawal, an end to the embargo, the return of refugees, and a political settlement. Clearly, the Russian Federation, headed by President Boris Yeltsin's special representative for the conflict, Vladimir Kazimirov, consistently preferred to pursue its own track. Eliasson expressed his concern on Russia's involvement in his diary:[19]

> There is competition and power ambitions at the heart of this. . . . The parties clearly feel pushed around and need us—possibly to play one negotiator against another.

Different ways had to be tried to gain entry into Russia's efforts. For instance, ahead of an important meeting, called by the Russians in Moscow in early 1994, the Swedes informed the primary parties—Azerbaijan, Armenia, and Nagorno-Karabakh—reminding them that they had officially welcomed a more active role for the CSCE. Faced with such a request from the primary parties, Kazimirov was upset but had little choice but to invite the CSCE to participate in the negotiations that hitherto had been conducted exclusively by Russia. The Eliasson team thus gained a role for the international community on this track, in addition to the deliberations at the CSCE headquarters in Vienna. This international presence was, as often is the case, particularly important to the weaker side, Azerbaijan.

For the international mediators, there was a constant danger of being sidetracked. For instance, one of the main texts of the negotiation process was the Russian-mediated cease-fire agreement of February 12, 1994. Although Russia officially was positive to the idea of coordination, the CSCE mediators were not shown the text of the agreement in advance. Still, the CSCE team persisted. In a letter to the Security Council on April 6, 1994, Eliasson again tried to assert the international role by stating that a cease-fire should not be the final move.[20]

The cease-fire agreement—still in force today—was concluded in mid-May 1994, after an initial agreement failed on May 9. Armenian forces had surrounded the Azeri town of Ter-Ter, and were ready to open artillery fire on its 60,000 inhabitants, when the president of Azerbaijan agreed to the cease-fire. The groundwork for this was made by a CSCE delegation led by Mossberg, who shuttled between the capitals in the Caucasus, achieving an agreement in principle among

---

18. The Swedish team consisted also of diplomats such as Carl-Johan Åsenius, Anders Bjurner, and Per Thöresson, and peacekeeping experts such as Jörn Beckman and others.

19. Eliasson, diary entry dated April 9, 1994.

20. See Eliasson's letter to the Security Council as chairman of the CSCE Minsk Group. "Letter Dated 6 April 1994 from the Chairman of the Conference on Security and Cooperation in Europe Minsk Conference and Minsk Group to the President of the Security Council," UN Security Council document S/1994/423 Annex, April 13, 1994.

the three parties. Russia was determined to have the cease-fire concluded under its auspices. This was done a few days later, on May 12, at a meeting of the CIS (the Commonwealth of Independent States) in Bishkek, Kyrgyzstan.

Kazimirov tried to keep the initiative and marginalize the CSCE team. This was demonstrated when talks over implementation were arranged in Russia's Ministry of Defense in Moscow. The talks were shown on Russian television on May 16, 1994. Russian defense minister Pavel Gratjov led the deliberations. There were no international representatives at this event, and no flags were displayed. In practice, the negotiations turned into Russia-led talks with the three parties (official representatives of Azerbaijan, Armenia, and Nagorno-Karabakh). Russia put the recalcitrant party, Azerbaijan, under strong pressure and was unwilling to give CSCE a role in the monitoring of the cease-fire.

However, the CSCE was still there and, in a joint statement to the press, Eliasson and Kazimirov "expressed their satisfaction that the present cease-fire, although fragile, is being respected" and that it was "the result of an agreement reached on May 12, 1994 . . . after mediation efforts by the CSCE and the Russian Federation." They also made clear that they had "proposed an agreement to consolidate the cease-fire through the deployment of international observers." Eliasson commented at the time:

> Nobody can say that we had been passive. In fact, we had speeded up the entire process and moved it in a direction that probably made "certain circles" in Moscow worried.[21]

In essence, Russia had ended the conflict in a way that was advantageous to Armenia, and the international efforts did not have a hearing in Moscow's Ministry of Defense. Politically, however, those efforts remained alive and significant. The Eliasson team now concentrated on having an international presence in the planned peacekeeping operations. This was stated in its letter to the Security Council that reported on Eliasson's and Kazimirov's visit to the region in June 1994:

> During this visit a draft agreement to consolidate the cease-fire was elaborated and accepted in principle by the parties. The agreement foresees deployment by monitors from CSCE, including the Russian Federation and/or the Commonwealth of Independent States. It also envisages that negotiations about the cessation of the armed conflict and the elimination of its consequences are expected to be concluded.[22]

Achieving this proved more difficult than expected. At the OSCE meeting in December 1994, OSCE agreed to send 1,500 monitors, but there was no funding. What could have become a first, major achievement for OSCE as a security organization did not come to fruition. There was not enough support.

---

21. Eliasson, diary entry dated May 19, 1994.

22. See Eliasson's correspondence with the UN Security Council. "Annex: Letter Dated 9 June 1994 from the Chairman of the Conference on Security and Cooperation in Europe, Minsk Conference and Minsk Group, Addressed to the President of the Security Council," UN Security Council document S/1994/687 Annex, June 9, 1994.

In essence, Russia made clear its superiority in the region. It had reluctantly accepted an international presence. As Kazimirov said in October 1994, "the real rationale behind attempts to appropriate a 'central role' to the Minsk Group . . . is to eliminate an independent mediation by Russia."[23]

This demonstrates the difficulty in mediating a conflict in the vicinity and strategic interest of a major power. The Eliasson team attempted to make itself relevant (by being party to the talks and agreements), by finding support (notably among the weaker parties), by creating transparency (through international observers), and by initiating a political process (which would enable a settlement as well as respect for principles of territorial integrity). There were some advances but the effort was—on the whole—more difficult than anticipated. However, the team remained on the scene and the OSCE process has continued to be a framework for a future settlement of the conflict.

We have seen that when there are different mediation efforts, mediators may compete for space. Such a situation may also risk forum shopping—that is, the primary parties may go to the mediator of their choice, for a better hearing or even a deal. This normally weakens a mediation effort. However, when a determined major power is involved, outcomes may be different. Azerbaijan's constant attempts to make the CSCE a strong third party were in reality an effort to reduce Russia's influence and to shop for a better deal. Finding a fitting forum is likely to be an approach for parties that are isolated and find themselves in an asymmetric situation. Azerbaijan's action echoes that of Iran in the 1980s and possibly some of the movements in Darfur in the 2000s, which pinned their hopes to UN special envoys. These actors will prefer a mediator they hope will serve their goals. However, to the mediator, there is a limit to the extent to which he or she can incorporate a particular party's ambitions without losing credibility on the opposite side. Being embraced by one can lead to refutation by the other. Forum shopping is likely to be an unavoidable option. For the mediator, it presents an additional incentive to make its particular role, approach, and standing the most attractive.

Styles in Mediation Context

The mandates of the mediator, with respect to actors other than the primary parties, are often unspecified. As Eliasson has been assigned by international organizations, it is natural to assume that the efforts should be as compatible with other interests as possible. Five of the six cases have been mandated or supported by the Security Council and/or the top international civil servant, the UN secretary-

---

23. This is illustrated in communication from Kazimirov to the chairman, Jan Eliasson, October 13, 1994, quoted in the report of the International Crisis Group, "Nagorno-Karabakh: A Plan for Peace," Europe Report No. 167, October 11, 2005, 9, 80.

general. Thus, Eliasson has been alerted to the significance of having the major powers on board. The support, however, has been varying. The Palme mission saw little supportive major power action, while the Iran-Iraq II mission witnessed greater consensus in the Council. In the two humanitarian issues, Eliasson operated as a top employee of the United Nations, and it seems to have caused little reaction among the major powers. In the Darfur case, Eliasson pointed to the lack of united Security Council support in his and Salim's final statement to the Council. Clearly the three Western permanent members were more concerned about the situation, while Russia and China only occasionally paid attention to it. China had the most tangible interests in Sudan and oscillated between different diplomatic positions. The bottom line was that the conflict would not affect power distribution in the country in a way detrimental to China's oil needs. Thus, the support from the Council was wavering.

The Nagorno-Karabakh case is an outlier and thus has warranted closer analysis. A major power, a permanent member of the Security Council at that, had a direct stake in the outcome. Among Eliasson's cases Nagorno-Karabakh was probably the most difficult experience. The multilateral mediators had to insert themselves into the situation and make themselves relevant.

An interesting observation can also be made regarding the operational mandate: the more "political" the dispute, the more forceful the interests of other actors trying to compete for influence. Ending wars affects the security of other states. They will act to protect or advance their interests. Humanitarian crises may often concern nongovernmental organizations. They may want more state action or be critical to such action. Yet, overall, tension and competition between mediators may be a more acute problem in political than humanitarian missions.

As to the scope, there was an emphasis on inclusion in Eliasson's approach, also in the Nagorno-Karabakh conflict. The Swedish diplomats argued that Russia involvement would benefit the process, even if it still might act unilaterally (as we have seen). Bringing in the Karabakh Armenians was also controversial: Eliasson made a dramatic and exhausting visit to the destroyed town of Stepanakert, their headquarters, as did Mossberg. This was a way to learn about their particular perspective. They ultimately convinced Azerbaijan on the value of this. Eliasson also paid visits to Turkey and Iran to bring in their views and keep them informed. The Eliasson team regularly reported back to the CSCE and sometimes to the UN Security Council.

There was a similarly inclusive and international approach in the Darfur case. The attempted international conference was a way to demonstrate this approach. In Iran-Iraq I and II, such an approach was less obvious, because the interactions were with the Council and the secretary-general, rather than with the public at large. Even the humanitarian cases had such a restricted approach. In those cases, there was a preference to deal directly with the parties and reduce media access to fairly technical and routine issues.

Another part of the international community—civil society organizations—has emerged and become important in peace processes. In the Darfur conflict, Eliasson connected to those other tracks, involving the nongovernmental community of actors. For instance, the Catholic community Sant'Egidio and the Center for Humanitarian Dialogue (based in Geneva) pursued "track two" mediation initiatives. Although these initiatives did not have an official mandate, their unofficial status was at times a strength. Eliasson himself has acknowledged the significance of international civil society in mediation.

Eliasson's mediation method in relation to the international dimensions of the Nagorno-Karabakh conflict was fostering rather than forcing in nature. He emphasized the primary parties, convincing them that there needed to be a significant CSCE role in the settlement. The international step-by-step approach became the strategy. Its strongest supporter was Azerbaijan: it wanted international oversight to compensate for its weakness, and it may have preferred a more comprehensive approach, including the withdrawal of Armenian forces from its territory. Although the mediators could not bring that about, they conveyed to the parties the urgency of ending the war. This may have been what the mediation effort was most successful in achieving. It helped to give CSCE a role in the continued process. More comprehensive ideas, such as the one of international peacekeeping, did not appeal to the militarily dominant parties.

In the other cases, the same fostering approach is apparent. There is reluctance to use threats or leverage, even in generating international support. Even in dealing with potentially competing mediation initiatives, the legal and political advantages for the UN track dominate. With our earlier example of the related negotiations on the hostages in Lebanon, we demonstrated that there may be leverage also for international mediators.

The mode obviously varies with the situation. When the task is to insert international mediation into a situation where the welcome is lukewarm, the use of media has been cautious. Generally speaking, there was considerable publicity surrounding the events in which Eliasson and his teams were engaged. It is, however, hard to see this as a regular form of public diplomacy. Attention was often on technical and narrow matters, although they affected the strategic equations. In the case of Nagorno-Karabakh, public statements were negotiated with Russia's special representative and referenced the various steps taken. Thus, they were not a part of an educational effort. Rather, they were a means to allow the big power to project the picture that it was in charge. In turn, the media was invited only to those meetings where Russia's strength was demonstrable. The mediators were clearly at a media disadvantage in such circumstances.

Openness was also restricted in the other cases. The appeal to public involvement was limited. The hope seems to have been to generate global support through meetings and exchanges of information rather than through media campaigns. In fact, public attention outside the concerned regions was limited in all cases except Darfur. As a whole, Eliasson's experiences illustrate a focus on peace, in a narrow sense. In the Nagorno-Karabakh case, there was little chance of raising the obvious injustices against Azerbaijan's territorial integrity or Armenians' self-determination rights. Concerns about war crimes, the return of refugees, and reparations were all deferred to the second and third stages of the imagined process. The question is whether it is actually possible to raise such issues in a highly asymmetric situation that also involves parallel mediating efforts by a major power. Eliasson made references to the return of refugees, for instance, but to no avail. The shadow of a strong neighbor affects all facets of the mediation style of an international go-between: it is not easy to go together under such circumstances. This illustrates the difficulties for collective and asymmetric mediation.

It is remarkable to find that international norms have yielded to other, more narrow concerns in several of the cases and, thus, in effect, stymied mediation efforts. Palme ran into an international reluctance to uphold the inviolability of borders in Iran-Iraq I; Eliasson could see some of the same in Iran-Iraq II, as well as in Nagorno-Karabakh. In Darfur, new norms dealing with war crimes were outside the mediation efforts and did not seem to generate strong support. Thus, the mediation environment may make mediators focus on a more narrow concept of peace.

7

Going Out:
The Diplomacy of Exit

A t some moment in time, the efforts of an international mediator must be terminated. The dynamics surrounding the cessation of mediation are as important for international mediators as those surrounding their entry and work during the mediation process. Remarkably, however, cessation dynamics have received substantially less attention. So we ask, under which circumstances do mediators decide to terminate a particular mediation effort? This section deals with three issues related to the diplomacy of exit. First, because a mediator may use the prospect of his or her withdrawal as leverage vis-à-vis the belligerent parties, we discuss when such a threat can be purposeful for the international mediator. Second, we examine the reasoning behind the termination of particular mediation initiatives, as seen from the mediator's perspective. Third, we raise the question of finding successors. A peace process seldom ends with the end of one mediation effort.

Threatening to Terminate

One strategy a mediator can use to achieve a desired outcome from negotiations, particularly if they appear stalled or protracted, is to threaten his or her withdrawal.[1] By suggesting that there is a limit to his or her patience, the mediator may increase the momentum for a settlement or bring about a breakthrough in the negotiations. When parties see the negotiation channel and the mediator as beneficial or even crucial for themselves, any indication that this channel will be closed may put the belligerents in a diplomatically more vulnerable position. This, then, is a way for a mediator to gain leverage over the parties.[2]

The termination threat is not the same as the mediator's use of deadlines. Rather, this concerns the ending of mediation efforts as such. Timing is essential.

---

1. Note that this value of mediation efforts can be due to an earnest wish to find a peaceful solution to the conflict, but it can also be strategic in the sense of gaining time for a new military attack or a better position in negotiations and thus greater concessions from the other, etc.

2. On the threat of mediation withdrawal as a tactic of mediation, see Zartman, *Ripe for Resolution*, 223; Touval and Zartman, "International Mediation in the Post–Cold War Era," 437; Crocker, Hampson, and Aall, *Taming Intractable Conflict*, 141; and Svensson, "Democracies, Disengagement and Deals."

A misplaced announcement may reduce, rather than intensify, urgency for a settlement. If parties expect the mediator to withdraw and the mediation efforts to be terminated, then the antagonists may have little incentive to invest time and energy in the mediation efforts. The mediator is at risk of becoming irrelevant without access to key actors.

However, Eliasson is doubtful about the utility of withdrawal threats in the diplomacy of exit. His comments illustrate his perspective in this regard:

> *Threats are dangerous to use for the mediator. You always have to be ready to implement them, or otherwise you will lose your credibility completely. Therefore, I am skeptical about using the threat of withdrawal as a mediating strategy. If I would threaten to withdraw, there is always the danger of becoming a "lame duck," reducing the relevance and importance of the mediator. Moreover, some actors sometimes also want the mediator to leave—it may be in their interest. To threaten to withdraw might play into the hands of the hawks.*

In this statement, Eliasson points to three dangers in using the termination threat in mediation: the risks of losing trust, credibility, and momentum. As a go-between, having the trust and confidence of the parties is essential. To use the threat of termination means trying to increase the mediator's leverage over the parties and putting pressure on them to make necessary concessions. In this way, it is more of a manipulative strategy.[3] Instead of using pressure on the parties, Eliasson's preferred approach generally is to emphasize the building of relationships between the antagonists themselves as well as between the antagonists and the mediator. To switch from a trust-building approach to one of threatmaking could undermine confidence created during the process.

Eliasson's second reason for skepticism is the loss of credibility. The mediator should not use the threat to withdraw if he or she cannot live up to it. If the belligerents continue to obstruct the process after a threat of mediation termination, the mediator must be ready to actually end his or her mediation effort. Eliasson's multilateral mandate makes such ultimate withdrawal difficult: the mediator is, so to say, bound by his or her appointment and assignment to stay in the situation if there is even the slightest chance of finding a solution to the conflict. The humanitarian incentives behind peacemaking compel the mediator to continue the effort. After all, the ultimate goal is to minimize human suffering. Ending it could be seen as leaving people to the mercy of war. Thus, when multilateralism and humanitarian concerns motivate the mediator, it is awkward to withdraw. It might have negative implications for those most exposed, the innocent and unprotected civilians. The parties might anticipate this, and thus the mediator's threat of withdrawal will not be credible.

The third factor in Eliasson's reluctance to use the termination threat relates to the public versus the more confidential mode of the mediation effort.

---

3.   More on the different mediation strategies of manipulation, formulation, and facilitation can be found in Zartman, "Dynamics and Constraints in Negotiations in Internal Conflicts."

There are often likely to be tensions inside the parties, what Eliasson refers to as "hawks" and "doves." There are those who question the utility of negotiation and mediation or even see them as resulting in dangerous concessions and those who support them. The termination threat can play into this intraparty dynamic.[4] In fact, the threat of withdrawal can empower those segments within a society that oppose any compromises and concessions toward the other side. Thus, if there are forces and actors that want the mediator to leave, a threat of withdrawal risks playing into the hands of such opponents.

Timing the Exit

Mediation processes sometimes appear endless. To continue negotiations requires great patience. There must be readiness to invest time and resources in processes that seem to lead nowhere. Indeed, Iran-Iraq I was the most protracted negotiation in which Palme had been involved, and this is also true for Eliasson.

Yet, sooner or later, an international mediation initiative must come to an end. All sides realize that. Often no party wants to be the one that ends the process. When, then, does it end? Some of the Eliasson negotiations have been short, notably the one on Nagorno-Karabakh. Others have been much longer. Eliasson was engaged in the Darfur issue from December 2006 until June 2008, and the Palme mission was most intensively pursued over four years.

The go-between needs to determine if there has been sufficient progress for him/her to end the mediation efforts. There are different yardsticks for success.

An agreement is a natural end point in the dialogue phase. In the two humanitarian mediation efforts, Eliasson's mediation ended with agreements. In Bangladesh and Burma/Myanmar in 1992, the parties issued a joint statement on repatriation, which was negotiated bilaterally, based on previous talks with Eliasson. Likewise, in Sudan the intervention ended with two bilateral agreements on war relief, one between the United Nations and the government in Khartoum and one with SPLA in Nairobi. The agreements provided a basis for humanitarian relief to previously inaccessible areas in the south.

Yet, when there is no agreement, the go-between needs to decide whether to continue the mediation efforts or terminate anyway. In Iran-Iraq I, the active mediation efforts were put on hold after 1982. The Palme mission presented to the parties a basis for a solution to the conflict. Yet, the parties did not agree to use this proposed solution as a starting point for a peace process. Palme and his team decided that a key factor for progress—a political willingness to seek a political solution—was missing. The mediators could not affect this and, therefore,

---

4. For a discussion on pro-continuation versus pro-conciliation, refer to C.R. Mitchell, *Gestures of Conciliation: Factors Contributing to Successful Olive Branches* (London: Macmillan, 2000).

further mediation efforts would be fruitless. In a letter to the secretary-general on February 28, 1982, Palme wrote,

> I do believe that we can see the beginning of a process that will ultimately lead to a settlement. The objective conditions, including a consolidated leadership on both sides, exist. What is lacking is a political decision to make a determined effort to reach such a settlement. No mission from the outside can provide this political will. It could happen overnight but will probably take considerable time. But I believe that the outline for a settlement that we have presented is reasonable and probably represents what will ultimately be an acceptable agreement.[5]

The suspension of the mediation efforts, thus, was driven by the idea of clarifying the responsibility for the lack of progress, and putting the responsibility into the hands of the parties. Similar reasoning was at hand when Eliasson considered terminating his involvement in Darfur. The main concern for Eliasson was to clarify basic responsibility for the continuation of the conflict. There was a risk that the parties, as well as people on the ground, would blame the mediators for the lack of progress. Yet, Eliasson argued, the determining factor behind the failed negotiation attempts was the lack of political will among the parties. He also added the lack of concerted pressure from the international community, in general, and the permanent members of the Security Council, in particular. Without political will among the parties, a serious effort to settle the conflict would not be possible. There is a limit to the ability of the mediator to create such "will" among the parties. As Palme had said sixteen years earlier, it cannot be created "from the outside."

Seeing no political will, Eliasson decided not to renew his mandate for the Darfur conflict when it expired in June 2008. He wanted to use his withdrawal as a way to make clear, in diplomatically well-formulated but still clear language, where the responsibility for the absence of a fruitful process toward peace rested. First, he and Salim went to the African Union and then to the United Nations with their shared evaluation, demonstrating to the conflicting parties, and the Security Council, who had the main responsibility for the conflict and its resolution. As Eliasson states,

> *I was going to lose my confidence capital if I would have stayed on in the Darfur conflict. In particular, when voices were raised blaming the mediators for absence of a political solution, the situation was becoming unacceptable. If a mediator is used this way and the parties are just playing games, withdrawal should be an option. Withdrawal is then a matter of clarifying who carries the responsibility for the lack of progress.*

Lack of political will also played a crucial role in Nagorno-Karabakh, when Eliasson decided to end his efforts as a mediator, despite the interest from the parties of seeing him continue in this capacity. In Eliasson's case this had to do with his other obligations (Eliasson became the state secretary of foreign affairs in Sweden in October 1994). But he also saw a lack of political will to settle the

---

5.   Letter to the UN secretary-general dated February 28, 1982.

conflict. When the parties themselves perceive the conflict as intractable, the possibilities for a mediator to move the parties toward peace are slim. Hence, the withdrawal from Nagorno-Karabakh was partly due to a realization that there was no will among the parties to seek a negotiated solution to the conflict. This conflict was moving from an intense phase into a frozen one, where the incompatibility could not be resolved. Hence, in Nagorno-Karabakh, the status quo situation was a sort of convergence of the parties' interests: a "no war, no peace" scenario, which both sides preferred above other alternatives.[6] Eliasson explains:

> *I remember a late night meeting with Levon Ter-Petrosyan, the leader of Armenia, who told me, leaning back in his chair and smoking his cigarette from a cigarette-holder: "Jan, you have many good ideas. But . . . this will be as Cyprus." At that moment, I realized that this was going to be an intractable conflict and that it was futile to continue to mediate.*

Here, the lack of commitment from the primary parties played into Eliasson's calculus to terminate his mediation efforts. As we discussed in chapter 6, the international environment was an important part of the dynamics of the conflict resolution process in Nagorno-Karabakh. Eliasson noted in his diary:[7]

> If I do not have the confidence of the Russians, I need to consider whether I should terminate my own role, or Sweden's role, as a mediator in this mission. However, first we need to know whether CSCE is ready to give a substantial contribution to the security of the region. If not, we should probably leave. To give our blessings to a solution that the parties do not want should not be a Swedish concern.

The mediation efforts can also come to an end because the whole dynamic of the conflict changes. In the case of Iran-Iraq II mediation, efforts became secondary after the Iraqi invasion of Kuwait in August 1990. The conflict with Iran moved to the background. Iran pledged neutrality in the conflict and thus did not exploit the opportunity to restart its war with Iraq. Eliasson remembers:

> *The chief negotiators from the Iranian side came to visit me at my summer home in Gotland, in the very end of July 1990. We discussed how the peace process was to proceed. The next evening they called me from the Sheraton Hotel in Stockholm. They had seen on CNN that Iraq had invaded Kuwait. After that, the peace process between Iran and Iraq was obsolete and lost its relevance.*

The conflict dissolved itself as the parties had other concerns. The parties actually opened direct negotiations outside the third-party mediation track. Thus, they regulated their remaining differences directly. Consequently, there was no need for further mediation.

---

6.   Charles King argues that a "no war, no peace" situation can reflect a convergence of elites' interests. King, "The Benefit of Ethnic War: Understanding Eurasia's Unrecognized States," *World Politics* 53, no. 4 July (2001): 524–552.

7.   Eliasson, diary entry dated September 23, 1994.

Finding Successors

We have seen that mediators can and do terminate their efforts. Yet, a mediator would be irresponsible if the parties were left drifting. The mediator will
attempt to pave the way for successors to continue peacemaking in the future.
Finding a successor becomes important. The ultimate decision is normally not
in the hands of the mediator. His or her advice, however, can be significant.

In Darfur, efforts to reinvigorate the peace process had not proved successful.
Eliasson's decision not to renew his mandate was coupled to efforts for finding
a new mediator who could (1) be jointly responsible toward the United Nations and the African Union and (2) be stationed permanently in the region. The
appointment of this particular type of mediator would address some of the concerns and limitations of the mission by Salim and Eliasson. The cooperation between Salim and Eliasson seems to have been close and constructive. However,
in the long run—in particular, when the parties are at the negotiation table—the
presence of two lead negotiators presents a risk. By appointing a mediator who
would be representing the United Nations and the African Union simultaneously, a coherent international approach could be enhanced:

> *Salim and I put a lot of effort into finding a suitable mediator that could take over from us in Dar-
> fur. We wanted to find someone from Africa and who could represent both the African Union and the
> United Nations—and minimize the risk that the parties played the mediators against each other.*

In other instances, the question of a successor was determined by organizational procedures unrelated to the mediation. In Nagorno-Karabakh, Eliasson's
mediation was done within the framework of the Swedish chairmanship of the
OSCE. Hence, when Sweden had fulfilled its presidency, Finland was elected
co-chair of the Minsk Group, while Italy resumed chairmanship of the OSCE.
Naturally, Finland then also took the lead for the mediation team and the Minsk
Group.

The process of succession after the humanitarian mediation efforts was different from the process of succession after political mediation. After Eliasson's
efforts between Bangladesh and Burma/Myanmar in 1992, the successor was
an agency within the UN system. UNHCR continued to negotiate with the
governments of Bangladesh and Burma/Myanmar and began to negotiate with
the Thai government as well, which was also affected by an influx of Rohingya
refugees.[8] Although Eliasson left the region with an immediate and positive outcome, there was no solution to the underlying problem:

> *In the case of the Rohingya refugees, it remains a problem. Maybe I should have followed up. The
> political problem has not been solved.*

---

8.   See HRW, "Human Rights Watch World Report 1992—Burma (Myanmar)."

In the same way, when Eliasson ended his efforts in Sudan in 1992, the humanitarian efforts of the United Nations Children's Fund (UNICEF) and its Operation Lifeline Sudan (OLS) were able to resume their activities.[9] The OLS continued to provide humanitarian relief to the war-affected populations as much as they could: expanding relief operations in 1993 from six to forty locations, thanks to the two agreements.[10] During 1993, the UN Commission on Human Rights also became engaged by appointing a special rapporteur for human rights in Sudan.[11]

In these ways, Eliasson's missions led to dynamics that continued under different auspices and with different actors. The missions were part of a process and the process continued.

Style and the Diplomacy of Exit

Mediation is, as we have discussed in this book, a voluntary activity, requiring the consent of the participating parties in conflict. This has implications also for the end phase of mediation. This ownership implies that it is up to the parties themselves to resolve the conflict.

The question of mandate is important in the diplomacy of exit. Eliasson, deriving his mandate primarily from the multilateral setting, needed to evaluate what was achieved through the mediation efforts from the viewpoint of what was the ambition of the third-party intervention. In Iran-Iraq I, the Palme mission aimed at facilitating authoritative communication. In other words, the mission was to lay the groundwork for direct negotiations between the parties on the highest political level. When the mediation efforts moved into a passive phase in 1982, the Palme team considered that they had exhausted all possibilities for direct negotiations. Its settlement proposal was, according to the team's perspective, the best possible basis for a fruitful and constructive negotiation aimed at resolving the conflict. Since the parties remained reluctant to negotiate on the basis of this proposal, the mediation team did not pursue its mediation efforts. It focused on confidence-building measures.

When Eliasson mediated in Iran-Iraq II in 1988–89, the mandate was to implement Security Council Resolution 598. The team attempted to create a jointly agreed-upon plan for the implementation of the resolution, but other events took over. In Nagorno-Karabakh, the mandate of the mediation efforts was initially to negotiate a comprehensive cease-fire agreement and later to dis-

---

9. Operation Lifeline Sudan at the time consisted mainly of UNICEF and the World Health Organization (WHO), as well as several NGOs.

10. See HRW, "Human Rights Watch World Report 1993—Sudan."

11. Gáspár Biro was appointed on March 10, 1993. Office of the High Commissioner for Human Rights, "Special Rapporteur on the Situation in Darfur," 2007.

cuss political aspects of the peace. The cease-fire agreement reached in May did stop the fighting and the Swedish mediation team did prepare the groundwork. In Darfur, the mandate was to reinvigorate a political process. As with Iran-Iraq I, it was a prenegotiation mission. When Eliasson and Salim terminated their mediation efforts, they thought that there was no way of moving the process further.

Thus, using the mandates as the baseline for evaluating outcomes, all the political mediation cases were difficult to bring to a natural end point. The humanitarian mediation efforts were quite different. In both cases, Burma/Myanmar and Southern Sudan, the operational mandates were fulfilled, and this provided a logical termination for Eliasson's mediation.

The scope of Eliasson's mediation efforts was quite important in the end phases. As is evident in the Darfur and partly in the Nagorno-Karabakh cases, the lack of commitment from the international community was one of the reasons that Eliasson decided to terminate his peacemaking efforts. The primary parties did not request that Eliasson end his efforts. A mediator is likely to end his or her mission in the same way that it has been pursued during its active phase. The inclusive aspect was present at this point as well: the issue was brought to a larger body that could continue the process, possibly with new instruments and new ideas.

To some extent, a more forceful method can be discerned in Eliasson's diplomacy of exit compared to his actual mediation efforts. At the end point, there was less concern with creating momentum and more with clarifying responsibility. In this way pressure was brought on the parties and on the outside world to take appropriate measures to end the conflict.

Mediation can also be ended on the supply side of the equation. In the midst of the Nagorno-Karabakh case, Eliasson was called to take on the position of the Swedish state secretary for foreign affairs, making it difficult to continue his operational responsibility for the continuation of the mediation process. Although Eliasson perceived that the parties had trust in him, he felt obliged to end his mediation effort. This also terminated Sweden's involvement. His withdrawal may have affected the course of the negotiations and illustrates the lack of an institutional setting for mediation. We will return to this theme in the next chapter.

The ending of mediation is, of course, a public event. In Iran-Iraq I, in the humanitarian missions, and in Darfur, the endings were used to make clear where the responsibility lay. The mediators wanted to put the responsibility squarely where it belonged and not be blamed for the lack of progress. In Iran-Iraq II and Nagorno-Karabakh, there were no such public endings. The mandates simply expired, notably those of the secretary-general and the Swedish presidency of the OSCE. A successor was found in the latter case and was unnecessary in the former. There is, in general, less public attention to the ending of mediation than to other phases of the peacemaking process.

At the end points, the mediators seem to have refrained from putting the conflict in a broader framework. The focus, in these cases, has been on the ending of the war and on the human suffering. Larger issues of justice have not been activated at this juncture.

Even so, the way a mediation mission ends is still likely to be remembered if it is associated with negative developments. For Eliasson this was not so. On the contrary, after each of his missions, the international community remained interested in his continued service.

8

Going Ahead: Lessons for Mediation Theory and Practice

Mediation is formed by the initial mandate. This has been overlooked in previous research. In this book we have demonstrated that it affects the styles of international mediators in managing and resolving armed conflicts and humanitarian crises. Through the experiences of Ambassador Jan Eliasson, we have seen how the mandate directs the way a third party enters a conflict, affects the mediation process, involves the international community, and finishes an assignment. In particular, we show how four basic styles in mediation—scope, method, mode, and focus—describe the challenges and opportunities in mediating international conflicts.

This constitutes a basis for formulating lessons for policy and research as well as for future inspiration and guidance. Thus, we highlight three main areas of how mediation can move forward. These concern the mandates, resources, and outcomes of mediation. Furthermore, we show how style plays out in the different components of Eliasson's mediation. This provides a tentative theoretical framework for future research on other mediators.

We also suggest that mediation has to be seen as a sequential selection process with different types of mediators playing different roles. This means, for instance, that the United Nations often is left to take care of neglected conflict situations or those where others have tried but failed. Paradoxically, states that want to mediate may be more restrictive than interstate organizations when choosing conflicts in which to be involved. The cases of armed conflict that reach the UN agenda are not a random selection. Rather, there is a notion in previous research that "the United Nations is saddled with the most intractable disputes."[1] In all the cases in our present study, mediation has stemmed from mandates, requests, and offers involving international organizations, not from individual states. Indeed, all the political conflicts Eliasson has dealt with can be defined as "difficult." Thus,

---

1. The citation comes from Saadia Touval, "Why the U.N. Fails," *Foreign Affairs* 73, no. 5 (September/October 1994): 51. Other scholars discuss the proposition that the United Nations gets to manage the tougher cases conflicts, such as Daniel Frei, "Conditions Affecting the Effectiveness of International Mediation," 26, 1976; and Jacob Bercovitch and Richard Jackson, *International Conflict: A Chronological Encyclopedia of Conflicts and Their Management 1945–1995* (Christchurch, New Zealand: Congressional Quarterly Inc., 1997).

they provide a set of exceptional situations from which lessons can be learned of relevance for all kinds of cases, whether "difficult" or "easy."

Mediation Mandate

In our analysis of Eliasson's mediation efforts, it became clear that the mandate is of crucial importance for what a mediator can do. It determines what strategies and tools a mediator may use. It sets the outer parameters of mediation, but still leaves some leeway for the mediator.

We have separated two elements of the mandate: its origin and its operational aspects. All of Eliasson's mediation efforts were based on a multilateral mandate (United Nations, African Union, or OSCE), although the requests for the humanitarian mediation efforts came from the realities in the field, the parties, or the local context, rather than from the international scene.

In general, a multilateral mandate gives mediators access to professional and communication resources, legitimacy, and informational clout. Moreover, it creates opportunities for cooperation and a division of labor between different actors. A multilateral mandate turns into a resource, as the efforts are part of what the international community wants to achieve in a particular conflict.

Yet, a multilateral mandate works as a restriction as well. Eliasson had no coercive power to use against the parties. Nor had he access to promises of resources to coax the parties toward peace. The multilateral setting also strained the efforts. The bureaucratic apparatus of multilateral organizations may prevent the peacemaker from acting quickly. It may also limit the go-between in the choice of tactics and strategies, as there is a constant need to anchor third-party efforts with significant countries from the mandating organization.

In the six cases we have studied, the mandate was formulated by multilateral bodies. The parties had a role in its formulation, but the mediator often did not have a corresponding impact. This is different from the cases of other mediators. For instance, Norwegian mediator Jan Egeland states that the Oslo peace process was initiated on a direct invitation from the parties themselves. Representatives of the PLO approached Norway requesting them to set up an informal channel of communication with the Israeli government.[2] Another Norwegian mediator, Ambassador Mona Juul, states the parties were "looking for alternatives" to the multilateral framework—the Madrid conference, co-chaired by the United States and the Soviet Union and with representation from most of the Middle East—that dominated the scene at the time: "we were in the position to offer a radically different approach."[3] There are advantages of getting

---

2.   See Egeland, "The Oslo Accord," 532.

3.   Mona Juul, "Israel and Palestine? Experiences of Mediation and Mediators in the Middle East," *Development Dialogue* no. 53 (November 2009): 34–35.

the mandate from the parties directly. There was confidence in the process from the outset and trust in the mediators by the parties. The difference in the way mandates are arrived at also sets parameters for mediation style.

A different approach to the mandate is reflected in the position of the OSCE high commissioner on national minorities. The first holder of the post, Dutch diplomat Max van der Stoel, held it for eight years from 1993 to 2001. According to the mandate, the commissioner could enter any country or region, without an invitation or even consent by the state or by OSCE. Such an overall institutional mandate provides freedom for independent initiatives. This definitely—as described by van der Stoel—was one of the "innovative elements" in the mandate.[4]

Generally speaking, however, the operational mandates of the mediator are intimately related to the phase of the conflict. Eliasson's six cases give many examples of this. For instance, we can see that in the cases that covered an early crisis phase, the operational mandate was limited to humanitarian issues. This is partly a result of the coordinating role of the UN secretariat (the cases of the Rohingya refugees, Southern Sudan). This conflict phase represents particular challenges for the mediator. The humanitarian imperative requires swift action with quick results. Yet, it is also important not to risk escalating the situation. After rapid interventions, Eliasson could hand over the process to other actors.

In a later crisis phase, when armed conflict is going on, the dynamics of the mediation efforts have been markedly different. Here the operational mandates have been to halt the fighting and provide space for a political settlement (for example, in Nagorno-Karabakh). The battle dynamics helped create a sense of urgency that made the parties willing to agree to a cease-fire. Yet, the challenge for Eliasson and for the mediation efforts was to try to expand the mandate to include political aspects in order to prevent agreements from resulting in an unresolved status quo—a frozen conflict. This turned out to be difficult.

The Eliasson-Salim mandate, in a very late, entrenched conflict phase (the case of Darfur), concerned finding ways to reinvigorate a virtually stalemated peace process. There was an opportunity to generate new momentum and energy with new strategies and new staff. Yet, the challenge for the two mediators turned out to be the need for unifying the divided opposition groups to facilitate substantive talks on concrete solutions.

In the one case with a postwar implementation mandate, Eliasson faced a conflict that had formally ended but lacked substantial agreements on the incompatible positions (Iran-Iraq II). Eliasson's challenge was to find common ground between parties with extreme levels of hostility and mistrust, and

---

4. Max van der Stoel, "The Role of the OSCE High Commissioner in Conflict Prevention," in *Herding Cats: Multiparty Mediation in a Complex World*, ed. Chester Crocker, Fen Osler Hampson, and Pamela Aall (Washington, DC: United States Institute of Peace Press, 1999), 68.

maintain the momentum of the political process so that the parties would not return to the battlefield.

With this in mind, we point to the need for researchers to study mandates, mediation objectives, and conflict phases for a more realistic understanding of the challenges and opportunities of the mediators. There is variation between mediators representing states and those coming from international organizations. But this distinction is not sufficient. What mediators are able to do will also depend on what they are requested to do by the mandating organization and by the conflicting parties.

This study is also meant to inform the thinking on how mediation mandates ought to be crafted. First and foremost, there is a difference between humanitarian and political mediation. Whereas humanitarian mediation can be short-term, immediate, and launched with limited resources and without regard to the phase of the crisis (although earlier phases would obviously be preferable), the same is not true for political mediation. Political mediation requires a more long-term commitment, more institutional support, and a coherent framework for cooperation within the international system.

Moreover, the optimal mandate must avoid crucial and damaging discrepancies. One of these is between mediation mandates and resources. Mandating a political mediation effort should be followed with substantial institutional backing that enables teams of experts and/or mediators, provides for links to research-based knowledge, and includes expertise on media relations. In most of Eliasson's mediation efforts (with Darfur being the exception), the institutional support the interventions received was remarkably limited, consisting of only a few individuals. This may be sufficient in humanitarian mediation efforts where the aspirations are narrow and precise. Yet, it is more problematic in political mediation efforts, which often concern more entrenched and difficult problems.

An imbalance can also occur between mediation mandates and expected outcomes. One may ask if the mediation commissioning bodies or parties have given sufficient thought to the preferred outcome already at the outset, or whether any outcome will be acceptable. For instance, in his work on Kosovo's status, Martti Ahtisaari followed guidelines that he interpreted to mean that Kosovo could not be returned to Serbia.[5] In other words, he followed the predetermined, preferred vision of the United Nations and its secretary-general, which was in effect incorporated in his mandate.

Finally, there could be discrepancy between mediation mandates and conflict phases. For instance, a mandate for negotiations when the parties are internally divided (as in Darfur and Iran-Iraq I) may be inadequate to achieve progress

5.   Martti Ahtisaari, "What Makes for Successful Conflict Resolution?" *Development Dialogue* no. 53 (November 2009): 42.

toward peace. The mandating organization needs to take parallel actions to ensure that the peace process can deal with the problem of who should be at the negotiating table, to consider the inclusion of civil society, and to assist in creating room in the mandate for mediation *within* some of the conflicting parties.

Mediation Outcome

An obvious lesson from the six experiences we have scrutinized is that mediation does not always result in complete and durable peace agreements between the parties. Such an outcome may not even be the purpose of mediation. This is a distinctive feature not only of Eliasson's work but of most mediators. Although there have been at least 175 peace agreements in the last twenty years, the number of mediators and mediation efforts is probably much higher. It is—no doubt—particularly rewarding to a mediator if a peace accord is solemnly signed in ceremonial circumstances. However, this is not necessarily as common as thought. In Eliasson's six mediation efforts, the goal was often to ease or keep communication between the primary parties, reduce the human suffering from the conflict, stop the fighting for a specific period of time, prevent a resumption or spread of conflict, and find elements for a final peace agreement.

The different measures of success may provide the first and most important lesson: it is not the mediator who stops the war, it is the parties. The parties, by accepting the mediator, indicate a willingness to find ways out of a particular conflict. However, the mediator cannot force the parties to end a conflict when one or the other does not want to end it. In our conversations, Eliasson often referred to the difficulty of getting horses to drink the water once they are at the waterhole. The six experiences all testify to the fact that the horses will drink when they are thirsty, not before. Wars end only when the warring parties are willing to end them.

However, we see that the go-between may be able to assist in increasing the awareness of the need to end a war. The go-between keeps reminding the parties of the expectations of changing their present behavior. The go-between also points to the bargaining range in which the parties find themselves. In the absence of direct communication between the parties, the mediator may be the one who is most informed on what options the other side has and thus what is potentially feasible and acceptable. Such information can be useful for primary parties when assessing their own preferred way of acting. We surmise that this is an important function in mediation, as often mentioned in the general literature.

Providing informed opinions may add new data to the fighting sides and may also, as we believe happened in the Iran-Iraq II case, result in direct contacts between the primary parties outside the mediation framework. Thus, it may be that a mediator can contribute to ending a war earlier than it would otherwise have ended. Of course, this is a hypothesis that is close to impossible to prove, at least with only six cases.

For the primary parties, as well as for their supporters and opponents, the puzzle may be different than the one pursued by the third party. Indeed, the negotiator is seldom the final decision maker for any of the parties. Only when negotiations directly involve a state leader is that the case. Eliasson has often had direct access to the leaders of the countries concerned, but most of his time has been spent with foreign ministers or high-level representatives of the parties. The leaders often prefer not to make personal commitments until late in the process. That provides for uncertainty in all mediation efforts.

Let us again point to the important distinction between humanitarian and political mediation. The two humanitarian efforts have involved quicker results, with governments agreeing to changes that facilitated solutions to humanitarian crises. At the time, the early 1990s, such crises seemed less politicized and were dealt with on the basis of a global consensus on the need to protect civilians.[6]

The political cases did not find easy ways out. In some of these cases, the mediator pointed to the humanitarian effects of the war, and some headway was made, notably an end to military attacks on cities and civilians in Iran-Iraq I. However, such a humanitarian consensus may be more difficult today, not least in Sudan. In retaliation for his ICC indictment, President Bashir decided in March 2009 to close down some international humanitarian efforts in Darfur, accusing international organizations of spying. This reduces the possibility of appealing to the need for international assistance as a way of reaching into a particular conflict.

An important difference between humanitarian and political mediation is also in the possibility of handing over implementation to other agencies. In the two humanitarian cases, Eliasson made the necessary agreements on a high political level. It was then left to humanitarian agencies to implement the deal, notably UNHCR in the Rohingya situation and UNICEF in Southern Sudan in the context of Operation Lifeline Sudan. This also made clear the practical and technical nature of the agreements. Professional, "neutral" agencies took over the issues.

In political cases, this is more difficult. After all, the war efforts have to be stopped by the parties themselves. It is difficult for third parties to monitor what actually takes place. However, organizations can be set up for this, and we have

---

6. Note, however, that some purely humanitarian mandates of actors within multilateral organizations, such as the role of Sergio Vieira de Mello at the UNHCR in the Cambodian mission after the Paris Agreement in the early 1990s, were indeed used for political objectives. Vieira de Mello, as head of the challenging task of managing the return of hundreds of thousands of Cambodian refugees, was one of the few UN staff in Cambodia that would start talking with representatives of the Khmer Rouge about humanitarian issues to solidify the fragile political process in post-conflict Cambodia, and in this way "use humanitarian successes to pursue political ends." Samantha Power, *Chasing the Flame, Sergio Vieira De Mello and the Fight to Save the World* (London: Penguin, 2008), 124.

seen this—for example, with cease-fire monitoring teams (as in the case of Iran-Iraq) and plans for a peacekeeping force (as was tried for Nagorno-Karabakh). Some issues could be handled by other agencies, notably the Iran-Iraq prisoner-of-war exchanges, through the regular procedures of the International Committee of the Red Cross. In the Iran-Iraq War, the secretary-general developed an unusual and innovative way to solve the question of responsibility for the war. Humanitarian issues may be "easier" to handle in less politicized ways, but even highly sensitive issues may find administrative, "neutral" solutions.

These practical examples point to an important insight long overdue in the scholarly literature. Researchers interested in understanding mediation and measuring outcomes and successes may need to broaden their horizons. It may not be enough to narrowly focus on peace treaties or cease-fire agreements. It may be necessary to incorporate more nuanced understandings of the operational objectives of international mediators and, particularly, those of the parties to the conflict. Finding ways to measure the success of ongoing mediation efforts might not be an easy task, but it appears nevertheless to be an inevitable next step for building more policy-relevant mediation research. It is even more urgent for fully professionalizing the process of mediation. A culture and practice of professional mediation requires accumulated knowledge and well-developed resources internationally, nationally, and locally. It also requires more realistic expectations for what a mediator can achieve.

Mediation Resources

A major lesson on resources from Eliasson's experiences is that multilateral mandates, their limitations notwithstanding, provide a fruitful basis for international involvement and support. In fact, there is a need to have the international community cooperating—"going together"—for mediation to be successful, particularly in political cases. An international body expresses its commitment to a peaceful outcome by appointing a third party. By continuously informing key actors, a mediator is able to exert pressure on the primary parties themselves. Eliasson clearly devoted much time to solicit the views of leading actors, notably the major powers, regional states, and parties themselves. This is a strategy for many mediators, of course, but particularly significant for the multilateral ones, which are accountable to the organization they represent.

In an ideal world, these leading actors would all rally behind the special envoy and supply him or her with all necessary assistance. In practice, this does not seem to be the case. The permanent members of the Security Council, for instance, may have their own objectives and pursue their own policy vis-à-vis the primary actors. Such activities, seen by major powers to be in their interest, also make clear to the primary parties that the mediation effort is *not* the only game in town—there are several others at the same time. Based on the six cases, we surmise that the stronger and more credible international support is for mediation, the more likely it will accomplish the set goals. The combined resources of the international community should indeed overpower what resistance any primary party could muster.

Another lesson pertains to the crucial need for sufficient human and material resources when entering, sustaining, and concluding mediation efforts—in other words, having a skilled and appropriately sized mediation team. A striking feature of the Eliasson cases is the limited size of the efforts. In all cases the mediation team consisted only of a handful of persons. Eliasson entered international mediation in 1980 as a personal adviser to Special Representative Olof Palme. The UN secretary-general also set aside time for some of his own associates (for instance, Diego Cordovez and Iqbal Riza). Although being a high-caliber team, all involved had other assignments at the same time.

The exception is the Darfur case, with a large office operating from Khartoum, which at moments in time has involved at least twenty persons. We see this as an encouraging sign of giving more emphasis to mediation in difficult cases. There may be circumstances unique to the Darfur case for this emphasis, however. This includes not only the guilt feelings of the outside world, but also the worries over the fate of the Comprehensive Peace Agreement in Sudan. Furthermore, there were many complications in getting this office to work smoothly, as it faced both the Sudanese authorities and the AU and UN bureaucracies.

By and large, international mediation efforts are provided with minimal financial resources from the sponsoring international organization. This seems to be the accepted practice for international mediation and not seriously questioned by our interviewees. As a result, efforts sponsored by the international community may be at a disadvantage compared to other mediation attempts. Henry Kissinger and Richard Holbrooke could draw on the U.S. State Department, Jimmy Carter and Bill Clinton on the entire U.S. federal government, and the third-party mediators in the Oslo channel benefitted from the diplomatic networks of the Norwegian foreign service. Only in 2006 did the United Nations set up a Mediation Support Unit, and only in 2008 was a team of external mediation experts recruited. This makes it inevitable for the go-betweens to rely on the resources of their home government. The efforts then run the risk of becoming "national" under an international heading. This is an argument for strengthening the international resources for mediation.

A possible solution to the chronically limited resources of international mediation teams could be to incorporate academic resources into the process. Eliasson improved his position by doing so, notably in the Nagorno-Karabakh and Darfur cases. As we demonstrated in chapter 3, Eliasson used his position as a visiting professor in a clever way to inject new ideas into the negotiations. In general, the academic community is likely to have considerable insights that are of relevance for the negotiations. It may also be possible to use the academic milieu as a possible framework for establishing separate channels of communication or for generating proposals for thorny issues.

There is even a need to have local representation for a mediation effort to be pursued with continuity and vigor. The lead mediator may have to travel extensively and perform the necessary diplomatic footwork associated with the efforts. However, there is also a need to be updated on what is happening among the primary parties. There may appear new opportunities that should be observed and acted on quickly. Having the full mediation team flying in at a particular juncture creates a lot of attention and expectation. Local representation may be a better way to capture the moment as well as prepare for the arrival of the team leader. Thus, not only having a high-caliber team based at the headquarters but also having a support team on the ground would strengthen mediation efforts.

To further assure continuity of mediation and to keep momentum in the process, there is a need for more in-house documentation as well as greater cooperation between international organizations, national foreign ministries, and nongovernmental organizations. These actors may benefit from having special offices for international conflict resolution efforts and policies for handing over "the file" to new envoys and mediators. Eliasson was appointed personal representative for the Iran-Iraq War, because "he knew the file." Similarly, Eliasson had experience with Darfur and Sudan prior to his appointment. On a more general level, Eliasson also was able to apply what he learned in one mission to the next one. However, in many other situations, a new third party comes in entirely "fresh" to the field. The UN special envoy to Burundi, Ahmedou Ould-Abdallah, experienced this lack of continuity in 1993 at the start of his mission. He scheduled briefings in Paris and Brussels on his way to Burundi to get an updated understanding of the situation on the ground before arriving.[7] Though it is not effective if time has to be used for relearning what has already been learned, we find, at this time, little evidence of the United Nations or other international organizations having clear procedures for making mediation efforts cumulative rather than sequential.

The lessons on mediation resources can all be connected to one key word—cooperation. Effective and sustainable international mediation requires the cooperation and support of crucial elements of the international community, complementing the international organization with the possibility of adding "drums in the background" to the process. It also calls for cooperation with local efforts and forces for peace as well as individual and personal cooperation between the lead mediator and his or her team. Mediation as a profession and a long-term process needs to accumulate knowledge over time. For researchers interested in

---

7. See Ould-Abdallah, *Burundi on the Brink.*

mediation, these lessons imply increased attention to research questions such as: How can multiple mediators cooperate to fulfill their objectives? What role do domestic conflict resolution resources play and how should the assets of the international community relate to them? What role do mediation support functions play and when are they effective in boosting mediation mandates and efforts? How can mediation knowledge be nurtured and transmitted among actors and across time?

The mandate, the outcomes, and the resources of mediation present intriguing lessons and inspiration for theory development. However, these concern the general framework of mediation. We have yet to see what lessons can be drawn about how international mediation might be pursued more fruitfully through the scope, methods, mode, and focus that are available to the mediator.

Styles of International Mediation

We have seen that Eliasson employed different styles of mediation over time and in different settings. Thus, the mediation style is likely to evolve for a particular mediator, but also vary with respect to the conflicts. We have identified four basic dimensions of mediation style: scope, methods, mode, and focus. In this section, we will pursue the discussion by first examining how the different dimensions played out in the case of Eliasson, attempting to identify his particular mediation profile. At the end of this section, we will turn to a comparative analysis of how his style compares to other international go-betweens and reflect on his style's strengths and weaknesses.

Scope: Inclusive or Exclusive

When entering as a mediator, there are basic decisions to be made regarding the scope of the mediation efforts. Eliasson did not intervene until he had secured support from key international actors and the acceptance of the main parties in the conflict.

The scope may also vary according to the conflict phase. When the operational mandate is about initiating processes, the scope can be more limited and centered on the main actors. During the mediation process, it is crucial to cooperate with others' initiatives, not least with those of regional actors. In the termination of mediation efforts, it is critical that the mediation efforts are followed by other actors, both within and outside the mandating organization.

A major debate in mediation literature is whether to include all parties or exclude some. In an interstate conflict, such as the one between Iran and Iraq, or even in the Nagorno-Karabakh issue, the parties are quite obvious. In the humanitarian cases, Eliasson's efforts were largely directed at the governments. The complications arise in internal conflicts. Interstate conflicts do not have this problem. In a regionally based conflict, such as the one in Darfur, it is also some-what more complex. The diversification of actors in Darfur was unprecedented, and the two mediators had to spend considerable time trying to bring the many different movements together. It did not help that the Sudanese government was also divided between the two parties to the 2005 Comprehensive Peace Agreement (covering the North-South conflict).

When Eliasson and Salim called a peace conference on Darfur, they decided to be inclusive. Yet, this created a process of self-selection among the different fac-tions. Only some wanted to participate, and several of the most important factions opted out since they questioned the legitimacy and representativeness of some that had accepted the invitation to attend. Some invited actors, who saw them-selves as obvious participants, refused to come because others were present whom they did not accept as legitimate, causing fragmentation within some groups.

Eliasson's scope in terms of the mediation process has been inclusive at dif-ferent levels. In the discussion of the diplomacy of entry (chapter 3), we outlined three levels that need to be ripe in order for the process to bear fruit. Obvi-ously, the scope of Salim's and Eliasson's mediation efforts, due to the mandate and the setting, had to incorporate all levels. For instance, in order to move the Darfur process forward, Eliasson and Salim shuttled between the international community, the regional actors, and the parties to the conflict. This was a way of trying to stimulate political will and forge the consensus needed for a peace process to materialize.

The first level relates the go-between to the international community. It is important to create international cohesion. The international community, par-ticularly the UN Security Council, must be united in its will to settle the conflict. Thus, it has to be in basic agreement on what the settlement process should look like. We have seen that Eliasson has gone to great lengths in order to include the major and most significant players at this level. In fact, the mediation process has often been just as much about going between the parties as going between them and the international actors.

A second important level is the regional context. Internal armed conflicts of-ten have important regional linkages. Likewise, interstate conflicts do not occur in a vacuum; neighborhoods are affected by and influence the dynamics of the conflict. Conflicts breed on other conflicts and interstate tensions. The primary parties need their neighbors in order to get access to arms, secure trade routes, build international prestige and reputation, and find political support. Primary parties need secondary parties. Therefore, protracted conflicts will not be ended unless there are accompanying peace moves on the regional level.

The primary parties form the third level of action for the international go-be-tween. First, there is the government side in the conflict. Its interest in a peaceful settlement and its internal cohesion are important prerequisites for progression toward peace. These factors can also be influenced by the actions taken by the international go-between. In civil wars, a second difficult and contentious issue is who will represent the nonstate actors fighting against the government. Here the international go-between has to work to get a coherent position from the movements to be present at the negotiation table.

There is increasing attention in mediation literature to the issue of inclusion versus exclusion. Some studies point to the significance of an inclusive approach.[8] Given that there has been a general proliferation of actors in conflicts at least since the early 1980s, such an inclusive approach may provide a strong challenge to the future conduct of mediation.[9] This certainly gives further support to the urgency of increased mediation resources, as mentioned earlier.

It may also point to the importance of incorporating other actors into the peace process. In the Darfur case, Eliasson and Salim reached out to humanitarian organizations. We have seen in other cases, such as in the Liberian peace agreement of 2003, that women's organizations played a significant role in pressing the primary parties toward an agreement.[10] It is important that a large number of actors understand an agreement and can monitor its implementation. However, we also think civil society should not be made responsible for the process as such. It may serve a more significant democratizing function by being a competent critical force in society.[11]

Method: Forcing or Fostering

Influencing the parties' perception of the process is key to Eliasson's style of international mediation. When entering as a mediator into a situation of humanitarian crisis or political conflict, Eliasson has tried to create a sense of momentum. The Palme team considered the possibility of demanding concessions from Iran and Iraq in 1980—making its acceptance of the mediation assignment conditional on initial progress in the peace process. However, the team did not pursue this forcing approach. Eliasson has not used conditionality in the entry

---

8. See, for instance, the conclusions of Kelly M. Greenhill and Salomon Major, "The Perils of Profiling—Civil War Spoilers and the Collapse of Intrastate Peace Accords," *International Security* 31, no. 3 (2006): 7–40; Harold H. Saunders, "The Multilevel Peace Process in Tajikistan," *Herding Cats: Multiparty Mediation in a Complex World*, ed. Chester Crocker, Fen Osler Hamspon, and Pamela Aall, 159–179 (Washington, DC: United States Institute of Peace Press, 2007); and Harmonie Toros, "'We Don't Negotiate with Terrorists!' Legitimacy and Complexity in Terrorist Conflicts," *Security Dialogue* 39, no. 4 (2008): 407–426. Desirée Nilsson comes to a somewhat different conclusion, finding that not all rebel movements in a conflict have to sign an agreement for peace to prevail between those parties who actually settle their conflict peacefully. Nilsson, "Partial Peace: Rebel Groups Inside and Outside of Civil War Settlements," *Journal of Peace Research* 45, no. 4 (2008): 479–495.

9. See the work of Harbom, Melander, and Wallensteen, "Dyadic Dimensions of Armed Conflict."

10. See Nilsson, "Partial Peace."

11. For more on this, see Peter Wallensteen and Mikael Eriksson, *Negotiating Peace: Lessons from Three Comprehensive Peace Agreements* (Uppsala, Sweden: Department of Peace and Conflict Research, Uppsala University, 2009).

phase of his mediation efforts. Instead, he has emphasized the creation of positive expectations to resolve the conflict or crisis.

During his different missions, Eliasson has primarily used a fostering style. The international go-between has limited possibilities of forcing an agreement on the parties. Other mediators may be at an advantage here. But for those working on international mandates, it is more difficult to exert consistent leverage on the parties. Instead, the go-between has to develop incentives. Eliasson is clear on the need to appeal to the parties by arguing that, for example, the conflict has gone on too long, the suffering is too high, military solutions will not work, and there is a fair settlement at hand.

Leverage can be generated, even artificially—for example, if one party has a specific need that only the international body can provide, such as recognition. However, Eliasson's style, in general, has not been based on developing leverage. Largely he has resorted to tactics of fostering agreement among the parties, rather than forcing it upon them. This means looking for ways of generating momentum and finding opportunities for reducing tension or building confidence, while at the same time striving to make the conflict less severe. Much of Eliasson's efforts have involved such a positive approach. The Palme mission suggested various confidence-building measures, some of which were actually implemented (ending the attacks on civilians in the border areas, for instance). In Iran-Iraq II, Eliasson developed concrete confidence-building measures, such as the release of prisoners-of-war. In the Nagorno-Karabakh case, Eliasson spent considerable time on creating a peace operation, though to no avail, and in Darfur he focused on persuading the parties to come to the negotiation table.

These examples again illustrate the central importance of the parties. If they are seriously interested in solving a conflict, confidence-building measures might not be necessary: they may move ahead anyway. Under such circumstances, the mediator's role is to build on the momentum. In several of Eliasson's efforts, there was little or no momentum to build on. Thus, confidence-building became a way forward: to create steps that would be tangible and generate the will to make peace. However the parties must know the direction that the steps will take them. Otherwise, they are unlikely to take the first step. A primary task of the mediator, in other words, is to assess the will and visions of the parties during all phases of the mediation and the conflict.

The personality of a mediator also affects the dynamics of mediation and affects whether a mediator is perceived as fostering or forcing. The mediator needs to be aware that his or her personal character is integral to the effective application of mediation style. A mediator may appear tough, rude, uncompromising, principled, and even dull, thus generating an image for the parties of being difficult to influence and move. Alternatively, the mediator may instead appear open, attentive, culturally sensitive, flexible, or even charming, thus generating a willingness among the parties to cooperate and compromise. One or the other style element may not appeal to the parties. Different mediators demonstrate different personality traits, which, of course, will color behavior.

However, as we have observed, mediation also requires a bit of artistry and acting skills. On this score, Eliasson is clearly focused on the significance of generating a good atmosphere, developing a positive, shared, and respectful problem-solving attitude that may turn a negotiation into a conversation without losing track of the ultimate purpose. Other mediators seem to take a different attitude. Some are described as chess players (to borrow a label used by Paul Kavanagh), implying a constant concern with moves, countermoves, and future moves. This gives little room for anything beyond normal courtesy. In our interviews, personality traits are often mentioned as important. Whether that actually is the case, however, is an open question.

Mode: Confidential or Open Mediation

In this study we have found that Eliasson employed different modes of mediation in different settings. At first, he was quite secretive and performed confidential mediation (Iran-Iraq), but later, he increasingly appreciated the value of openness and public attention (Darfur, in particular). Having realized that the media can either enhance or hurt mediation efforts, he may be one of the first media-conscious go-betweens.

In all of the cases of mediation explored in this book, Eliasson has been public and open about the initiation of his mediation efforts. Whereas other go-betweens may have worked secretly, far away from the public arena, Eliasson has been in the limelight when entering a situation of humanitarian crisis or political conflict.

The use of the media has varied across the mediation efforts. During Eliasson's first experience, he could see how Palme considered its role. However, a member of the Palme team, Iqbal Riza, described Palme as very careful in first fully informing the Security Council before talking to the media. This makes sense for maintaining support for the mediation effort. At the same time it was also important to engage the media, because the primary parties make their own public statements. It is important for a mediator to convey a "correct" understanding of the mediation efforts. This engagement involves an educational element.

The importance of media also appeared in another way. In 1993 Eliasson was criticized by the nongovernmental organization Human Rights Watch for only privately condemning the forced relocations of people in Southern Sudan. He was said to continue "the failed policy of 'quiet diplomacy.'" At his first mediation effort as a special representative to the Iran and Iraq conflict, in September 1988 in Geneva, Eliasson would also keep what the media referred to as a "low profile." Conflict engages the primary parties, who watch the mediator very carefully. The humanitarian aspects will, however, activate other actors, who may also bring their perspective to bear. Thus, the mediator will have to be observant of many such interests.

The actual conduct of negotiations, however, remains confidential. It is difficult for the mediator to publicly reveal much beyond that to which the parties can agree, if the mediation is to continue. This may cause the mediator to face many charges, including accusations of being partial or being blamed for the lack of results. All mediators are exposed to such dangers. But the multilateral mediator may suffer more, as his or her efforts are likely to be more public, thus making it more important for the parties to "win" the public relations battle. The mediator, in such circumstances, needs strong support primarily from the head of the mandating organization. For the prospective mediator, it is important to have such support from the outset. Furthermore, by being accessible, the mediator seems more convincing and trustworthy when encountering the media.

The go-between can also utilize other actors in the multilateral system in order to maximize his or her weight on the parties. In fact, while go-betweens show an open attitude, they may at the same time cooperate closely with more confidential channels. In Darfur, perhaps Eliasson's most public intervention, he cooperated with the Geneva-based Center for Humanitarian Dialogue, which held confidential workshops with the movement leaders.

The endings of the international mediation efforts in which Eliasson has been engaged have varied in terms of their public or confidential modes. An interesting comparison can be made between the scaling down of the Palme mission in 1982 and the termination of the Eliasson-Salim Darfur mission. In the first case, the mediation team chose not to visit the region. It did not put forward new suggestions after finding that there was no political will to settle the conflict. After his fifth visit to the warring parties, Palme suggested disengaging from the mediation effort. Thus, this was going to be his last visit to the region. Palme, however, communicated this disengagement confidentially to the secretary-general. The secretary-general, however, asked Palme to remain special representative to the conflict between Iran and Iraq. By contrast, in Darfur, Eliasson and Salim decided to publicly reveal the lack of political willingness among the actors and thus clarify the parties' own responsibility for the lack of progress in the process. This was done in a UN Security Council meeting. They pointed to the parties and, in effect, also to members of the Security Council.

Thus, Eliasson demonstrates a mediation style that is unusually open and accessible. We suggest that this is consonant with the times: the media world today requires such an attitude, though it may not have been equally required in the 1980s.

Focus: From Narrow to Wide Peace

Throughout his career as a third party, Eliasson has encountered the problem of "narrow or wide" peace—that is, whether the focus should be on the immediate war-related issues or on broader dimensions, including justice. In Darfur, this question became particularly acute after Eliasson ended his mission. A reason for his involvement in Darfur was Eliasson's belief that the world had to react to the atrocities in the region. Thus, ending the conflict would be a way also to end the suffering of the population in the region. The injustices could end once the war ended. However, the negotiations were making slow progress.

In all the cases, there are basic moral dilemmas through which the mediator has to navigate. Peace—even in the narrow sense of ending war, building conditions for durable peace, and undoing some of the effects of war—may contradict justice in a number of ways. First, there are the underlying reasons for the war (based on ethnic cleansing, genocide, marginalization of regions, etc.) and the issue of whether they need to be addressed in the peace process. Second, there are issues stemming from the conduct of the war (weapons used, targeting of civilians, treatment of prisoners of war, etc.), which all relate to issues of humanitarian law, in some cases even to war crimes, that fall under the auspices of the International Criminal Court. Third, there are the issues of initiating and ending the war. Does the peace agreement correspond to principles of legality and justice (the justification for the first attacks, the violation of borders, the keeping of territory, etc.)? This also relates to the outcome itself. For instance, does the peace agreement correspond to legally enshrined principles (the status of refugees, for instance)?

The mediator, obviously, cannot pursue a justice-based approach when talking directly to the parties. It is unlikely that regimes would pursue mediation in the face of public criticism from a mediator; the mediator would be regarded as partial. For a mediator, there seems to be a difficult choice between a broader concept of peace including "justice" and a more narrow, traditional peace of ending a war. At the same time, Eliasson believes that the "moral high ground" should belong to the mediator. After all, the mediator represents an organization based on international law and humanitarian rules, which is committed to end a war that generates mass suffering. Mediation builds on the principles of peaceful settlement of disputes and the non-use of force between states. In Iran-Iraq I, the Palme mission also emphasized the nonacquisition of territory by force, which was welcomed by the Iranians and difficult for the Iraqis to reject. Thus, international law provides a principled standard beyond the interests of the parties.

Eliasson and his mandating organizations addressed the challenges mainly by separating wider issues from the mediation effort. To Iran, the war was unjust as it was started by Iraq. Thus, it was important for Iran to establish the responsibility for the war. This remained its approach throughout the war and was referred to in Resolution 598 of 1987, which led to the cease-fire of August 1988. For the secretary-general, it was a delicate issue to handle. The Kuwait War in 1990–91 in a way simplified the matter as it seriously weakened Iraq's standing. Still, Iraq did not want to be branded as the aggressor or face the prospect of compensation. Remarkably, it did not supply information to the panel of academics that investigated the issue in the second half of 1991. The report was submitted to the secretary-general, who made it public on December 9, 1991.[12] It recognized Iraq's responsibility. Iran had probably expected compensation, but it was not forthcoming. Instead, Iran kept the aircraft that Iraq had based in Iran to prevent the United States from attacking them during the Kuwait War. To Iran, peace was, in the end, accompanied by an element of justice. The secretary-general turned this matter into a separate process, outside Eliasson's mandate.

There were also other moral issues activated by the conflicts and to which mediators have to relate. A particular concern in the Iran-Iraq War was the use of indiscriminate weapons and the deliberate targeting of civilians, primarily by the Iraqi side. The use of chemical weapons is banned in international law. When Iran strongly criticized the use of such weapons, the international community had to react. The secretary-general gave the task of heading a mission to one person, Iqbal Riza, who was also a member of the mediation team. Formally, however, it was a separate undertaking, thus isolating the mediation efforts from the chemical weapons issue.

Riza made a thorough investigation on both sides of the front lines. His report demonstrated that such weapons had been used by Iraq, but it could not conclude the same for Iran.[13] Clearly, Iraq was trying to win the war through illegal weapons, with horrible effects. For a mediator, this created a further dilemma: such weapons clearly increased human suffering and would also prolong the war, even causing escalation. In retrospect, Eliasson believes he and the Palme mission should have been more active on this issue, mobilizing, albeit discreetly, other governments and opinion leaders. Riza, however, did what he believed was the right thing to do. He handed his report to the organization which could—and should—do something: the UN Security Council. It decided to do nothing.

---

12. See "Further Report of the Secretary-General on the Implementation of Security Council Resolution 598 (1987)," UN Security Council document, S/23273, December 9, 1991.

13. See the reports emanating from the later missions of Iqbal Riza and his colleagues in 1987 and 1988 ("Report of the Mission Dispatched by the Secretary-General to Investigate Allegations of the Use of Chemical Weapons in the Conflict between the Islamic Republic of Iran and Iraq," UN Security Council document S/17911, March 12, 1986, and "Report of the Mission Dispatched by the Secretary-General to Investigate Allegations of the Use of Chemical Weapons in the Conflict between the Islamic Republic of Iran and Iraq," UN Security Council document S/18852, May 8, 1987), as well as documents without Riza ("Report of the Mission Dispatched by the Secretary-General to Investigate Allegations of the Use of Chemical Weapons in the Conflict between the Islamic Republic of Iran and Iraq," UN Security Council document S/20134, August 19, 1988).

After this report had been presented, Riza was exposed to Iraq's displeasure. In a campaign, he was accused of being partial. The secretary-general allowed Riza to leave the mediation team and initiated an investigation that fully cleared Riza. He later became *chef de cabinet* under Secretary-General Kofi Annan.

Also the Nagorno-Karabakh issue presented moral issues apart from the need to stop the armed conflict. The fact was that Armenian and Karabakh forces had, by mid-1994, occupied one quarter of Azerbaijan's territory and that this created an exodus of people. The cease-fire merely froze the status quo. It left Azerbaijan dismembered and with a large refugee population. International law would rule that the displaced persons have the right of return following the ending of warfare. This was clearly not in the cards. The peace negotiations certainly would take up the issue, but they had to work from a basis of a de facto occupation. Eliasson criticized Armenia and Nagorno-Karabakh for this, something the parties did not object to, since it was done on a humanitarian basis.

To this we may add that many mediators will have to deal with regimes that do not adhere to values such as democracy, human rights, equality, and transparency. Iraq and Sudan were ruled by dictatorial or authoritarian regimes during Eliasson's missions, Iran was under a theocratic system, democracy was weak in Armenia and Azerbaijan, both just coming out of seven decades of Soviet rule, and Burma/Myanmar was under military rule. The common values to which mediators may appeal, may have had little resonance in such ruling circles.

Such a dilemma may be particularly pronounced for a mediator coming from an international organization espousing such values. This would be the case with third parties from the United Nations, OSCE, and the African Union. Depending on the conflict, this dilemma will be more or less acute for the mediator, who will have to find ways to deal with it while keeping to his or her main mission, ending the war. For a mediator, the continuation of the war may be the greatest injustice of all.

Comparing Mediation Styles

In this discussion, we have tried to analyze the style of one go-between, Jan Eliasson, in terms of scope, method, mode, and focus. Building on this analysis, we can draw a tentative picture, a profile, of Eliasson's mediation style. He is a go-between who has moved from confidential to open diplomacy, kept to a fostering rather than forcing method, worked more for inclusion of actors than exclusion, and given priority to a narrower peace focus. This particular style is in some sense unique to Eliasson, although he shares similarities with other go-betweens and other international mediators. The reasons for his choices of style are not necessarily only due to his personality but also to the mandates, the resources, as well as the types and the phases of conflict in which he has been active.

Being a public go-between in the international arena, Eliasson has increasingly shown a preference for being open about his mediation. He has consistently preferred to move talks forward through a fostering method. This particular combination is very interesting. Its advantage is the possibility to create positive, public expectations and build on such a momentum. At the same time, it lacks the advantages of access to leverage. Other mediators, notably Holbrooke, when engaged in former Yugoslavia, chose a more forcing approach. For instance, Holbrooke explicitly threatened the Serbian side during the negotiations with coercive measures, and could enforce the credibility of those threats with NATO bombing on Serbian targets.[14] By contrast, the American mediator in Northern Ireland, George Mitchell, applied a more fostering method, by stressing the joint political and economic gains that could be earned through a negotiated agreement. He also engaged the parties for a long (and tiresome) period, and his approach has even been described as "relationship therapy."[15]

Our analysis points to the importance of how mediation ends, not only how it starts. Eliasson has made conscious decisions to withdraw from mediation, but refrained from doing so strategically. True to his fostering style, he has not created artificial deadlines and has not capitalized on real deadlines (although in principle he is in favor of the idea). Other mediators act differently. At crucial points during the negotiations over the former Yugoslavia, Holbrooke threatened to terminate his mediation effort when confronted with intransigence by the Bosnian-Serb leader Radovan Karadzic.[16]

A second way to use termination dates for negotiations is to agree to or clarify end points. This is expected to sharpen the minds of the negotiators. Mitchell, who largely pursued a fostering method in Northern Ireland in the 1990s, still used the threat of his withdrawal if the parties did not meet a final deadline. Interestingly, this date was not unilaterally imposed but was carefully negotiated with the parties and governments.[17] Another example stems from U.S. assistant secretary of state Chester A. Crocker, who mediated in southern Africa in the late 1980s. He was able to use the real deadline of U.S elections and change of administration—clarifying for the negotiators that this would imply change of personnel and basic policy review. In Crocker's words, "the U.S. mediators pressed the Angolans, Cubans, and South Africans not to waste years of effort. The

---

14. See Kurran, Sebenius, and Watkins, "Two Paths to Peace," 519.

15. Ibid.

16. See Richard C. Holbrooke, "The Road to Sarajevo," in *Herding Cats: Multiparty Mediation in a Complex World*, ed. Chester Crocker, Fen Osler Hampson, and Pamela Aall (Washington, DC: United States Institute of Peace Press, 1999), 341–342.

17. Kurran, Sebenius, and Watkins, "Two Paths to Peace," 525.

agreements were signed ten days later."[18] In this way, Crocker and his team were able to create a sense of urgency that pressed the parties to an agreement.

An entirely different approach is for the mediator to not terminate the mediation efforts. The Vatican mediation team in the Beagle Channel case (a dispute between Argentina and Chile) underlined that it would stay on and would not terminate the mediation efforts. "The mediator's repeated statements that it would never abandon the mediation put the burden on the parties to withdraw."[19]

A question is which of these styles will achieve an ending to war and a lasting peace. Clearly, building on positive momentum and finding steps of agreement can be significant in the early phases of a peace process, when the parties are unwilling to engage in peace diplomacy. It means, however, that negotiations will take time, as they did in Northern Ireland. The more forceful approach may thus be more appropriate when one wants quicker results, as was the wishes of the United States and the West in the Bosnia case. In Northern Ireland, the outcome is largely a self-sustained peace, while in Bosnia the international presence remains heavy fifteen years after the agreement.

Another conclusion that can be drawn from this study is that Eliasson achieved humanitarian goals with his style. His pure humanitarian mediation efforts in Burma and Sudan can both be considered quick and successful. Also, he gained achievements in the humanitarian dimensions of the political mediation efforts, such as the agreements between Iran and Iraq not to attack border villages and to exchange prisoners of war, and the cease-fire agreement of 1994 in the Nagorno-Karabakh conflict. As a public go-between on the international area, Eliasson was able to create breakthroughs on the humanitarian front, where the parties may also have been concerned about demonstrating a positive image. Getting agreement on the central political issues, however, turned out to be more difficult. One may wonder if more forceful methods would have been needed to make the parties abandon long-held positions and patterns of behavior and whether these could have come from the mediator.

An aspiration for Eliasson has been to create opening and positive spillover effects from the humanitarian issues to the political sphere, "a foot inside the door," as he has told us. This dynamic has rarely materialized, however. Humanitarian accords have been important, but remain isolated islands of agreement in a sea of disputes and animosity. On the positive side, they have decreased the suffering of affected civilians. On the negative side, some may argue, these measures may also have taken away an urgency to settle these conflicts by lowering the incentives for finding a solution. Other mediators have not sequenced their

18. See Chester Crocker, "Peacemaking in Southern Africa: The Namibia-Angola Settlement of 1988," in *Herding Cats: Multiparty Mediation in a Complex World*, ed. Chester Crocker, Fen Osler Hampson, and Pamela Aall, 207–244 (Washington, DC: United States Institute of Peace Press, 1999), 229.

19. Thomas Princen, *Intermediaries in International Conflict* (Princeton, New Jersey: Princeton University Press, 1992), 175.

mediation efforts in a similar manner. For instance, Alvaro de Soto, mediating in El Salvador, built his efforts on the premise that a cease-fire agreement should not come until the parties had agreed to substantial societal changes.[20]

Eliasson's open mediation style has attractions but also weaknesses. One is that public mediation may make parties reluctant to reveal information to each other or jointly seek creative solutions based on such information. Other mediators that also work with a fostering method still have preferred confidentiality. For instance, in Burundi, the Sant'Egidio made progress by establishing a confidential negotiation channel once the official, public negotiations had reached an impasse.[21] Moreover, the initially secret Oslo channel used an academic cover, because the parties' demanded deniability and thus created a confidential process.[22] This may have been strategically important at that time, whereas all the following agreements in the Oslo process were negotiated in almost complete openness.

An aspect of openness is the relationship to media. We have observed an evolution in Eliasson's approach. There are interesting alternatives. The Vatican mediation effort in the Beagle Channel case had a very different approach to media. Right from the onset of the negotiation, the Vatican insisted that public press releases should only be made through the mediator. Thus, the parties were not allowed to issue press statements separately.[23] In this way, the Vatican go-betweens ensured strict control over information flow, minimizing the risk, in effect, of having to negotiate through media. Norway's facilitators in Sri Lanka had another approach to public media. They worked with press releases (often done in cooperation with the primary parties) to avoid rumors and clarify misunderstandings, but left it to the parties themselves to generate public support for the peace process. Since the parties did not take on such a responsibility, this resulted in a thwarted public image of the peace process and an increasing public mistrust toward the mediation effort.[24]

The public international mediator can mobilize the international community and generate political will. Yet, the open mode may make it difficult to maintain confidentiality. The direct negotiations at the table may be confidential, but they are made in an atmosphere of publicity, the press waiting outside the negotiation room. With such international attention, each side knows that they will have to face their own constituencies after making any concessions. The confidential setting could be more beneficial for concession making, but on the other hand, any

---

20. de Soto, "Ending Violent Conflict in El Salvador," 374.

21. Fabienne Hara, "Burundi: A Case of Parallel Diplomacy," in *Herding Cats: Multiparty Mediation in a Complex World*, ed. Chester Crocker, Fen Osler Hampson, and Pamela Aall, 135–158 (Washington, DC: United States Institute of Peace Press, 1999), 147.

22. See Egeland, "The Oslo Accord," 530–531, and Juul, "Israel and Palestine?" 35.

23. See Princen, *Intermediaries in International Conflict*, 175.

24. See Kristine Höglund and Isak Svensson, "Fallacy of the Peace Ownership Model."

mediator engaging in such activities will have problems creating public support. This dilemma has been recognized by the OSCE high commissioner on national minorities (HCNM), who worked in a strictly confidential mode.[25] One possible "solution" to this dilemma could be for the mediator to be attentive to the particular phase of the conflict. Secrecy could be more important in the (earlier) phases where concessions need to be made. When the potential for an agreement exists, however, it could be more important to create commitment. At this stage, a publicly oriented mediator can help to build public support for peace and get the parties to publicly bind themselves to such agreements. Given that the international media have grown increasingly important in the field of peace diplomacy, knowing when to communicate and having the skills and resources to communicate correctly and effectively to the public is becoming more important.

Thus, there is a potential problem for a multilateral go-between in combining a fostering method with openness. Eliasson's mandate did not generally give him the clout to make the parties change positions, nor did the mandating multilateral organizations provide a sufficiently protected atmosphere of confidentiality, where the parties could feel safe to share information on their underlying interests and possible openings. Back-channel mediation, such as the Oslo process, is interesting from this perspective, as it had a particular ability to combine fostering and secret elements.

There is also another area where there are potential contradictions among different elements of mediation style. We have characterized Eliasson's style as exclusive in scope with a focus on a narrow concept of peace. The multilateral HCNM also varied between an exclusive and inclusive scope, but with a preventive mandate HCNM also had the luxury of being broader in focus. Since the disputes on the HCNM agenda had not yet become violent, the focus was often on finding institutional approaches that satisfied minorities, thereby in effect contributing to more just societies.[26] Other mediators have been more narrowly focused on peace. Lakhdar Brahimi, the international mediator in Iraq in 2004 and before that in Afghanistan, criticized "human rights purists" for failing to understand that peacemaking implied talking to people with blood on their hands. His focus was on reaching peace, not establishing justice. That does not imply that he did not care about human rights issues, just that he thought that it was not the mediator's role to focus on human rights.[27] Eliasson had to deal with authoritarian primary parties to reach an end to violence or solve humanitarian problems.

Inclusion is an important but difficult dimension of international mediation style. Backed by his mandate, Eliasson opted for a more inclusive scope over

---

25. Van der Stoel, "The Role of the OSCE High Commissioner in Conflict Prevention," 71–72.

26. Ibid.

27. See Martin, *Kings of Peace, Pawns of War*, 25.

time. The invitation to negotiations from Eliasson and Salim to the Darfur rebel factions was open, broad, and inclusive. As we have seen, this created a difficult process of self-selection. Relevant actors contested the legitimacy of other factions. Intrarebel tension halted the process. The Norwegian mediators faced a related problem in Sri Lanka. Deriving their mandate from the parties themselves, they saw the LTTE and the government of Sri Lanka as the main parties, and thus allowed them to determine who should be at the negotiation table. This resulted in an exclusive process, where large segments of the society were not represented at the table.[28]

The scope has implications for the mediator's focus. With an exclusive scope, the agenda will also be affected. As mediators are tied by their mandates, a number of options are likely to be difficult to develop. In a sense, they are connected to the realities of the balance of power at the time. Mediators will have to accept the powers that be in order to achieve the more limited objectives of mediation—for instance, preventing deteriorating conditions or diffusion of conflict, or ending ongoing violence. Achieving thorough social change is outside the reach of most mediators. At a minimum, however, we conclude that mediators must make sure that agreements make an allowance for the creation of more just societies—such as by allowing the presence of civil society groups, freeing popular movements, protecting freedom of media, etc.

A final observation is the remarkable consistency in Eliasson's mediation style. It is likely to be the same for many other mediators. A mediator may develop a particular way of acting. When being selected, previous performance is likely to be a criterion. We note that Eliasson has changed primarily only with respect to scope, where he has moved toward a broader inclusion of actors, and to mode, where he grew more open to the media and the public at large. With respect to focus on peace, he has also demonstrated greater willingness to incorporate broader conceptions. However, his emphasis has continuously been on a fostering approach: trying to persuade the parties rather than to force them into agreement. The record of progress in this regard is mixed. This points to the importance of learning from other mediation efforts to find the right methods for a particular case: can fostering and forcing approaches be combined and would that enhance effectiveness? Eliasson's mediation experience, as well as those of many other mediators, are ad hoc and do not build on institutionalized resources for mediation. The limited successes of mediation in actually ending wars suggest the importance of a closer link between mediation research and mediation practice. This is what our final section deals with.

---

28. See Svensson and Höglund, "Fallacies of the Peace Ownership Approach."

Ten Implications for Mediation Research and Mediation Practice

Let us now attempt to draw some general conclusions on international mediation from this study that are applicable to mediation in practice and mediation research. We have identified ten significant conclusions.

1. Incorporate Learning into the Mediation Process

This book has put in focus one mediator, Ambassador Jan Eliasson. His six different experiences of international political and humanitarian mediation demonstrate unique characteristics as well as the general aspects of mediation. Eliasson belongs to a small set of persons in the world with such extensive experience in international mediation. The group also includes personalities such as Martti Ahtisaari, Lakhdar Brahimi, Jimmy Carter, and George Mitchell. However, the pool of experienced mediators is remarkably small.

Yet, how experiences and insights, fruitful approaches, and failures are transmitted from one setting to another is an arena of study that has been little explored. There is an evident need of more knowledge on the longer-term developments of different types of third-party mediators. The question of how different—positive as well as negative—experiences are accumulated by the third-party mediators remains to be examined.

In many conflict situations, diplomats, politicians, or representatives from the civil society engage themselves as mediators. Often they have no previous experience in mediating serious armed conflict. There are risks associated with a lack of the professionalism that may be needed in order to manage the extreme complexities of today's armed conflicts. To our knowledge there are no studies comparing such committed mediators to the more experienced ones. For the development of the field this seems a highly urgent task.

The protracted nature of many peace processes—with negotiations and peace agreements breaking down, followed by new attempts to settle conflicts—underline the importance of finding ways for learning the optimal ways of mediation. Today's many ad hoc mediation attempts may lead to ineffective, or even counterproductive, third-party interventions. There is a need to create systematic approaches to learning, sharing, training, and knowledge production in the field of international mediation.

A way to gain such insights motivated the writing of this book. Following one mediator acting in several different contexts turns out to be a very fruitful exercise. Such analyses hold potential for the future. Lessons from other experienced mediators are highly valuable. Together such work may also constitute the basis for comparative and statistical analysis, thus giving us generalized understandings of the art and science of mediation.

However, learning can also be achieved in a more direct way than focusing on particular individual "stars" in negotiations. We advocate that mediation efforts should be formulated as teams of individuals combining different competences, experiences, and backgrounds, operating under one mandate. That would make it possible to cover, in a competent way, the many different aspects involved in mediating an armed conflict or a serious international crisis. Mediation quality might improve.

Another advantage of such a mediation team is that it gives opportunities to train third-party mediators through actual participation in a real-life experience. Involvement as a junior diplomat or expert in a mediation team may yield valuable insights to be used in other efforts in the same conflict or even elsewhere. This helps to deepen knowledge, practice, and insights in the third-party mediation profession.

Certainly, experienced and world-renowned mediators have some clear advantages: they bring public attention to the situation, they have access to world political leadership, and their presence can help to create positive momentum for a process toward peace. Yet, the complexities of today's conflicts and crises point to the need for broader approaches that can manage the multidimensional aspects of conflicts. There are more parties to handle, an increased need for public relations, more regional powers to be included, and a more active role for civil society. Forming mediation teams is a way of meeting these new complexities.

2. Craft the Mandate with Care

The mediators' mandate is the cornerstone of mediation. This study has shown that the particular style of the mediators is largely driven by the mediation mandate. Previous research and policymaking debates have given surprisingly little attention to mediation mandates—how they are shaped and changed, as well as their strengths, weaknesses, and effects. This is a neglected field of study. This lacuna is even more striking when compared to peacekeeping, where the mandates are obvious starting points for analysis and action.

Thus, we argue that more study is needed of the mandate. No mediator operates without one. There is always someone "sending" the mediator to a particular situation, whether this is a government, an intergovernmental organization, a nongovernmental body, or some other type of organization. The mandate gives space to the mediator, but also restrains his or her choices. To some extent, we think, a mediator can affect the mandate. The "stronger" or more attractive a particular mediator is, the more there is a possibility of having an impact on the mandate. If a mediator appears successful, his or her space may become wider. However, there is never complete freedom for a third party. The primary parties and the mandating body will make that clear. Thus, there is a need for would-be mediators as well as mediation researchers to scrutinize the mandates.

The implication for policymakers is the importance of carefully crafting the mediators' mandate. It has to resonate with the context, the phase of the conflict, and the resources that the mediators have at their disposal. In this regard, a particular problem is that there may be opposition to mediation by parties who see their vital interests threatened. The opposition can come from the parties in conflict but also from outside states, neighbors, or big powers. Thus, there will be a tendency to restrict the mandate or limit the actions of the mediators. This provides a particular challenge in the process of shaping mediation mandates.

One insight of our analysis is the importance of minimizing discrepancies between mandates on the one hand, and available resources, anticipated outcome, and phases of conflict on the other hand. In some circumstances it may be important to give the mediators a wider mandate—for instance, to decide on the relevant actors of a peace conference—in order to avoid self-selection processes. Giving stronger mediation mandates on inclusion criteria can prevent dominant primary parties from vetoing participation by civil society and other actors deemed important by the mediator.

Individuals, governments, and international organizations do not always intervene in the same types of conflict. There is a selection process, which can create problems for mediation. It may lead to a mismatch between the request for particular mediators and the willingness of mediators to supply mediation. Finding the optimal fit between the parties' willingness to invite particular third-party mediators and the appropriate mediators to intervene is a crucial question in designing mediation mandates.

3. Make Way for Specific Styles in Mediation

As we have shown, mandates interact with styles in mediation. The styles of mediators vary with the mediators as well as the conflict situation that they are facing. The framework for analyzing the stylistic dimensions that we have presented in this book—scope, method, mode, and focus—is likely to be useful for the study of other mediation efforts. Clearly, the style used by a particular mediator is not just a reflection of personality, but is determined by the situation in which the mediator finds himself or herself. In addition, the style chosen may impact the mediation process, resulting in different outcomes. It is important for would-be mediators, as well as analysts who are examining mediation processes, to be aware of the style.

The discussions on style in the mediation literature have been dominated by the distinction between trust and power mediation and the typology of facilitation-communication-manipulation. This is akin to what we describe as the "method," in terms of either fostering or forcing the parties toward peaceful relationships. Yet, this distinction is too simplistic to be analytically fruitful. Styles have many more dimensions. The scope in terms of inclusiveness, the mode as the degree of openness, and the focus in terms of the broadness of the peace desired are other pivotal aspects of mediation style.

This typology makes mediation style a new research agenda. A systematic comparative approach, where the styles in mediation are empirically measured, could shed light on conditions under which different mediation styles are effective in bringing about peaceful resolution of conflicts and crises.

After understanding styles in a broader sense, third-party mediators should be able to create their own particular style depending on the mandate and the overall conflict situation in which they are involved. This implies that the style can, and in many cases should, vary over time, depending on the phase of the process. For instance, mediation could be more exclusive in the beginning of the process (mediation focusing only on the parties with armies, for instance) in order to pave the way for more inclusiveness at a later stage (incorporating civil society, neighbors). Hence, paying careful attention to the basic dimensions involved in mediation styles, policymakers can find new profiles in mediation and thus new ways of managing contemporary situations of conflicts.

4. Assess the Humanitarian Aspect of Mediation

One important distinction in this book is between political and humanitarian mediation. They are quite different in their mandates and processes as well as outcomes. Political mediation has dominated mediation study and policy debates while leaving aside humanitarian mediation. Still, humanitarian mediation is an important aspect of international mediation, both in terms of frequency and its likelihood of success. Humanitarian mediation is underrated.

As judged from this study, there is a marked difference in how humanitarian and political mediation efforts are initiated. The parties themselves or local actors directly affected by the crisis request humanitarian action in order to reduce acute suffering and/or prevent further deterioration of a situation. Humanitarian organizations play an important role in generating attention. Political mediation efforts, on the other hand, tend to stem from processes in the international arena. The international community needs to show the parties as well as their own constituencies that they are "doing something" about a particular political situation. The difference in how an operation starts has implications for how the process unfolds and for the prospect of reaching constructive solutions.

Humanitarian mediation efforts are more likely to be productive: temporary cease-fires may be negotiated, sufficient assistance delivered, and, thus, an emergency may be managed. Humanitarian mediation gains from its distance to the highly sensitive political sphere. This may make it politically attractive to turn to humanitarian mediation. That said, however, the challenges and problems with humanitarian mediation should not be glossed over. One of the most promising but also problematic aspects of humanitarian mediation is its relationship to politics. It appears from our study that humanitarian mediation efforts rarely move the parties closer toward settlement of the underlying political issues. There is some immediate remedy, which is to be applauded, but political mediation faces very entrenched interests that are more difficult to shift.

We have seen such dynamics in this study, but the general patterns need to be discerned. In particular, there is an urgent need to examine the relationship between political and humanitarian processes in conflict settings. For instance, can humanitarian mediation efforts create a momentum that spills over into the political sphere? Or are humanitarian mediation efforts merely waiting games in order to gain good will and buy time in order to pursue the armed conflict with renewed ferocity?

5. Focus on the Chance for Direct Dialogue

Efforts by a third party to depoliticize issues, for instance, through humanitarian mediation, in order to affect the political process is not necessarily a way to move forward. The intractability of political conflicts in general and armed conflicts in particular underlines the importance of finding constructive ways of managing sensitive political issues. Using clout to get the parties to negotiate the political issues rarely leads to constructive and sustainable solutions. This points to a third alternative that is neither nonpolitical nor power-based: to get a direct, political dialogue process between the parties themselves and to help sustain it. Many mediation efforts testify to the difficulty of achieving this but also demonstrate that this is the core of conflict resolution. Thus, political mediation should be seen as a dialogue process where the parties maintain a straightforward but constructive direct dialogue. In this the strengths of political and humanitarian mediation efforts are combined. Creating a channel where the parties can negotiate directly on their political incompatibility seems to be the hallmark of successful mediation efforts.

6. Create Institutional Support for Mediation

The individual mediators at the international scene are well-known and their capabilities tested in several different conflicts. Yet, the institutions of peace diplomacy are less developed. In order to be successful, third-party mediation cannot depend only on individuals and their talents. In addition, there has to be an institutional setting for international mediation. Much of this structure has yet to be developed. An example is the following.

International mediation sometimes tends to work in a "fly-in/fly-out" pattern, implying that mediation is not always initiated when it is most opportune. A local mediation presence in a conflict arena could maintain a more continuous process of dialogue and, thereby, increase the chance for an effective and peaceful outcome. Permanent offices of mediation and facilitation could lower the audience costs for initiating dialogue. It would be more of a routine operation and, thus, less dramatic if part of the mediation team was always at hand near the capital or the headquarters of the parties. It would also provide a way for mediators to react quickly when there seems to be an opportunity for them to act.

Another example is to develop the institutional capability of media relations. The mediator is an important source of information for media on the dynamics and obstacles of a peace process. We have noticed that the media play an increasingly important role in how a mediation effort is perceived. Thus, it is important to provide a correct message. Some individual mediators may have the capacity to engage in such public diplomacy, but in the long run there has to be a more institutional basis for public relations.

7. Be Alert to the Proliferation of Parties

One of the most important tasks for a mediator is to make a proper diagnosis. A thorough assessment of the situation—its complexity in terms of issues and actors—lays the basis for all further mediation efforts.

The mediator's first task when entering a conflict is to assess the situation in terms of whether the conditions are right for a successful effort. For that the international and regional scenes have to be favorable, as do the primary parties and their supporters. The mediation agenda has become more complex. During the Cold War, internal conflicts were polarized into blocks confronting each other. Since the Cold War, the number of conflict parties has increased. The creation of new groups is more common than the forging of united fronts. The relative ease with which groups can get access to arms, funds, and loyalty is surprising, but it is a fact with which the mediator has to grapple.

This is a problem that has not been part of previous experiences and only recently been covered in the literature. There is even the possibility that the onset of mediation sparks the proliferation of groups. As the mediation teams cannot necessarily reach all groups at the same time, this may fuel suspicion among some and appear to favor others. New groups are quickly created. It is also difficult for the mediators to set the criteria of who should be invited to negotiations and who should not. Such decisions should most appropriately be made by the mandating organization rather than by the mediator. This would be a way to keep the integrity of the mediation intact: the mediator is following decisions by others in this regard. An alternative is to empower the mediator to deal with the selection of negotiation parties, but then the support of the mandating organization is crucial.

8. Relate to Other Third Parties

In recent political mediation, there is a plethora of third parties. By contrast, humanitarian mediation efforts seem mostly to be conducted by single mediators without parallel or competing mediation efforts. The political mediation draws the attention and involvement of many actors who work in sequence or in parallel efforts.

The study of styles can help identify how different types of mediators can complement one another. In many instances, a variation of styles may be needed. For instance, both fostering and forcing the parties could be used as methods simultaneously. Likewise, both a more inclusive and more exclusive scope can run parallel in the process. Some mediators may focus more on justice and the broader types of peace, while others can focus on the task of getting a more narrow peace in the form of an end to violence.

The exact composition of mediation teams—how it should be created in order to maximize the possibility for success—is a potential avenue for future research. Different mediators may bring different types of leverage to the process. Some may bring sticks, others carrots, and still others may contribute more intangible resources such as information, trust, and the ability for face-saving. The circumstances under which these different resources strengthen and complement rather than counteract one another deserve to be examined.

9. Find a Way to Intraparty Mediation

One major obstacle that hinders progress in mediation processes is internal tension within the primary parties. Mediators try to bridge the gap between the parties, but oftentimes the stumbling block exists within the parties themselves. Tensions between doves and hawks, moderates and fundamentalists, or competing centers of power can stand in the way of any movement toward peace. Mediators tend to prioritize the relationship between the parties. Yet, there is a lack of focus on intraparty mediation. Thus, there is a need for mediators to mediate between the factions within the sides in conflicts. If mediators can play different roles, working in different relationships but toward a common goal, then the whole mediation effort would be more likely to be successful.

An important field for further exploration is, therefore, to examine how indigenous resources can be brought to bear in peacemaking processes. Actors within a conflict setting can play a fruitful role in mitigating intraparty tensions. The jury is still out on how this can be done and how it can complement interparty mediation.

10. Be Open to Different Outcomes and Exits

Success of mediation is an elusive concept. Looking for agreements, mandates, and long-term effects provides three ways for evaluating mediation success. One should, however, bear in mind that the outcome of the process is not the only way to think of success. In intense conflicts with high levels of hostility and mistrust, the fact that the process is carried out has its own intrinsic value. Keeping negotiation and mediation channels open can be a success in itself. In fact, it is common that mediation processes are associated with periods of reduced levels of fighting between the parties.

An agreement may at first seem to be an appropriate indicator of success. After all, some mediation efforts end when the parties have reached an agreement. Yet, even an agreement does not guarantee a positive outcome. Agreements can be abandoned or left unimplemented, and implementation can be slow, delayed, partial, or biased.

The question of scope is an important aspect of the diplomacy of exit. Many actors in the conflicts open up the possibility for partial peace. Factionalism within the sides may create increased complexity for the end phase of the mediation efforts. When there are several factions, the go-between can choose between making partial peace with those that were ready to come to the negotiation table. Alternatively, the mediator can wait until more actors are onboard—and, if they are not, withdraw from mediation.

Another basis for evaluation is the mandate. The mediator, deriving his or her mandate primarily from the multilateral setting, needs to evaluate what is achieved in the mediation efforts according to the goal of the third party.

Success can also be categorized on a short-term to long-term continuum. Some types of outcomes can be more sustainable in the longer run; others can be effective but only in the short term. There is a potential tension between short-term and long-term international mediation outcomes.

Important in this regard is the cumulative aspect of international mediation, meaning that initial progress can pave the way for further success down the road. Even seemingly unsuccessful attempts can build the basis for progress later in the process. Hence, earlier mediation attempts may lay the groundwork for later success.

Real failures in mediation would be if the process leaves the parties frustrated with the mediation, the mandate, or the mandating organization, or gives the parties a pretext for escalating the conflict. Mediators seldom see such effects. Often mediation aims at keeping the process going, with the hope of preventing conflict escalation and fostering direct dialogue and solutions. The hope can often remain just that. This book provides lessons that will enable mediators to better realize that hope.

APPENDIX
Chronologies of the Six Cases

Compiled by Mathilda Lindgren

CASE 1: Iran-Iraq I

1980

November 11

Olof Palme is appointed as the special representative of the secretary-general to Iran-Iraq.

November 17

Eliasson joins the Palme team. He visits Geneva and meets with the Cuban chargé (Ortiz), the Iranian chargé (Dabiri), and the Iraqi ambassador.

November 18–24 (first visit to the region)

November 19–20, Tehran, and November 21, Dezful and Kermanshah, Iran

Meets with the Swedish and Cuban ambassadors, presidential advisers (Farangh and Sanjabi), Prime Minister Mohammad Ali Rajai, and President Abolhassan Bani-Sadr; dines with the Algerian ambassador and meets with Foreign Minister Saadoun Hammadi.

November 21–24, Baghdad

Meets with Deputy Prime Minister Tariq Aziz and President Saddam Hussein; dines with Aziz and meets with Hammadi.

November 26, New York

Palme has separate meetings with representatives of Iran, Iraq, and Mexico.

December 15, London

Palme meets with the Cuban mediator (Malmierca) for the Non-Aligned Movement (NAM).

December 3–6 and 10, New York

Assistant Secretary-General Diego Cordove and Palme meet with the secretary-general to come up with ways to break the impasse on the Shat al-Arab waterway.

1981

January 13–19 (second visit to the region)

January 13–15, Baghdad

Palme and team meet with Deputy Prime Minister Aziz, Foreign Minister Hammadi, and President Hussein.

January 16–19, Tehran

Palme and team meet President Bani-Sadr, Prime Minister Rajai, Speaker of the Majlis Hajoteleslam Rafsanjani, a delegation of expelled Iraqis, the Indian foreign secretary, the Cuban Ambassador, and Ayatollah Beheshti.

January 20–21, New York

The secretary-general and Palme meet to discuss the recent visit to Iran and Iraq, after which Palme holds a press conference.

February 16–24 (third visit to the region)

February 17–19, Baghdad

Palme and Eliasson meet with Aziz and Hammadi several times.

February 19–22, Tehran

Palme and Eliasson meet with President Bani-Sadr, Ayatollah Beheshti, and Speaker of the Majlis Rafsanjani; Cordovez meets with Sanjabi; Palme dines with the Algerian ambassador; and Cordovez and Palme meet with the International Committee of the Red Cross (ICRC) representative in Tehran (Josseron).

February 23, New York

Palme meets with the secretary-general, holds a press conference, and has separate meetings with the ambassador of Iraq, the president of the Security Council (France), the Pakistani chargé, and Bernard Nossiter of the *New York Times*.

February 24, New York

Palme meets with the ambassadors of Algeria, the United Kingdom, India, Mexico, and Panama.

March–April

Low-key communication continues between the Palme team and representatives of Iran and Iraq.

May 11, Geneva

Palme meets with the secretary-general.

May 26, New York

Palme and Eliasson have separate meetings with the ambassador of Iraq and the Iranian chargé and with the secretary-general.

May 28

Palme meets with the president of the Security Council (Japan).

June 17

Palme and Eliasson meet with the foreign minister of India in Visby, Sweden.

June 19–28 (fourth visit to the region)

June 20–25, Tehran

Palme and Eliasson meet with Prime Minister Rajai, members of the Supreme Defense Council, Ayatollah Beheshti, and Speaker of the Majlis Rafsanjani.

June 26–27, Baghdad

Agenda unknown.

June 28–29, Geneva

The Palme team meets with the secretary-general and the president of NAM (Malmierca).

July–December

Due to lack of interest in mediation from both parties and political turmoil in Iran, the mediation effort was tuned down during the summer and the fall. Not until December, when Ali Akbar Velayati was appointed foreign minister in Iran, did interest in a cease-fire again surface. Thus, the secretary-general approached Palme and his team to continue their mediation.

1982

January

Preparatory meetings with representatives of Iran and Iraq, before Palme's fifth, and final, visit to the region.

February 24–March 1 (fifth and final visit to the region)

February 24–26, Baghdad

Palme and Eliasson meet with representatives of Iraq.

February 27–March 1, Tehran

Palme and Eliasson meet with representatives of Iran.

March, New York

Palme informs the secretary-general that active mediation is no longer relevant and the mission from now on focuses on informal low-key contacts between the parties.

September 19

Palme wins the Swedish elections and remains the main mediator of the Iran-Iraq conflict.

October–December

Low-level contacts continue between representatives of Iran and Iraq and the United Nations.

1983

Low-level contacts continue between representatives of the parties at the United Nations and UN staff throughout the year. No formal attempts at mediation.

1984

June 11, New York

Iran and Iraq separately commit to the UN secretary-general to stop attacking civilian targets.

July–December

No formal political mediation. The secertary-general remained involved, maintaining confidence-building measures and discussions to achieve a cessation of hostilities.

Fall

Iran again welcomed mediation delegations—including from the United Nations—to pursue their efforts.

1985

March

The secretary-general presents representatives of Iran and Iraq with an eight-point peace plan on which intense discussions follow throughout March.

April 7–9 (visit to the region)

Secretary-General Pérez de Cuéllar visits the region to facilitate an end to the conflict. Both sides agree to proceed with the eight-point plan presented in March.

April 7–8, Tehran

The secretary-general meets with President Sayed Ali Khamenei, Speaker of the Majlis Rafsanjani, Prime Minister Hosein Mousavi, Foreign Minister Velayati, and Deputy Foreign Minister Hossein Kazempour-Ardebili.

April 8–9, Baghdad

The secretary-general meets with President Hussein, Deputy Prime Minister and Foreign Minister Aziz, and Deputy Foreign Minister Ismat Kittani.

May–December

No formal political mediation. The secretary-general remained involved, maintaining confidence-building measures and discussions to achieve a cessation of hostilities.

1986

February 28, Stockholm

Olof Palme is murdered.

March–December

The Secretary-General and the permanent five members of the Security Council (P5) intensify their diplomatic efforts at ending the war from this point, paving the way for Security Council Resolution 598 (1987). For instance, between October 3 and 8, the Security Council met five times to discuss the Iran-Iraq War.

1987

January–July

The P5 negotiate back and forth between the parties and facilitate the adoption of Security Council Resolution 598 (July 20, 1987).

September 11–16 (visit to the region)

The secretary-general presents a framework for the implementation of Security Council Resolution 598 to representatives of both parties.

September 11–13, Tehran

The secretary-general meets with President Khamenei, Speaker of the Majlis Rafsanjani, Prime Minister Moussavi, and Foreign Minister Aziz and other senior officials.

September 13–15, Baghdad

The secretary-general meets with President Hussein, Deputy Prime Minister and Foreign Minister Aziz, and senior Foreign Ministry officials.

September 25

The secretary-general meets with members of the P5, who all agree to assist in ending the armed conflict between Iran and Iraq.

October–December

The secretary-general, supported by the Security Council, discusses ways to implement Security Council Resolution 598 and to initiate mediated talks with the parties. This type of communication continues until August 20, 1988, when both parties enter a formal cease-fire.

CASE 2: Iran-Iraq II

1988

August 20

The cease-fire officially enters into force.

August 25–30, Geneva (first round of talks, foreign-minister level)

The secretary-general holds face-to-face talks with Iranian Foreign Minister Velayati and Iraqi Foreign Minister Aziz.

September 1–13, Geneva (first round of talks continued)

September 1

Eliasson is officially appointed special representative of the secretary-general to Iran-Iraq.

September 2–13 (formal talks)

Eliasson meets with Velayati and Aziz and their delegations, the P5, and Saudi Arabian envoy Prince Bandar bin-Sultan.

September 14–30

Informal contacts continue between meetings.

September 30, New York

The secretary-general meets with the two foreign ministers.

October 1–2, New York (second round of talks)

The secretary-general, Giandomenico Picco, and Eliasson meet with Velayati and Aziz in New York a face-to-face meeting, and Picco and Eliasson meet with Velayati and Aziz.

November 1–12, Geneva (third round of talks)

The secretary-general, Eliasson, and Picco meet with Velayati and Aziz in direct talks. In separate negotiations with the ICRC, both parties agree to exchange sick and wounded prisoners of war by December 31.

December

Low-level contacts and communication continue.

1989

Late January, Tehran and Baghdad (first visit to the region)

Eliasson visits Iran and Iraq, meeting with Mousavi, Hussein, Aziz, Velayati, and other senior officials of the two countries. Eliasson also visits military observers in the field.

February 10, New York (fourth round of talks)

The secretary-general meets with Velayati and Aziz—first separately, then jointly.

Early March–March 10, New York

Preparatory talks with Eliasson and representatives of Iran and Iraq continue before the next round of ministerial meetings. Implementation of Resolution 598 is discussed.

ca. March 25–early April, New York

More preparatory talks are held between Eliasson and representatives of Iran and Iraq.

April 20–23, Geneva (fifth round of talks)

Secretary-general meets three times with Velayati and Aziz together, after holding a separate meeting with each official. Eliasson remained in touch with both sides to prepare for future meetings.

Early May, New York

Eliasson and the ambassadors to Iran and Iraq hold preparatory meetings.

Mid-May, Geneva

Eliasson meets with the parties separately.

May 19, Washington, DC

Eliasson briefs U.S. Deputy Assistant Secretary of State Peter Burleigh.

May 25, New York

Eliasson holds several informal preparatory meetings with representatives of the two sides on the ambassadorial level.

Early June, New York

Several informal meetings at the ambassadorial level are held.

July 4, Geneva

The secretary-general and Eliasson meet with Velayati.

July 6, Rome

The secretary-general and Eliasson meet Iraq's Aziz.

July 17, New York

Eliasson reports to the secretary-general and Security Council in an informal session.

Early August, New York

The secretary-general meets with an emissary of the Iranian foreign minister (Ambassador Xarif) to create momentum for the upcoming NAM meeting in September.

Early August, Geneva

Eliasson holds separate meetings with the foreign ministers of Iran and Iraq.

August 23–25, Geneva

Eliasson meets with representatives of both parties in Geneva to present and discuss some new ideas, constructed as "signals for momentum."

September 8, Beograd, Serbia (fifth round of talks)

Eliasson meets both parties at the ministerial level.

End of September, New York

Eliasson meets with representatives of the parties at the time of the General Assembly.

September 29–October 3, New York

The secretary-general and Eliasson consult informally with Velayati and Aziz.

October 11–12, New York

Eliasson meets with representatives of Canada, Kuwait, and Cuba.

October 30–November 17 (second visit to the region)

October 30–November 3, Baghdad

Eliasson, together with Picco, Raymond Sommereyns, and Judy Karam, meets representatives of Iraq.

November 3–5, Tehran

Eliasson meets with Rafsanjani and Velayati.

November 5–10, Baghdad

Eliasson meets with President Hussein, Aziz, and other senior officials.

November 10–15, Tehran

Agenda unknown.

November 15–17, Baghdad

Agenda unknown.

November 28, New York

The secretary-general and Eliasson report to the Security Council.

December 18, New York

The secretary-general and Eliasson have separate meetings with the foreign ministers of Iran and Iraq.

1990

March 13, New York

The secretary-general presents a new plan for Iran and Iraq.

March 29, New York

The secretary-general consults informally with the Security Council, and Eliasson is in close contact with representatives of the parties.

ca. April 24, New York

Eliasson and the secretary-general meet with Velayati and Deputy Foreign Minister Zahawi in separate meetings to prepare for direct talks.

May, New York

Eliasson and the secretary-general meet with Aziz.

May 14, Rome

Aziz informs Secretary-General de Cuéllar of the recently established direct written communication between Iran and Iraq, which is to complement the efforts of the United Nations in resolving the conflict and implementing Resolution 598.

July 3, Geneva

For the first time since talks in Geneva in 1988, Velayati and Aziz meet face-to-face, together with the secretary-general, Eliasson, and Picco, as well as other Iranian and Iraqi officials.

July–December

Low-key discussions continue on the full implementation of Resolution 598.

1991

January 6, New York

Iran and Iraq sign an agreement on the withdrawal of forces, demining, and the creation of a buffer zone, among other things.

March 12, Sweden

Eliasson receives a visit from Iranian Ambassador Kharassi, who reiterates and defines the Iranian position.

End of March (visit to the region)

The secretary-general and Picco visit Tehran and Baghdad to install the United Nations Office of the Secretary-General in Iran (UNOSGI) and the United Nations Office of the Secretary-General in Iraq to take over after the United Nations Iran-Iraq Military Observer Group (UNIIMOG).

May

Eliasson is in close contact with representatives of both Iran and Iraq concerning increased accusations of violations of the cease-fire agreement.

September 10–14 (third visit to the region)*

September 10–13, Tehran

Eliasson and the secretary-general talk to Iranian officials and make a preliminary evaluation of the war damages.

September 13–14, Jeddah, Saudi Arabia

Eliasson and the secretary-general talk to the Gulf Cooperation Council (GCC) on their recent peace plan.

---

* Visit number corresponds to Jan Eliasson's visit to the region as a mediator. Other visits listed in this chronology refer to official UN visits.

End of September, New York

Eliasson and the secretary-general again meet with representatives of the GCC.

December 9, New York

The secretary-general presents his report (S/23273) on the issue of responsibility of the start of the Iran-Iraq War.

December 24

The secretary-general issues his second report, based on Under-Secretary-General Farah's report on the issue of reconstruction in Iran.

1992

Eliasson ends his mediation mission between Iran and Iraq and is appointed under-secretary-general and head of the newly established Department of Humanitarian Affairs.

CASE 3: Burma/Myanmar—Bangladesh and the Rohingya Refugees

1992

Early March

The United Nations High Commissioner of Refugees (UNHCR) tries to assess the situation of the Rohingya refugees.

Late March

Eliasson, as the first UN under-secretary-general for the coordination of humanitarian affairs, is commissioned by the secretary-general to assist the governments of Bangladesh and Burma/Myanmar in finding a solution to the humanitarian crisis in Bangladesh.

March 29–April 12 (visit to the region)

March 3–Apri l1, Dakha, Bangladesh (first round)

Eliasson meets representatives of the governments of Bangladesh and Burma/Myanmar, visits some of the Rohnigya camps, and meets with Bangladeshi prime minister Zia.

April 1–April 4, Rangoon, Burma/Myanmar

Eliasson meets representatives of the two governments in talks for four days.

April 10

Secretary-General Boutros-Ghali announces that the two governments are about to agree to begin a process of voluntary and safe repatriation.

End of April

Bangladesh and Burma/Myanmar officially agree to several steps for repatriation, outlined in the "Joint Statement by the Foreign Ministers of Bangladesh and Mynamar, Issued at the Conclusion of the Official Visit of the Myanmar Foreign Ministers from 23–26 April."

May and forward

The UNHCR resumes the initiative of Jan Eliasson and the United Nations Department of Humanitarian Affairs, continuing to negotiate with the governments of Bangladesh and Burma/Myanmar.

September

Voluntary repatriation begins into the Arakan province, even though Burma/Myanmar has not yet agreed to allow UNHCR presence in the province to monitor safe and voluntary repatriation.

1993

November

UNHCR and the government of Burma/Myanmar finally agree to station UNHCR personnel in the Arakan state to monitor repatriation.

CASE 4: Southern Sudan

1992

August

The humanitarian NGO Norwegian Church Aid calls the United Nations' attention to the deteriorating humanitarian situation in Southern Sudan.

September 9–21 (first visit to the region)

Eliasson visits Somalia, Kenya, Sudan, Djibouti, and Zimbabwe to inspect relief operations throughout the region. Together with James Grant, director of the United Nations Children's Fund (UNICEF), and other UN officials.

September 14–20, Khartoum and the Juba area of Sudan

Eliasson meets with military strongman Lt. Gen. Omar Bashir and other Sudanese officials; Eliasson sees the forced relocations of populations and assesses the humanitarian crisis in the region.

September 17

Eliasson announces that he and the government in Khartoum and the SPLA rebels in Nairobi have come to an agreement for war relief to previously nonaccessible areas in the South.

September 18

Talks still in progress to work out more access to aid.

September–December

Operation Lifeline Sudan (OLS), headed among others by UNICEF, continues its humanitarian relief work in Southern Sudan.

CASE 5: Azerbaijan (Nagorno-Karabakh)

1993

November 30–December 1, Rome

The Council of Ministers meet and Sweden takes over the chairmanship of the Minsk Conference and the Minsk Group from Italy.

Mid-December

The Conference for Security and Cooperation in Europe (CSCE) Minsk Group meets with delegations from Azerbaijan and Armenia.

December 21–22, Åland Island, Finland

The parliamentary delegations of Azerbaijan, Nagorno-Karabakh, and Armenia partake in a seminar visit to the Åland Islands. (The Russian Ministry of Foreign Affairs, the Commonwealth of Independent States Inter-parliamentary Assembly, and the Åland Institute of Peace organize the meeting.)

1994

February 10, Vienna

Eliasson meets with former chairman of the Minsk Group, Italian Mario Sica, the IOPG (peacekeeping planning group), and Simon Fuller (UK) and speaks at the Organization for Security and Cooperation in Europe (OSCE) Permanent Council.

February 28–March 7 (first visit to the region)

March 1–2, Baku

Eliasson meets with President Heidar Alijev, Assistant Prime Minister Abbas Abbasov, the Azeri representative in the Minsk Group, Vafa Goulizadeh, Head of Parliament Rasbul Ghoulijev, and Foreign Minister Hasan Hasanov (Gasan Gasanov).

March 3–4, Stepanakert, Nagorno-Karabakh

Eliasson meets with the chairman of the Nagorno-Karabakh defense committee, Robert Kotjarian.

March 5–6, Baku

Eliasson meets with President Alijev, Foreign Minister Hasanov, Armenian foreign minister Vazgen Papazian, Armenian defense minister Serge Sarkissian, and Armenian president Ter Petrosian.

March 9, Vienna

Eliasson holds a press conference on his visit to the region.

March 21–25, Moscow

Eliasson attends a meeting with representatives from both parties in a joint mediation effort with the OSCE and Russia.

March 23–25, Vienna

Eliasson attends a meeting with the OSCE.

March 24–25, Vienna and Graz

The Minsk Group chairmen meet with representatives of the parties and Eliasson also consults relevant international actors about his mediation.

April 11–12, Prague

Eliasson's team meets with the parties. Armenia launches an attack in Azerbaijan.

April 14–15, Vienna

The Minsk Group has an internal meeting.

April 19–20, Stockholm

Eliasson meets with the Russian special envoy for Nagorno-Karabakh, Vladimir Kazimirov.

April 26–May 2 (visit to the region)

April 27, Baku

The OSCE meets with Hasanov, Alijev, and Goulizadeh.

May 2, New York

Eliasson informs the Security Council on the situation.

May 11, Vienna

Eliasson meets with the "Minsk Group 9" (MG9) and updates the CSCE Permanent Council.

May 12–15 (second visit to the region)

Eliasson, Mossberg, and Kazimirov visit Baku and Yerevan in a joint effort. Eliasson meets with Goulizadeh and Aliev (Azerbaijan), Ter Petrossian and First Deputy Foreign Minister Zhirayr Liparityan (Armenia), and Robert Kotjarian (N-K).

May 17, Vienna

Eliasson meets with the Chairman-in-Office (CiO), MG9, Initial Operations Planning Group (IOPG), and the Permanent Council.

May 19, Vienna

Eliasson holds a press conference.

June 14–19 (third visit to the region)

June 14–15, Baku

Eliasson and Thöresson meet with Goulizadeh, Hasanov, Aliev, and Speaker of Parliament Mamedov.

June 16, Yerevan

Eliasson meets with Armenian first deputy foreign minister Zhirayr Liparityan.

June 16, Stepanakert, Nagorno-Karabakh

Eliasson meets with Kotjarian and dines in the mountains.

June 17, Yerevan

Eliasson meets with Ter Petrossian.

June 18, Baku

Eliasson meets with Goulizadeh and Aliev.

June 19, Yerevan, Armenia

Short meetings are held before returning to Vienna.

July 4, Vienna

Eliasson meets with Kazimirov, Höynck, and Gouliev.

July 7–8, Vienna

The MG9 meets and Eliasson is mandated to try to negotiate a comprehensive cease-fire agreement.

July 13–14, Stockholm

Eliasson meets with Kazimirov.

August 5, Moscow

Eliasson participates as an observer in Russian-mediated talks.

August 16–18, Vienna

A meeting with MG9 mandates Eliasson to travel to the region to discuss political (not only technical) aspects of the peace. Russia and OSCE fail to reach a consolidated peace proposal due to parallel Russian negotiations in Moscow.

August 23–29 (fourth visit to the region)

August 23, Baku

Eliasson meets with Goulizadeh, Hasanov, and Aliev.

August 24, Yerevan

Eliasson has a short meeting with Liparityan.

August 24–25, Stepanakert, Nagorno-Karabakh

Eliasson meets with Goukhasian, the self-proclaimed foreign minister of Nagorno-Karabakh and Kotjarian.

August 25, Yerevan

Eliasson and Mossberg meet with Liparityan and Ter Petrossian.

August 26, Baku

Eliasson meets with Goulizadeh and Aliev.

August 27–28, Yerevan

Eliasson meets with Ter Petrossian, the Armenian First Deputy Foreign Minister Zhirayr Liparityan, and the head of the Karabakh Armenians, Karen Baburyan.

August 28, Baku

Eliasson meets informally with Aliev.

September 1, Moscow

The OSCE participates as observers in Russian-mediated negotiations.

September 12–14, Vienna

The Minsk Group meets and Eliasson is recommended to (1) work for an international security force and (2) mediate a "political package."

September 20–22, Tehran

Eliasson meets with representatives in Iran.

September 22–23, Vienna

Eliasson meets with the CSCE.

September 27–30, New York

Eliasson negotiates with the parties (Sergei Lavrov, Ter Petrossian, Aliev, Goulding, Derek Boothby, Madeleine Albright, Joe Presel, Sir David Hannay, and Klaus Kinkel).

October 24–25, 31, Vienna

Eliasson holds meetings with the CSCE.

November 9–15 (fifth visit to the region)

November 9–10, Baku

Eliasson meets with Hasanov, Aliev, and Gouliev.

November 11, Stepanakert, Nagorno-Karabakh

Eliasson meets with Kotjarian and the head of the Karabakh Armenians, Karen Baburyan.

November 12–13, Yerevan

Eliasson meets with Ter Petrossian, Kotjarian, and Baburyan.

November 14, Baku

Eliasson meets with Hasanov and Aliev.

November 18, Budapest

OSCE meeting is held.

November 28–December 4, Budapest

Numerous meetings on an OSCE peacekeeping mission to Nagorno-Karabakh are held.

1995

January 12–13, Vienna

Meeting of the "Minsk Group 10."

January 26–February 2 (sixth visit to the region)

January 26–27, Baku

Meetings with Aliev, Goulizadeh, and Commander-in-Chief Mamedov are held.

January 28, Yerevan

Meetings with Libaridian and Ter Petrossian are held.

January 30–31, Stepanakert, Nagorno-Karabakh

Meetings with Kotjarian are held.

January 31, Yerevan, Armenia

Meetings with Ter Petrossian are held.

January 31–February 2

Meetings with Abbas Abbasov, Aliev, and Goulizadeh are held.

February 6–11, Moscow

The OSCE Minsk Conference co-chairs draw up an agreement among Azerbaijan, Nagorno-Karabakh, and Armenia on a mechanism for possible settlement with the aim of strengthening the cease-fire agreement; negotiations among Azerbaijan, Nagorno-Karabakh, and Armenia are under the auspices of the OSCE Minsk Conference co-chairs.

February 28 (seventh visit to the region)

Eliasson and his co-chair meet with representatives in the region.

March 13–14, Vienna

OSCE meetings with the Minsk Group are held.

May

Eliasson's mission ends.

CASE 6: Sudan (Darfur)

2006

December 19

Eliasson is first appointed interim special representative of the Secretary-General to Darfur and later officially mandated to succeed Dutch special envoy Jan Pronk.

2007

January 5, New York

The secretary-general meets with Eliasson and Salim on the humanitarian crisis.

January 6–8, Addis Ababa

Eliasson meets with AU officials.

January 8–12 (first joint visit to the region)

January 9–11, Khartoum

Eliasson and Salim meet with representatives of the government, such as President Bashir and Foreign Minister Lam Akol, as well as New Mexico Governor Bill Richardson.

January 12, Al-Fasher, Darfur

Eliasson and Salim meet with representatives of the government of North Darfur State.

January 27–29, Khartoum

Secretary-General Ban Ki-Moon visits Sudan on the sidelines of the Africa Union meetings.

February 12–17 (second joint visit to the region)

January 12–13, Khartoum

Eliasson and Salim meet with President Bashir, Foreign Minister Lam Akol, presidential adviser Dr. Khalifa, and Intelligence Chief Salah Abdallah Gosh.

January 14–15, Darfur

Eliasson and Salim meet with the African Union Mission in Sudan (AMIS), the field commanders of nonsignatories to the May 2006 agreement, representatives of internally displaced persons (IDPs), the representatives of the Justice and Equality Movement (JEM), and some of the tribal chiefs. They then hold a press conference.

January 16–18, Khartoum

Eliasson and Salim meet with President Bashir.

February 27, Wadi Anka, Darfur

Reunification conference of the Darfur rebels is held.

March 6, New York

Eliasson briefs the Security Council on the Darfur peace talks is held.

March 22–28 (third joint visit to the region)

March 22, Asmara, Eritrea

Eliasson meets with President Issaias Afeworki.

March 24–27, Khartoum

Eliasson and Salim meet Foreign Minster Lam Akol, other senior government ministers, and opposition leaders (Hassan Turabi of the Popular Congress Party, Sadiq al-Mahdi of the Umma Party, and Ibrahim Nugud, leader of the Communist Party.) They also meet with representatives of Darfur Arab tribes and hold a press conference in the city.

April 16–17, New York

Eliasson and Salim brief the Security Council.

April 23, Europe

Eliasson holds discussions with foreign ministers of the European Union.

April 28–29, Tripoli, Libya

Eliasson and Salim attend a peace conference hosted by Libya, attended by representatives of the United States, Britain, Sudan, Chad, Eritrea, the African Union, and the European Union.

May 8–19 (fourth joint visit to the region)

May 8–11, Khartoum

Eliasson and Salim meet with representatives of the government and hold a joint press conference.

May 13–19, Juba

Eliasson and Salim visit Southern Sudan and prepare for official talks with first vice president and president of the government of Southern Sudan, Salva Kiir Mayardit.

June 3, Darfur

A delegation of the Joint Mission Support Team to the AU-UN Special Envoys for Darfur meet with the JEM.

June 8, New York

Eliasson presents a "road map for peace" to the Security Council, which is later discussed with all rebel movements.

June 25, Paris

The secretary-general attends the Paris Conference, designed to consolidate the efforts of the international community in a Contact Group for Darfur.

June 8, New York

Eliasson and Salim present a joint road map for Darfur to the Security Council.

July 4–14 (fifth joint visit to the region)

July 4–6, el-Genina, West Darfur

Eliasson holds a series of meetings with representatives of the rebel movements. Salim arrives on July 7. The UN-AU Joint Mediation Support Team, led by the United Nations' Pekka Haavisto and the African Union's Sam Ibok, holds talks with groups based in North Darfur and in Asmara.

July 6–7, Khartoum

Eliasson meets with senior officials in the hybrid AU-UN peacekeeping team, representatives of the UN Development Programme (UNDP), the World Bank, and NGOs, and the senior assistant to the Sudanese

President, Minni Minawi. Eliasson and Salim hold talks with senior Sudanese government figures, including Foreign Minister Lam Akol, as well as with civil society groups and tribal leaders.

July 8, Kariarii

Eliasson and Salim meet with JEM and other movements.

July 9–10, Khartoum

Salim meets with Foreign Minister Lam Akol.

July 13, Asmara, Eritrea

Eliasson, with the UN-AU Joint Mediation Support Team, meets with Darfur rebel groups and Eritrean president Isaias Afewerki in preparation for the Libyan conference.

July 15–16, Tripoli, Libya

Eliasson and Salim jointly chair a conference with key regional and international players. Attending the talks are Egypt, Eritrea, Libya, Britain, Canada, Chad, China, France, the Netherlands, Norway, Russia, the United States, the Arab League, and the European Union, as well as Sudan (eighteen countries represented in total).

July 19–August 3

Eliasson and Salim, with teams, work on making as many movements as possible to participate in the Arusha talks, scheduled for August 3.

August 3–5, Arusha, Tanzania

Eliasson and Salim host a meeting with leading rebel groups of the nonsignatories to the Darfur Peace Agreement (DPA) to prepare for formal negotiations.

August 12, Juba

SPLM holds a follow-up consultation meeting in Juba with the nonsignatories to further discuss the agenda produced in the Arusha talks.

August 23–28, Sudan (first independent visit of Salim to the region)

September 3–7, Sudan

The secretary-general discusses the deployment of peacekeeping operations and visits Darfur for the first time and agrees with the Sudanese government to start official talks in Libya on October 27.

October 10–12, Khartoum (first independent visit of Eliasson to the region)

Eliasson talks to government representatives, such as presidential assistant and top negotiator, Nafi Ali Nafi; rebel leaders; and civil society representatives to prepare for scheduled talks in Libya. Eliasson also chairs a high-level meeting with the regional partners to the talks (including Ali Triki, Libya's minister for African affairs).

October 27–30, Sirte, Libya (first formal round of talks)

The Darfur peace talks officially begin. Sudan announces a unilateral cease-fire at the start of the talks. Eight groups are absent due to boycott. Eliasson and Salim hold a press conference on October 28. Peace talks are delayed until December.

October 31–November 12, Darfur

Eliasson and Salim meet with JEM chairman Khalil Ibrahim of Justice and Abdalla Yahya, the leader of the Sudan Liberation Movement (SLM)–Unity Faction. An AU-UN delegation visits Juba to convince other rebel groups, such as SLM-Ahmed Abdelshafi and SLA–Unity Command, and some other commanders.

November 13–15, Asmara, Eritrea

Eliasson and Salim meet regional actors in the peace process (Chad, Eritrea, Libya, and Egypt).

November 14, Juba

Nine factions announce they are uniting under the SLM.

November 18

Salim announces that talks are further stalled and will resume next year.

November 30, Juba

Darfur rebels unite into two rebel groups.

December 4, Sharm el-Sheikh, Egypt

Eliasson and Salim meet with regional partners and discuss peace talks.

December 5–12 (second independent visit of Eliasson to the region)

December 5–7, Khartoum

Agenda unknown.

December 7–10, El Fasher, Darfur

Eliasson meets with JEM, Minni Minawi Minni Arkou Minawi, leader of the SLM–Minawi faction, tribal leaders, and many others.

December 11–12, Khartoum

Eliasson holds a press conference.

2008

January 13–20 (eighth visit to the region)

January 13, Khartoum

Eliasson and Salim head off to Darfur.

January 14–20, Darfur

Eliasson and Salim meet with SLM–Unity, which agrees to participate in talks with SLM–Abdelshafi. Eliasson holds a press conference on increased violence in the region. Eliasson and Salim meet.

February 8, New York

Eliasson reports to the Security Council and holds a press conference.

March 11–18, Geneva (international conference)

Eliasson and Salim host talks with regional partners Chad, Egypt, Eritrea, and Libya and later also other countries, including the P5. Representatives of the P5 meet with the SLM in the presence of Eliasson and Salim.

April 17–18 (joint visit to the region)

April, El Fahser, Darfur

Eliasson and Salim meet the leadership of the SLA.

April 18, Khartoum

Eliasson and Salim hold a press conference on the progress of the peace process.

May 22, Paris

Eliasson meets with Abdel-Wahid al-Nur, the leader of the SLM.

May 31, Stockholm

Eliasson meets with the secretary-general and discusses his future as special envoy.

June 2, Khartoum

Eliasson cancels the Geneva meeting, scheduled to be the second round of talks, and announces his resignation as special envoy for Darfur.

June 12, Addis Ababa, Ethiopia

Eliasson and Salim hold a press conference on the peace process.

June 27

It is announced that Burkina Faso foreign minister Djibril Bassole will take over the peace process as the new special envoy.

INDEX

Aall, Pamela, 13
Aboke girls from St. Mary's College boarding
    school, 22
academic community, 113
accepting mediation, 25
Aceh, 14, 23
actors. *See* parties
Addis Ababa, meeting in Nov. 2006, 49
admission of guilt, 22
African Union, and Darfur, 78, 100
Agence France-Presse, 83
agenda, as mediation issue, 46
agreement. *See also* cease-fire agreement
    as natural mediation endpoint, 97
    and positive outcome, 135
Ahtisaari, Martti, 14, 108
Algiers Accord, 75
Aliyev, Heydar, 39–40
amnesty, 23
Annan, Kofi, 14
Arab world, and Iran-Iraq War, 41
arbitration, xiv
Argentina, 124
armed conflicts
    ending, vs. justice issues, 23
    identifying issues, 43–46
    intractability of, 132
    role for mediation impacting, 2–3
    UN on agenda, 105
Armenia, 41
    view on mediation, 51
Arusha, Tanzania, 45
atrocities, mediator reaction to, 67
Australia, 14
autonomy, 44
Azerbaijan, 6, 8, 28–29, 41. *See also* Nagorno-
    Karabakh conflict
    efforts to strengthen CSCE, 90
    interest in solution, 39–40
    occupation by Armenian and Karabakh
        forces, 122
    support for step-by-step approach, 92
    view as victims of aggression, 65
    view on mediation, 51

back-channel mediation, 126
Baghdad
    Eliasson travel to, 1
    shuttle diplomacy between Tehran and, 5
Bahr el Ghazal region, 5
balance of power, 127
Bangladesh, 26. *See also* Burma/Myanmar (1992)
    chronology, 147–148
    statement on repatriation, 97
    successor for mediation, 100
Bashir, Omar, 18, 22, 80, 110
Bassolé, Djibril Yipènè, 78
battlefield, and political will, 39
Beagle Channel case, 124, 125
Berlin talks (2003), 20
Bigombe, Betty, 16–17
bilateral negotiations, third party intervention,
    3n3
Bosnia case, 124
Bougainville, Papua New Guinea, 11
Brahimi, Lakhdar, 126
Burma/Myanmar (1992), 8
    call for mediation, 26
    chronology, 147–148
    Eliasson results, 124
    Eliasson's use of humor in negotiating, 55
    focus of mandate, 35
    humanitarian diplomacy in, 5
    mandate fulfillment, 102
    other mediation efforts, 100
    statement on repatriation, 97
    other mediation efforts, 74
Burundi, 14, 19, 125
    UN special envoy, 113

Cambodian mission (1990s), 110n6
Carter, Jimmy, 14, 18, 22, 112
Carter Center, 14
cease-fire agreement
    between Iraq and Iran, 56, 60
    in Nagorno-Karabakh, 39
    Russian-mediated in 1994, 88–89
Center for Humanitarian Dialogue (Geneva), 92,
    119

Chad, and Darfur, 40–41, 78
chemical weapons, 121
    Iraq's use of, 66
    UN secretary-general and Iraq's use, 67
Chile, 124
China
    and Darfur, 91
    and Sudan, 42
    and UN, 31
Chissano, Jaquim, 14
civil society organizations, 92
civilians, efforts to stop targeting, 59
Clinton, Bill, 112
coercive intervention, xiv
cohesion of government, and mediation progress,
    39
Commission on Conciliation, for settling Shatt
    al-Arab issue, 60
Commonwealth of Independent States (CIS), 89
communications. *See also* media
    of mediation invitation, 13–14
compensation, Iran's demand for, 64
competition, in mediation efforts, 73, 86
comprehensive mediation method, vs. step-by-
    step approach, 18
Comprehensive Peace Agreement (2005), Sudan
    division, 115
conduct of war, 21
    and humanitarian issues, 120
    justice in, 65
Conference for Security and Co-operation in
    Europe (CSCE), 28, 87
    Azerbaijan efforts to strengthen, 90
    Eliasson team report to, 91
confidence
    creating, 53–57
    measures to build, 117
    termination threat and, 96
confidentiality, 19–20, 63
    vs. openness, 118–19, 125
    and withdrawal threat, 96
Conflict Management Initiative (CMI), 14
conflict managers, 21n29
conflict region, direct interactions, 86
conflict resolution, core problem of, 50
conflict ripeness, 3n4
conflicts, change in dynamics, 99
Congo, Democratic Republic of, 14
context of mediation, styles in, 90–93
cooperation, 113
coordination of mediation, 77
Cordovez, Diego, 28, 112
cost of conflicts
    and mediation request, 30
    and offering mediation, 33–34

credibility of mediators, termination threat and,
    68, 96
Crocker, Chester A., 13, 123–24
CSCE. See Conference for Security and
    Co-operation in Europe (CSCE)

Darfur, 8, 29, 77, 119
    accusations of spying, 110
    chronology, 154–59
    diversification of actors, 115, 116
    efforts to find new mediator, 100
    Eliasson as special envoy of UN secretary-
        general, 6
    Eliasson end to mission, 120
    Eliasson's effort in, 65, 117
    Eliasson's statements on, 34, 45, 78, 82, 83–84
    end of mediation, 98, 102, 120
    fear of fractionalization, 68
    focus for, 36
    humanitarian issues, 33–34, 80
    inclusive scope for mediation, 91, 127
    internal power disputes, 44–45
    international norms impact, 93
    issues in conflict, 45
    mandate for mediation, 102
    media role in, 63, 70
    mediation team, 112
    meetings for, 85–86
    other mediation efforts, 74
    potential for military solution, 39
    principles of territorial integrity, 57
    Security Council and, 91
    shuttle diplomacy, 75
Darfur Peace Agreement, 49
de Soto, Alvaro, 17–18, 125
deadlines, mediators' use of, 17, 95
demands, unrealistic, 56
democratic mediators, 3n3
Democratic Republic of Congo, 14
democratizers, 21n29
"departing train" strategy, 63
diagnosing situation, 37
    assessing initial solution, 37–43
    identifying actors, 46–47
    identifying issues, 43–46
    style and, 49–51
directive strategies, 6n4
disaggregation, 43n12
documentation, in-house, 113
domestic affairs, interference in, 15

East Timor, 19
Egeland, Jan, 18, 106
Egypt, and Darfur, 78
El Salvador, 17–18, 125
Eliasson, Jan, xiv

as chair of Minsk Conference, 6
and conditions for mediation entry, 116–17
consistency in style, 127
in Darfur talks, 45, 49, 77
discussion away from negotiations, 85
face-to-face meetings, 76–77
focus of, 118
fostering method of mediation, 117
humanitarian mediation by, 124
with Hussein, 1
initiative for mediation efforts, 25–29
international mediation experiences, 8
mandates and style of, 35
media use by, 62, 118
mediation methods, 69–70
on mediation team in Iran, 32
and Minsk Group, 29, 41
negotiations on Resolution 598, 54
open mode of mediation, 119, 123
other mediation efforts in cases, 74
on Palme mission, 28, 112
personality of, 53
political mediation efforts, 50
as professor at Uppsala, 44
question to begin Iran-Iraq mediation, 64
reputation, 32
in Southern Sudan, 69
support for, 34
time soliciting views of leading actors, 111
travels in cases for ending war, 76
Eliasson, Jan, statements
on agendas, 46
on Burma/Myanmar refugees, 26
on chemical weapons, 66
on climate for mediation, 53
on conversation with Nyunt, 61
on Darfur conflict, 34, 45, 78, 82, 83–84
on Darfur humanitarian needs, 80
on Darfur inclusive talks, 47
on effects of war, 76
on hinderances to talks, 56
on importance of media to meditation, 62
on Iran-Iraq conflict, 42
on Iran-Iraq I, 56–57, 59
on Jarring, 19
on justice issues, 65
to media on Iran-Iraq cease-fire
    implementation, 82–83
on mediator as moral authority, 67
on Nagorno-Karabakh, 34, 58
on peace dividend, 79
on regional relations, 41
on risk of withdraw from Iran-Iraq II, 68
on Russian involvement in Nagorno-
    Karabakh, 42–43, 88
on scorched-earth tactic, 66
on starting negotiations, 49
on Sudan, 42, 58
on threats, 79
on timing of mediation, 37
on utility of withdrawal threats, 96
Eliasson team, Picco's mission and, 81
entry phase, leverage of mediator in, 47–49
Eritrea, 77
and Darfur, 78
ethnic groups
    in Burma/Myanmar, 26. *See also* Rohingya
        ethnic group
    vs. political borders, 40–41
European Union, 79
exclusive scope for mediation, 16–17, 114–16
exit diplomacy
    finding successors, 100–01
    importance of, 123
    openness to different options, 134–35
    style and, 101–03
    threat to terminate mediation, 95–97
    timing the exit, 97–99
external source for mandate, 13

factionalism, 135
Finland, in Minsk Group, 100
focus of mediation
    narrow vs. wide, 20–23, 120–21
    scope implications for, 127
forcing method of mediation, 17–18, 116–18
foreigners, suspicion of mediation role, 11–12
fostering method of mediation, 17–18, 92, 116–18
    by Eliasson, 123
fractionation, 43n12
    fear of, in Darfur, 68

Al-Gaddafi, Muammar, 83–84
Garang, John, 27
global attention, generating, 82–83
global support for mediators, 75–77
go-between. *See* mediators
goals
    of armed conflicts, 43
    of mediation, 109
Gratjov, Pavel, 89
Griffiths, Martin, 23
Gulf Cooperation Council (GCC), 79

Haiti, Carter in, 22
Hammarskjöld, Dag, 31
Hampson, Fen Osler, 13
Hassan al-Bashir, Omar, 65
Helgesen, Vidar, 19, 20
Henri Dunant Center for Humanitarian Dialogue
    (HDC), 14
historical grievance, unilateral apology, 21

Holbrooke, Richard, 12, 112, 123
hostage negotiations, Lebanese, 80–81
human resources, in mediation efforts, 112
human rights violations, 22
    mediator reaction to, 67
Human Rights Watch, 118
humanitarian consensus, difficulty reaching, 110
"humanitarian corridors", 69
humanitarian issues, 43
    and conduct of war, 120
    discussion without mandate, 70
    gradual vs. comprehensive approaches, 61
    and keeping talks going, 68
    Sudan need for aid, 27
humanitarian mediation, 15, 58, 74
    Eliasson entry, 50
    inclusive or exclusive scope, 114–15
    limitations, 35
    mandates, 108
    results, 110–11
    succession process after, 100–01
    and withdrawal threat, 96
Hume, Cameron, 16
humor, 55
Hussein, Saddam, 1–2, 27–28, 48, 64

inclusive scope for mediation, 16–17, 47, 114–16
    Eliasson and, 126–27
Indonesia, 14
informal discussions, 55
information assymmetries, 2n1
institutional mandate, 107
interdependence, xi
internal armed conflicts, discussion on
    responsibility, 22
International Committee of the Red Cross, 111
international community
    go-between relationship, 115
    lack of commitment from, 102
    readiness for mediation, 41–43
international conferences, 85–86
International Criminal Court (ICC), 65, 80, 120
international environment, and Nagorno-
    Karabakh conflict, 99
International Herald Tribune, 62
international legal principles, 58
international mediation. See mediation
international norms, 83–84
international principles, significance of, 22
intraparty mediation, 134
Iran
    delegation in NY 1988, 85
    Eliasson as personal representative of UN
        secretary-general to, 1
    resistance to accepting peace agreement, 51
    territorial integrity position, 84

    UN Security Council loss of credibility, 31
Iran-Contra affair, 84
Iran-Iraq case I (1980, 1982), 4, 5, 8. *See also* Palme
    mission
    chronology, 137–42
    end of mediation, 102
    focus for, 36, 70
    internal division in Iran, 46
    international norms impact, 93
    justice as issue, 64–65
    media complications in, 63
    mediators' image as neutral, 56
    and nonacquisition of territory by force, 120
    other mediation efforts, 74
    Palme mission approaches in, 59–60
    proposal for comprehensive solution, 60
    risk of return to war, 67
    Saudi Arabia and, 82
    Security Council view, 42
    shuttle diplomacy, 75
    United Nations and, 79
Iran-Iraq case II (1988–91), 5, 8, 107
    chronology, 142–47
    Eliasson's methods in, 117
    end of mediation, 102
    impact of Kuwait invasion, 99
    informal discussions and, 55
    international norms impact, 93
    mandate to implement Resolution 598, 101
    other mediation efforts, 74
    threats of withdrawal, 68
    verbal cease-fire, 70
Iranian News Agency (IRNA), 63
Iraq
    chemical weapons use, 66, 121
    Eliasson as personal representative of UN
        secretary-general to, 1
    resistance to accepting peace agreement, 51
Israeli government, and PLO, 18

Janjaweed (Sudan militia), 29
    disarmament, 45
Japan, peace treaty with United States (1950), 22
Jarring, Gunnar, 19
Juba, 5, 77
jus ad bellum, 21
jus in bello, 21–22
jus in deliberatione, 22, 23
justice, 20n29, 64–67
    norms evaluation related to, 83
    vs. peace, 120
    in peace negotiations, 21
Juul, Mona, 106

Karabakh Armenian minority, 28, 40
    inclusion in negotiations, 91

Karadzic, Radovan, 123
Karlsson, Klas-Göran, 44n13
Kavanagh, Paul, 28, 54
Kazimirov, Vladimir, 88, 89, 90
Khomeini, Ayatollah, 28
Kissinger, Henry, 112
Kittani, Ismat T., 55
knowledge
    accumulation over time, 113–14
    need for increasing, 128
Kony, Joseph, 22
Kumaratunga, Chandrika, 16
Kuwait War
    impact on Iran-Iraq conflict, 99, 121
    Iraq air force in Iran during, 65

language, understanding, 68
lead mission, 73
League of Nations, 58
LeMoyne, James, 19
leverage of mediator
    in entry phase, 47–49
    generating, 117
Liberation Tigers of Tamil Eelam (LTTE), 16
Libya, 77
    and Darfur, 40–41, 78
    talks in 2007, 47
Lidén, Anders, 28, 86
linkage politics, 81
local representation, for mediation effort, 113
Lord's Resistance Army (LRA) soldiers (Uganda), 17, 18

Madrid conference, 106
major powers, Palme mission and, 91
mandate for mediation, 11–15, 25, 51, 106–09
    by conflicted parties, 13
    content of mandate, 15
    and Eliasson's style, 35, 50
    and exit diplomacy, 101
    vs. expected outcome, 108
    and mediation function, 105
    need to study, 108
    official vs. unofficial, 14
    origins, 12
    responsibility for, 11–14
    and style, 24
    and success evaluation, 135
    and withdrawal threat, 96
Mandela, Nelson, 14
Marker, Jamsheed, 19
material resources, in mediation efforts, 112
media, 118
    complications from, 63
    Eliasson use of, 70
    mediator as information source, 133

mediator credibility with, 82
mediator use of, 61–63, 92
openness and, 125
and public interest, 82
mediation, 19
    back-channel, 126
    breakdown, 67–68
    clusters of strategies, 5
    coping with other conciliators, 73–75
    entry to and exit from assignment, 7. See also
        exit diplomacy
    inserting, 86–90
    leading, 77–82
    nature of, 2
    outcome of, 8, 109–11
    practice vs. theory, xiii
    value of, xi
mediation conclusions, 128–35
    humanitarian aspects, 131–32
    institutional support, 132–33
    intraparty mediation, 134
    learning as part of process, 128–29
    mandate created with care, 129–30
    openness to different outcomes and exits, 134–35
    parties' proliferation, 133
    styles of mediation, 130–31
    third party relations, 133–34
mediation initiative, 25
mediation team, 129
    size of, 112
mediators
    belligerents' choice of, 48
    cultural sensitivity, 54
    danger of being sidetracked, 88
    differentiating, 4n4
    effectiveness, 2n1
    global support for, 75–77
    initial assessment when entering, 133
    neutrality, 56
    personality, 117–18
    public profile of, 31
    setting conditions for involvement, 48
    task of, xii
    war-adverse, 48n15
Melander, Erik, 44n13
Minsk Conference, 29, 85
    Eliasson as chair, 6
Minsk Group, 29, 34, 87
    Finland in, 100
    Russians and, 43
missions, multiple with different mediators, 74
Mitchell, George, 17, 23, 123
mode of mediation, 19–20
Moi, Daniel Arap, 18
moral issues, 66–67

Mossberg, Mathias, 76, 87
Mozambique, 16, 23
multilateral mandate, 106
     scope for, 35
multilateral mediator
     credibility with media, 82
     risk of blame for lack of progress, 119
     and withdrawal threat, 96
Museveni, Yoweri, 18, 22
mutually enticing opportunities, 3n4
mutually hurting stalemate, 3n4, 38, 50

Nagorno-Karabakh conflict, 6, 28–29, 76, 91
     cease-fire agreement in, 39
     chronology, 149–54
     clash in legal principles, 58
     efforts to find new mediator, 100
     Eliasson's methods in, 92, 117
     Eliasson on, 86
     Eliasson results, 124
     end of mediation, 102
     focus for, 36
     humanitarian issues, 66
     internal tensions, 46–47
     Karabakh Armenian minority, 28, 40
     lack of political will, 98–99
     mandate for mediation, 101–02
     moral issues, 122
     most sensitive issue, 44
     other mediation efforts, 74
     public statements, 92
     rationale for CSCE mission, 33
     reframing issues, 68–69
     Russia and, 41, 84
     Russia competition with Eliasson team, 86–90
     shuttle diplomacy, 75
     status issue at center, 61
     UN Security Council resolution, 42
Nairobi Agreement, 18
narrow focus for mediation, 20–23, 120–21
Nasseri, Sirious, 55
national sovereignty, international mediation
     and, 31
negotiation room, organizing for conversation, 54
negotiations. See also mediation
     designing, 84–86
     establishing principles for, 54
     laying ground for, 37
Neu, Joyce, 18, 22
neutrality, of mediators, 56
New Zealand, 14
non-paper, 60
Nordquist, Kjell-Åke, analytical matrix, 44
Northern Ireland peace process, 17, 23, 124
     Mitchell in, 123
Norway, role in Palestinian question, 14

Norwegian Church Aid, 27
Norwegian mediators, 18
Nossiter, Bernard, 62
Ntaryamira, Cyprien, 20
Ntibantunganya, Sylvestre, 20
Nyerere, Julius, 14
Nyunt, Khin, 55, 61

obstructions, dealing with deliberate, 56
offering mediation, reasons for, 32–35
open mode of mediation, 19–20
     vs. confidentiality, 118–19
     by Eliasson, 123
     and media relations, 125
     restrictions on, 93
Operation Lifeline Sudan (OLS), 101, 110
operational definition of mandate, 35, 107
Organization for Security and Co-operation in
     Europe (OSCE), 6, 28, 33, 107
high commissioner on national minorities
     (HCNM), 126
Oskanyan, Vardan, 44
Oslo peace process (1993), 14, 18, 106
Ould-Abdallah, Ahmedou, 19, 20, 113
outcomes of mediation, 8, 109–11
ownership, issue in mediation processes, 62

Palestine Liberation Organization (PLO), 18
Palme mission, 27, 31, 32. See also Iran-Iraq case I
     (1980,1982)
     connection with Iran religious leaders, 54
     distancing from Security Council, 57
     end of mediation efforts, 119
     international norms impact, 93
     major powers and, 91
     and nonacquisition of territory by force, 120
     potential for concessions demand for entry,
     116
     suspension of mediation efforts, 97–98
Palme, Olof, 4–5, 27–28, 48
     chronology in Iran-Iraq case I, 137–42
Papua New Guinea, 11
parties. See also primary parties
     keeping at table, 67–68
     readiness for mediation, 38–40
     regional, 40–41
     relationship with mediator, 53
patience, 17
peace, 20n29
     vs. justice, 120
peace agreement, 109, 120
peace process
     rationale for, xi
     threat of withdrawal, 67
Peking formula, 31
"people diplomacy", of Iran, 63

People's Republic of China. *See* China
Pérez de Cuéllar, Javier, 17, 57, 81
   negotiations on Resolution 598, 54
permanent member states in UN, perceived
   national interests, 42
personality, of mediator, 117–18
persuasion, 19
Picco, Giandomenico, 28, 57, 80, 81
PLO. *See* Palestine Liberation Organization (PLO)
Poitras, Jean, 21n29
political mediation, 15, 51, 131
   focus on direct dialogue chances, 132
   involved parties, 75
   limitations, 35
   mandates, 108
   other states and, 91
   results, 110–11
political will
   absence, and mediation suspension, 98
   and battlefield, 39
post-Cold War, typical conflict situations, 6
power, 79
   struggle for, 45, 130
primary parties
   internal tensions, 134
   mediator action and, 115–16
   readiness for mediation, 38–40
principles, 56–58
private initiatives, in African conflicts, 14
proposals, formulating, 58–61

Ramberg, Agneta, 63
Red Cross (International Committee), 111
reframing issues, 68–69
refugees
   in Azerbaijan, 122
   from Burma/Myanmar, 26. *See also* Rohingya
     ethnic group
regime change in Iraq, 64
regional actors, 40–41
regional context, 115
regional spoilers, preventing rise, 77
relationship, between mediator and parties, 53
requesting mediation, 30–32
resources for mediation, 108, 111–14
   limitations, 34
   mandate related to, 24
responsibility, acknowledgment in treaty, 22
restorative justice, 21n29
retributive justice, 21n29
Riza, Iqbal, 28, 63, 67, 112, 118, 121, 122
Rohingya ethnic group, 26. *See also* Burma/
   Myanmar (1992)
   chronology, 147–48
   Eliasson on use of media during crisis, 63
   as refugees, 61

UNHCR and, 110
rumors, news media to reduce, 20
Russia
   and Darfur, 91
   and Nagorno-Karabakh, 41
   and Sudan, 42
Rwanda, 14

Salim, Salim Ahmed, 45, 49, 100
   leadership in Darfur case, 77, 98
Sant'Egidio (Catholic community), 16, 23, 92, 125
Saudi Arabia, 41
   and ending of Iran-Iraq War, 82
scapegoat, efforts to make mediator, 56
scope of mediation, 16–17, 69, 114–16
   as exit aspect, 135
secrecy. *See* confidentiality
Security Council. *See* United Nations Security
   Council
self-determination, 58
self-fulfilling prophecy, mediator entry for
   creating, 48
Shatt al-Arab waterway, 59, 65, 79
   commission for settling, 60
shuttle diplomacy, 40, 82, 86
   in Nagorno-Karabakh, 87
   between Tehran and Baghdad, 5
side payments, 2n1
Sirte, Libya, 85–86
Solheim, Erik, 19, 20
Southern Sudan, 27
   chronology, 148–49
   mandate fulfillment, 102
SPLA. *See* Sudan People's Liberation Army
spokesperson, 38
Sri Lanka, 14, 16, 19
   Norway facilitators in, 125
start of mediation, 25
state sovereignty, 84
step-by-step approach, vs. comprehensive
   mediation method, 18
Stepanakert, 91
Strait of Hormuz, 59–60
styles of mediation, xiii, 4, 15–23, 114–22
   comparison, 122–27
   conclusions, 130–31
   context, 90–93
   and diplomacy of entry, 35–36
   exit diplomacy and, 101–03
   focus, 120–21
   forcing or fostering, 17–18, 116–18
   inclusive or exclusive scope, 114–16
   and instruments of mediation, 69–71
   mandates and, 24
   and mediation diagnostics, 49–51
success, 134–35

measuring, 97, 109, 111
possibility, and offering mediation, 34
Sudan, 6–7, 8, 110. *See also* Darfur
    Carter mediation between Uganda and, 18
    chronology, 154–59
    demands for sanctions, 80
    Eliasson and, 67, 124
    focus of mandate, 35
    humanitarian diplomacy in, 5
    international community views, 42
    other mediation efforts, 74
    regional context, 40–41
    territorial integrity of, 57–58
Sudan Liberation Movement/Minni Minawi
    faction (SLM/MM), 49
Sudan People's Liberation Army (SPLA), 18, 27
Sumbeiywo, Lazaro, 19
suspicion, 11–12, 50
Sweden, 33
    Palme in, 48
Swedish International Development Authority
    (SIDA), 12
Swedish Ministry for Foreign Affairs, 34

Tehran, shuttle diplomacy between Baghdad
    and, 5
Ter-Petrosyan, Levon, 99
territorial integrity
    as Darfur mission principle, 57
    Iran's position on, 84
third parties, relating to, 133–34
threats
    to force mediation, 17
    from international community, 80
    of withdrawal from peace process, 67, 95–97
timing
    of engaging in conflict, 17, 18
    of mediation, 33, 37
    of mediators' exit, 97–99
transparency, 19
travel by mediators, 76
trust, 19, 53, 54, 130
    and acceptance of mediator, 31
    termination threat and, 96
Turkey, 87

Uganda, 16–17
    Carter mediation between Sudan and, 18
United Nations, xi, 105
    Charter, 42
        Article 99, 79
    Commission on Human Rights, 101
    Department of Humanitarian Affairs
        (UNDHA), 5, 110
    for humanitarian aid support, 27
    mandate by, 78

Mediation Support Unit, 112
    support from, 75
United Nations Children's Fund (UNICEF), 101
United Nations General Assembly, 85
United Nations Mediation Support Office, 34
United Nations secretary-general, 79
United Nations Security Council, 28, 41, 87
    agreement on mediation objectives, 115
    and Darfur, 91
    history of bias against Iran, 56–57
    and Iraq chemical weapons, 121
    lack of unity and political will, 42
    loss of credibility, 31
    mandate to secretary-general, 81
    objectives and policy, 111
    report on Eliasson and Kazimirov visit 1994,
        89
    Resolution 479, 56–57
    Resolution 598, 1, 5, 28, 42, 61, 64–65, 101, 121
        negotiations on implementation, 54
United States
    and Nagorno-Karabakh conflict, 42
    peace treaty with Japan (1950), 22
    relations with Iraq and Iran, 84
Uppsala Conflict Data Program, xi
Uppsala University, xiv
urgency, in conflict resolution process, 39

van der Stoel, Max, 107
Vatican mediation team, 124, 125
Versailles Treaty, 22
Vieira de Mello, Sergio, 110n6
violent conflicts. *See* armed conflicts

Waldheim, Kurt, 27, 42
Wallensteen, Peter, 44n13
war-adverse mediators, 48n15
war crimes, 22
wars. *See also* armed conflicts; conduct of war
    end of, 109
weapons, introduction of new, 66
Wickremasinghe, Ranil, 16
wide focus for mediation, 20–23, 120–21
words
    making changes, 68
    risk from misinterpreted, 2

Yeltsin, Boris, 88

Zarif, M. Javad, 55
Zartman, I. William, 3n4
Zulfugarov, Tofiq, 44

About the Authors

Isak Svensson is associate professor in the Department of Peace and Conflict Research at Uppsala University (Sweden), and postdoctoral visiting fellow at the National Centre for Peace and Conflict Studies at Otago University (New Zealand). His areas of expertise include religion in conflict resolution, unarmed insurrections, and international mediation. His main focus has been on how mediation can help to overcome bargaining problems, including those related to the role of biased mediation in civil wars, issues of power and trust in mediation, and third-party security guarantees. His work has been published in several high-ranking journals, such as *Journal of Peace Research, Journal of Conflict Resolution, Negotiation Journal*, and *International Negotiations*. In addition, he has explored Norwegian mediation efforts in Sri Lanka.

Peter Wallensteen has held the Dag Hammarskjöld Chair of Peace and Conflict Research at Uppsala University (Sweden) since 1985 and has been the Richard G. Starmann Sr. Research Professor of Peace Studies at the Joan B. Kroc Institute of International Peace Studies at the University of Notre Dame (United States) since 2006. He directs the Uppsala Conflict Data Program (www.ucdp.uu.se), whose data on conflicts and peace efforts is published annually in *Journal of Peace Research, SIPRI Yearbook, Human Security Reports/Briefs*, and *States in Armed Conflict*. He also leads the Special Program on the Implementation of Targeted Sanctions (www.smartsanctions.se), which has contributed to reforming the use of sanctions in the United Nations and the European Union and presented a study of arms embargoes to the United Nations in November 2007. His *Understanding Conflict Resolution* explains the basics of conflict resolution and is used in classrooms worldwide. He edited (with Carina Staibano) *International Sanctions: Between Words and Wars in the Global System*, which examines the theoretical and empirical dimensions of targeted sanctions, and (with Anders Mellbourn) *Third Parties in Conflict Prevention*. He has also published a number of works on third parties, conflict resolution, and mediation, most recently a coauthored article in *Negotiation Journal*.

United States Institute of Peace

Since its inception, the United States Institute of Peace has published over 150 books on the prevention, management, and peaceful resolution of international conflicts—among them such venerable titles as Raymond Cohen's *Negotiating Across Cultures; Leashing the Dogs of War*, edited by Chester A. Crocker, Fen Osler Hampson, and Pamela Aall; I. William Zartman's *Peacemaking and International Conflict*; and *American Negotiating Behavior*, by Richard H. Solomon and Nigel Quinney. All our books arise from research and fieldwork sponsored by the Institute's many programs. In keeping with the best traditions of scholarly publishing, each volume undergoes thorough internal review and blind peer review by external subject experts to ensure that the research, scholarship, and conclusions are balanced, relevant, and sound. As the Institute prepares to move to its new headquarters on the National Mall in Washington, D.C., the Press is committed to extending the reach of the Institute's work by continuing to publish significant and sustainable works for practitioners, scholars, diplomats, and students.

—VALERIE NORVILLE

DIRECTOR

About the Institute

The United States Institute of Peace is an independent, nonpartisan institution established and funded by Congress. Its goals are to help prevent and resolve violent conflicts; promote post-conflict peacebuilding; and increase conflict-management tools, capacity, and intellectual capital worldwide. The Institute does this by empowering others with knowledge, skills, and resources, as well as by its direct involvement in conflict zones around the globe.

Chairman of the Board: J. Robinson West

Vice Chairman: George E. Moose

President: Richard H. Solomon

Executive Vice President: Tara Sonenshine

Board of Directors

J. Robinson West (Chair), Chairman, PFC Energy, Washington, D.C.

George E. Moose (Vice Chairman), Adjunct Professor of Practice, The George Washington University

Anne H. Cahn, Former Scholar in Residence, American University

Chester A. Crocker, James R. Schlesinger Professor of Strategic Studies, School of Foreign Service, Georgetown University

Ikram U. Khan, President, Quality Care Consultants, LLC

Kerry Kennedy, Human Rights Activist

Stephen D. Krasner, Graham H. Stuart Professor of International Relations, Stanford University

Jeremy A. Rabkin, Professor, George Mason School of Law

Judy Van Rest, Executive Vice President, International Republican Institute

Nancy Zirkin, Executive Vice President, Leadership Conference on Civil Rights

Members ex officio

Michael H. Posner, Assistant Secretary of State for Democracy, Human Rights, and Labor

James N. Miller, Principal Deputy Under Secretary of Defense for Policy

Ann E. Rondeau, Vice Admiral, U.S. Navy; President, National Defense University

Richard H. Solomon, President, United States Institute of Peace (nonvoting)